Silent No More

Confronting America's
False Images of Islam

Paul Findley

amana publications

First Edition
(1422AH/2001AC)
© Copyright 1422AH/2001AC
amana publications
10710 Tucker Street
Beltsville, Maryland 20705-2223 USA
Tel: (301) 595-5777 / Fax: (301) 595-5888
E-mail: amana@igprinting.com
Website: www.amana-publications.com

Cover page photo credits:
Muhammad Ali *(Stan Jennings)*
Ahmed Zewail *(CalTech Public Affairs)*

Cover design: Ken Tiessen

Library of Congress Cataloging-in-Publications Data

Findley, Paul, 1921-
  Silent no more : confronting America's false images of Islam / by
  Paul Findley.
      p. cm.
  Includes index.
  ISBN 1-59008-000-9 -- ISBN 1-59008-001-7 (pbk.)
    1. Islam--Apologetic works. 2. Islam--Public opinion. 3. Public opinion--
  United States I. Title.

BP170.F56 2001
297.2'9--dc21

                                                                2001022275

Third Printing 2002

Printed in the United States of America by
International Graphics
10710 Tucker Street
Beltsville, Maryland 20705-2223   USA
Tel: (301) 595-5999 Fax: (301) 595-5888
Website: igprinting.com
E-mail: ig@igprinting.com

Contents

To
all who prize liberty
for all people
in all lands
everywhere.

Our defense is in the preservation of the spirit which prizes liberty
as the heritage of all men, in all lands, everywhere.
Destroy this spirit and you have planted the seeds of despotism
around your own doors.

-ABRAHAM LINCOLN

Speech at Edwardsville, Illinois, October 11, 1858

Acknowledgments

This is my fifth book, by far the most challenging, complex, and enthralling. Assisting me were most of the people listed in the index. They supplied anecdotes, personal experiences, and priceless insights. They did so enthusiastically, hoping the final product will help clear away misunderstandings of Islam.

At the editorial level, my chief benefactor was Shirley Cloyes. In past years, she edited my two books on the U.S.-Israeli relationship and now helps alleviate the human suffering that is the aftermath of civil strife in Kosova. Helping with detailed editing were Dr. Nour Naciri, a lay Islamic scholar; his wife, Zainab Elberry; Andrew Patterson, a teacher and linguist; and Dr. Wolf Fuhrig, a neighbor and retired political science professor.

Lucille, my wife and best critic, clarified muddled prose while proof-reading. Asked to read several drafts of the same chapters, she surely wondered if this book would ever be completed. Both of our children, Craig and Diane, helped to sharpen the text. Like their parents, both enjoy circles of friends that are multicultural and multireligious. The staff of Amana Publications provided unstinting cooperation and patience.

I feel a touch of sadness as the manuscript, compressed into a single, small diskette, leaves my hands. Its preparation has deepened my respect for Islam and enriched my life with Muslim friendships. As the diskette departs, I want the friendships to remain.

Cover:
Among Those Who Challenge Stereotypes

Pictured on the front cover and on the insert placed inside this book are some of the remarkable American citizens I encountered during my journey through the World of Islam. They represent various vocations. Not all are Muslims, but each challenges in a significant way the stereotypes of Islam. They do so by example, word, or deed.

They are typical of the thousands of people who deserve recognition for advancing interfaith understanding. I wish I could meet—and list—them all.

Across the top of the front cover (from left to right): Muhammad Ali, the most popular Muslim in the world; U.S. Representatives David Bonior and Thomas Campbell, champions of the civil rights of Muslims; April Szuchyt, an American convert to Islam who works in the Peace Corps; New Hampshire State Representative Saghir Tahir, a Republican Party leader and Muslim activist; Ahmed Zewail, a Muslim scientist who won the 2000 Nobel Prize in chemistry.

Across the bottom of the front cover (from left to right): Agha Saeed, founder-chairman of the American Muslim Alliance (AMA) and the organizer of presidential bloc voting by Muslims in the 2000 presidential election; Salam Al-Marayati, national director of the Muslim Public Affairs Council (MPAC); Abdurahman Alamoudi, an early pioneer in Muslim political activism; Rima Nashashibi, a Muslim who is prominent in Democratic Party leadership; Yahya Basha, president of the American Muslim Council (AMC); Nihad Awad, national director of the Council on American-Islamic Relations (CAIR).

Introduction:

An Unexpected Journey

These days, I find it hard to believe that my unplanned exploration of the World of Islam began twenty-five years ago in a small, remote country that no U.S. official had visited for years. I was there on a rescue mission that had nothing to do with Islam but everything to do with the plight of Ed Franklin, a constituent who had been imprisoned on false charges of espionage. In 1974, midway in my twenty-two-year career in the U.S. House of Representatives, I found myself traveling alone deep into an unfamiliar world—the Arab Middle East—where I would seek Franklin's release.

My destination was Aden, the capital of the People's Democratic Republic of Yemen, then a Marxist state situated a third of the way around the world at the southwestern tip of the Arabian peninsula. You won't find it on current maps, because its government collapsed and the country united in 1990 with the Yemen Arab Republic to form the Republic of Yemen.

When I set out to win Franklin's release, he was already in his sixteenth month in solitary confinement, enduring what I imagined were harsh, primitive circumstances. His distraught parents, who lived near my home in Western Illinois and were convinced that their son had been wrongfully convicted, appealed to me for help. In a letter from prison, Franklin explained that the commercial plane which was taking him to his teaching position in Kuwait developed engine trouble and made an emergency landing in Aden.

While waiting for the plane to be repaired, he took photographs of the airport and the nearby harbor, not realizing that this violated security regulations. The local police, suspicious that the British might be planning a commando raid like the one they had carried out six years earlier, took Franklin into custody. After several weeks of interrogation, a court sentenced him to five years in prison.

Like most Americans at the time, my image of the Middle East was gloomy, and official Washington did nothing to relieve my foreboding. The U.S. State Department viewed the government in Aden as the most radical of all the regimes in the Arab world. No American official had entered the country since the June 1967 Arab-Israeli War, and this meant that I would be without the protection of the U.S. government and would have no diplomatic assistance once I arrived. While pondering whether to make the trip, I asked a senior diplomat what the State Department would do if the South Yemen regime put me in jail too. His unsettling answer, "We would try to find another congressman willing to go there to try to get you out."

Communications with the British Foreign Office, which had an embassy in Aden, convinced me that I represented Ed Franklin's only hope for release. So, despite a deep foreboding, I flew from Washington to New York, then took a direct flight to Beirut, Lebanon, where I boarded a plane to Aden. As the plane approached Aden, I wondered what lay ahead—perhaps unfortunate consequences for me, as well as the family I left behind, and even negative consequences for U.S. foreign policy. What would I do if no one met me at the airport?

To my surprise, a delegation of Aden officials welcomed my arrival. I was escorted to a government guesthouse and provided with a car and driver for the duration of my stay. After three days of discussions with cabinet officials, sight-seeing and anxious waiting, I met President Salim Rubay'a Ali on the evening before my scheduled departure. He detailed Aden's complaints about U.S. policy in the Middle East and then announced good news. My constituent—whom Ali referred to as "the prisoner"—would be released into my custody that night and permitted to join me on my departure the next morning.

The rescue mission was more than just an unusual example of constituent service. It proved to be a major milestone in my life. Looking back, I realize that Aden was my first stop on a long, exciting and instructive journey of exploration into the Islamic world. At subsequent stops, my eyes would be opened to a culture based on honor, dignity and value of every human being, as well as tolerance and the quest for learning—standards that I learned later are deeply engrained in the Islamic religion. These are goals that my Christian forebears would have applauded.

In that faraway land I received my first introduction into the faith of more than a billion people worldwide, a religious community exceeded in number only by Christians who number over two billion. At the time, I did not realize that Muslims were already becoming a substantial and growing minority in America. Nor did I realize that among them were leaders in business, science, arts, academia, the professions, and sports. And I was unaware of the fact that, despite their impressive contributions to American society, widely-held stereotypes grossly distorted public perceptions of Muslims and left their great potential for public service unrecognized and scarcely tapped.

Six years later, during my tumultuous but successful re-election campaign for Congress in 1980, I learned from personal experience how painful stereotyping can be. My opponent portrayed me in nationwide advertising as anti-Semitic—a charge arising from my efforts to bring justice to the Palestinians.

Several Jewish colleagues, both Democrats and Republicans, publicly defended me against the charge, but the stain had spread so widely that I concluded it was impossible to erase. To this day, whenever I meet a Jew for the first time, I wonder if he or she has prejudged me on the basis of a partisan epithet. This personal experience with stereotyping left me with a firm resolve to protest when others suffer false characterizations, and it is one of the factors that led me to write this book.

My discovery of Islam did not happen through a sudden revelation, like discovering a box of treasures in the dark corner of an attic. Instead, gems of understanding surfaced one after another over time, with each discovery provoking new curiosity and questions. My journey did not include the formality of classroom instruction, the perusal of study manuals or reading lists, or even—

with a few exceptions—discussions with Muslims who are known to be Islamic scholars. I learned about Islam from scores of lay Muslims who are engaged in various occupations and reside throughout the United States and beyond. In this book, I present the religion as it is understood and practiced by these ordinary Muslims. I report their disagreement on some points of doctrine and practice but their overriding unity on fundamentals.

B efore my journey began, I held ominous concerns about a looming clash of civilizations—East against West. All my life I had heard about the Judeo-Christian ethic, but no one spoke of the Judeo-Christian-Muslim ethic. In this process of exclusion, Islam became, in my mind, something strange, distant and disquieting. In the absence of corrective messages from Muslims or others, I believed that Christianity and Judaism were linked together as the civilized and progressive West on one side of a great divide. On the other side of this divide was Islam, which I wrongly viewed as a backward and menacing force in the Arab East. These stereotypes flourished in everyday life in America. They formed a worldview that I now recognize as false and misleading.

This is not to suggest that I now put all Muslims on a pedestal. I realize that the misbehavior of some, like that of some professed Christians and Jews, violates their religious pledges and, by any standard, is hypocritical and reprehensible. But I find most Muslims to be good people that I would welcome as next door neighbors. Islam is not purely Eastern, nor is it mainly Arab. Muslims are now more numerous in the United States than the followers of Judaism. This means that, in the demographic sense, Muslims should be considered as American as Jews.

During my visit to Aden, I discovered that Islam, Judaism, and Christianity have common Abrahamic roots and share important beliefs, traditions, and standards of conduct. At subsequent milestones of my journey, I would learn that Islam, like my own Christian faith and the faith of Jews, is rooted in peace, harmony, family responsibility, interfaith respect, humility and equal justice for all humankind under one God. Islam is a universal, multicultural and multiracial religion. It proclaims the brotherhood and equality of all people, regardless of race, nationality, or religious faith.

D espite these fundamental, shared doctrines, Muslims face daily difficulties in America's predominantly Christian society. Most Americans are unacquainted with any Muslim and remain unaware of the fast-growing presence of Muslims in the United States. They have never discussed Islam with anyone informed about the religion and have never read a verse from the Quran. Their perceptions of Islam arise mainly from the negative, false images that emerge from news accounts, movies, television dramas, and talk shows on radio and television.

Most Americans do not deliberately ignore Muslims or harbor hostile opinions of their religious practices and customs, but the challenges Muslims face are at least as severe as the discrimination Jews faced in the United States in the recent past.

In writing this book, my goals are interfaith understanding, tolerance, and cooperation. I am not an evangelist, trying to convert non-believers to the Islamic faith. Nor am I an authority on Islam. I seek only to advance the correct understanding of the religion, an objective that will require sustained, competent leadership, especially by Muslims. The leadership must be provided at every level of society—the family, the neighborhood, the schools, the media, and—most importantly—in the realm of political action. In increasing numbers, Muslims must become active participants in the American political arena.

A promising beginning is under way. As I assembled material for this book, I became impressed by the number of Muslims who are moving, with little fanfare, into community leadership, where they work for interfaith harmony and other civic advances. Some are taking part in partisan electoral campaigns. In my view, these are parallel, complementary undertakings that hold the promise of a better life for all citizens.

I have spent almost my entire life in politics, so political endeavor is never far from my thoughts. I began early. In 1935, at the age of fourteen, I purchased a used mimeograph for five dollars, modest equipment that enabled me to earn income by printing programs and bulletins and lured me into becoming a pamphleteer on a small scale, of course. I distributed to schoolmates and neighbors a series of juvenile commentaries. A year later, in the fall of 1936, I played the cornet with fellow students on the streets of my hometown, where we literally tooted the horn for the Republican candidate for president, Kansas Governor Alf M. Landon. Despite our tooting, Landon failed to defeat President Franklin D. Roosevelt's first bid for re-election. Landon lost every state except Maine and Vermont.

But Landon's defeat only quickened my interest in politics. Ever since, I have followed the political world with keen interest and, except for military service in World War II, I have taken a role in every biennial general election. From personal experience, I know what it's like to lose, as well as to win. In my first quest for public office, in 1952, I made an unsuccessful bid for the Republican nomination for state senator. In 1960, I was elected to the U.S. House of Representatives. My name has been on election ballots twenty-five times. I won eleven of twelve general election campaigns and lost the last one by only a narrow margin. Democrats strongly contested my candidacy in all twelve elections, and Republican candidates challenged me in three of the thirteen primary campaigns. I won all primary election campaigns except the first one. Beyond these personal contests, I often worked on behalf of other candidates and, between elections supported a variety of public causes—delivering speeches, canvassing neighborhoods, and writing articles and books.

I have experienced the personal satisfaction that activists often feel, even when they fail to reach their immediate election-day goals. On the two occasions when I lost, the campaigns opened doors to other important challenges. For example, my failed campaign for state senator established friendships and provided experiences that helped in my successful bid for election to Congress eight years later. I viewed my failure to win a twelfth term on Capitol Hill in 1982 as a dark cloud, but it soon displayed a silver lining. If I had won re-election that year, I probably would never have explored Islam or written this book—or two books on U.S.-Israeli relationships.

M y long endeavors for human rights were inspired by childhood experiences in a small college town in central Illinois, where I witnessed racism that was still conspicuous seventy years after Abraham Lincoln signed the Emancipation Proclamation. I watched as African-Americans were refused service in restaurants, hotels, and barbershops, and required to sit in a corner of the balcony at the local movie theater. And all of this in the Land of Lincoln!

Later, as a teenager, I visited Washington, D.C., and found racism flourishing a few blocks from the Capitol dome. One afternoon during that visit, I boarded a bus that took me across Memorial Bridge. When the bus reached the Virginia side, the driver stopped it and refused to continue until all African-Americans aboard moved to seats in the rear. I was upset at this demeaning relic of slavery.

During service in World War II, I encountered racism deeply rooted in the U.S. Navy. African-Americans were kept separate and usually given menial tasks. All officers were white. I made a mental note to put the advancement of human rights on my postwar agenda. Racism had to go.

I n 1944, the Seabee battalion in which I served took part in the enormous invasion that liberated Guam from the Japanese. Fifteen months later, after the Japanese surrender, my battalion took part in the occupation of Japan. Soon after landing there, I drove a jeep to nearby Nagasaki where a single U.S. atomic bomb had killed over 60,000 civilians a few weeks earlier and forced Japan to end hostilities. I explored the circle of rubble more than two miles in diameter, all that remained of that large industrial city after the single bomb exploded, and reflected on the awesome power of the atom.

My visit to Nagasaki convinced me that if an atomic war should erupt in the future, it could trigger the destruction of all humankind. I resolved that those of us who had struggled successfully against the forces of Adolf Hitler and the Japanese military junta were morally obligated to invest the same sustained commitment in a quest for a new international order that would assure permanent world peace. I remembered that World War I was sometimes called "the war to end all wars." But, instead, it was only the prelude to another, more devastating conflict. The next war, I feared, would be even worse. I entered another goal for my postwar agenda. War, too, had to go.

I became convinced that another war could be averted if the experienced democracies formed a federal union, as proposed in *Union Now,* a book written by *New York Times* foreign correspondent Clarence K. Streit. He proposed a great new government that would transform the principal self-governing, industrialized nations—the United States and fourteen other democracies—into a federation large enough and strong enough, Streit argued, to deter aggression anywhere in the world. It would, at the same time, safeguard basic individual liberties everywhere. Streit and I corresponded during my Navy years, and after the war, I helped him establish in Washington, D.C., the short-lived monthly magazine called *Freedom and Union.*

Eighteen months later, I took a step that ultimately opened the way to elective office. I became editor and part owner of a small weekly newspaper in rural Illinois, a position that provided a medium through which I could vent my political views. It also helped me establish close acquaintances throughout West Central Illinois. These proved to be crucial assets when, in 1960, I conducted a successful campaign for Congress.

When I took the oath as a member of the U.S. House of Representatives in January 1961, none of the issues that I felt needed attention concerned Muslims or the Middle East. At the time, I had no idea what the words Islam or Muslim meant, and if anyone had asked me to name the countries in the Middle East, I would have been able to list only a few. I had little awareness of the complex issues and powerful interests converging in the region, and the few impressions I had of Islam and the Middle East were inaccurate. At the time, most of my colleagues on Capitol Hill shared similar levels of ignorance and disinterest about the Muslim world.

Still, my goals arose from idealism on a grand scale. I wanted to help enact legislation to advance human rights—especially for African-Americans—and to promote a new international institution that would prevent war. I worked enthusiastically for the enactment of the civil rights legislation of the 1960s, even though I knew my votes for these proposals were generally unpopular in the district I represented. As I look back, these votes stand out as the most satisfying of my entire career on Capitol Hill.

In 1963, I began working to mend strained U.S. relations with France, a key North Atlantic Treaty Organization [NATO] ally. In 1965, I caused a mini-storm on Capitol Hill and in my district by leading a small group of Republican colleagues on a controversial week-long fact-finding mission to Paris. In 1966, I stirred even wider protest when, in a speech at Harvard University, I urged normalization of diplomatic relations with the People's Republic of China.

In 1967, my seventh year in Congress, I was appointed to the Foreign Affairs Committee. Later that year, with the help of a bipartisan coalition, I witnessed progress in the Atlantic Union resolution, which was inspired by Clarence Streit's federation proposal. Even though the resolution was denounced as un-American by groups I called misguided patriots, it cleared the House of Representatives Committees on Foreign Affairs and Rules. But, despite strong supportive debate which included endorsements by two future presidential candidates—John B. Anderson of Illinois and Morris K. Udall of Arizona—the resolution was defeated by eighteen votes.

Udall and Anderson, I must note, had exceptional qualities—courage, a delightful sense of humor, and political vision. Years later, in the spring of 1976, when Udall's bid for the Democratic nomination for the presidency had failed, he brought a gale of laughter when he told reporters, "The people have spoken, the stupid bastards."

He must have had the same reaction seven years earlier, in 1973, when our bipartisan group decided to put the federation dream on the shelf. Despite the added support provided by Paul Simon of Illinois, another future presidential candidate, the "misguided patriots" had chipped away at our base of support and the resolution was defeated by a larger margin than before.

T he controversies surrounding these early legislative initiatives may have conditioned me for the challenges that confronted me when I worked for a balanced U.S. policy in the Middle East, one that would be fair to both Arabs and Israelis. I became a member of the Foreign Affairs Committee only a few months before the outbreak of the June 1967 Arab-Israeli war. At that time, I had no acquaintance with anyone I knew to be a Muslim. That would not happen until three years later, and even then, it was a fleeting experience.

During a conversation with Egyptian Ambassador Ashraf Ghorbal, with whom I had developed a close friendship, I casually asked if he was a Muslim. He responded with an amused glance but a cordial affirmative. I was 51 years old. Up to that point, Muslims had been nonexistent in my life. No Muslims lived in my hometown in Illinois. None had been in the student body or faculty at the college I attended. During my three years in the Navy in World War II, and thirteen years as editor of a weekly newspaper, I never encountered—to my knowledge—even one Muslim.

In 1972, Ghorbal invited the Findley family—my wife, Lucille, me, and our two children, Diane and Craig—to visit Egypt. We accepted, and in July 1972 spent an exciting week there, during which we saw Egypt's glorious antiquities and observed its present-day security problems. We were received hospitably in homes and offices and met a number of Muslims, of course, but all conversations centered on the politics and the threat of war, not religion.

At the time, Cairo displayed reminders of the June 1967 Arab-Israeli war in which Egypt suffered heavy losses. Concerned that Israel might resume its air attacks, the Egyptian government had placed protective sandbags at all vital buildings and museum treasures throughout the city. Full diplomatic relations between Egypt and the United States, severed by the war five years earlier, had not been re-established, and Israeli troops still occupied the Sinai peninsula, which was historically a part of Egypt.

On a brief visit to war-battered Suez City on the west bank of the Suez Canal, we glimpsed Israeli soldiers patrolling the East Bank. Warned about land mines, we noted only an occasional sign of human life—laundry hanging out to dry—amid the rubble that once was a large, bustling Egyptian resort community. Nearby, we saw the bombed-out remnants of an oil refinery, once prized as an example of Egyptian economic progress. At the time, we did not realize that the devastation was a grim by-product of a war motivated largely by religious intolerance.

Fifteen months later, in October 1973, the Arab-Israeli conflict flared up again. The conflict was initially perilous to Israel, when its forces, short on equipment and supplies, faced the possibility of defeat. Later, the tide turned against Egypt, when Israeli forces, quickly re-supplied by the United States, approached Cairo.

The war's aftermath prompted me to begin speaking out. I lamented the neglected plight of uprooted Palestinians. These statements put me in the center of a controversy so absorbing and intense that the study of Islam had to wait.

I gave no thought to Islam, the religion of most Palestinians, nor did my colleagues discuss the Islamic facet of the Arab-Israeli conflict. The subject of Islam was largely ignored on Capitol Hill, partly because no Muslim had ever served in Congress. I cannot recall an occasion when Islamic views were presented to a congressional committee. As I reflect on the 1970s, I doubt that even one Muslim could have been found among the more than six thousand people employed in staff positions on Capitol Hill at that time.

As far as I knew, no Muslim resided in my constituency of 450,000 people. My ignorance of Islam was appalling. Despite my deep interest in NATO, I would not have recognized Turkey, a key member of the alliance, as a Muslim country. Perhaps this was because I assumed at the time that Islam was confined to the Arab world.

M y rescue mission to the People's Democratic Republic of Yemen in 1974 had involved stops at two other Muslim countries, Lebanon and Syria. In discussions in Beirut and Damascus, as well as Aden, I gained my first direct insight into Arab grievances over U.S. policy and broadened my understanding of Arab-Israeli politics.[1]

These experiences prompted me to protest against the anti-Arab bias in U.S. Middle East policy when I returned to Capitol Hill from Yemen. I criticized our government's failure to reestablish diplomatic relations with the Aden government and several other Arab states, relations that were severed at the time of the June 1967 war. I urged the U.S. government to suspend all aid to Israel until it stopped violating Palestinian human rights and halted military assaults against Lebanon. I argued that, in the long term, bias against Arabs would be unhealthy and damaging to the interests of the United States and to those of Israel as well.

M y protest campaign against this bias ultimately covered eight years, during which I encountered a mounting level of opposition. I was a lonely advocate for an even-handed policy, a position strongly opposed on Capitol Hill as well as in my home state. It ultimately became a major factor in my defeat on election day in November 1982.

This long, intense experience on the Middle East political firing line was followed by two years of equally intense research, during which I gathered information and wrote my book, *They Dare to Speak Out: People and Institutions Confront Israel's Lobby*. To my astonishment, it became an immediate bestseller with sales exceeding 300,000. It elicited heavy, enthusiastic correspondence from readers. Over nine hundred letters arrived within the first few months after publication. Beginning in the summer of 1985, I made more than forty media appearances on both coasts and in major cities in between. During a three-year period, I accepted numerous invitations, some of them arranged by Arab student groups, to lecture on the campuses of American colleges and universities. I also spoke at events in Canada, Yemen, Jordan, the United Arab Emirates, Saudi Arabia, Iraq, England, and Egypt. These lectures were interspersed with participation in many gatherings, large and small. During informal discussions in several cities, citizens of Arab ancestry explained to me the social and political problems they confronted in daily life.

The book brought profound changes in my life and opened fascinating new doors. Because of it, Muslims came to me, and I to them. In 1989, enthusiasm for the theme of my book motivated a group of men and women to help me establish the Council for the National Interest (CNI), a Washington-based organization of about five thousand Americans who seek balanced U.S. Middle East policies. Muslims, along with Christians and Jews, assisted in CNI's organizational meeting and remain prominent in its leadership and support. Gene Bird, a veteran of the U.S. State Department's foreign service, is CNI's president.

Later that year, a Muslim student sent a videotape of my lecture at Kansas State University to the Islamic Propagation Center International in Durban, South Africa, an organization that distributes Muslim documents and videotapes worldwide. In May 1989, a message arrived from Ahmad Deedat, president of the center. He invited Lucille and me to Cape Town where he wanted me to join him in addressing a public gathering.

We accepted and in July traveled half way around the world to South Africa. It was one of many times that Lucille has shared my journey through Islam, experiences that have enriched our lives, beyond our own religiously mixed marriage, through friendships with people of other religions. Lucille was reared a Roman Catholic, an inheritance of her father's French ancestry and her mother's Irish forebears. My Presbyterian roots go back to Scotland. In recent years, close friendships with Hindu neighbors, the Prabhakar and the Ayyagari families, have broadened our religious horizon even further, making us comfortable with people of other faiths and disinclined to be self-righteous about our own.

T he meetings with Deedat and his staff proved to be a major learning experience. I had talked with a number of Muslims in the United States during book promotion events and lectures, but, until my discussions in South Africa, I did not recognize the extent of false stereotypes about Islam. Nor was I aware of the rapid growth of the Muslim population in the United States. Despite my deep, sustained involvement in Arab-American and Middle East politics, I had overlooked these developments.

The talks in Durban related to Muslim practices as well as principles. During one conversation, a member of Deedat's staff took pains to correct my pronunciation of the word Muslim. I had been mispronouncing it as mooz-lim, or maaz-lim. Ever since, I have encouraged others to say moos-lim, the correct pronunciation. This undertaking may seem trivial, but I learned long ago that pronouncing names correctly communicates respect for a person's identity, and it follows that one's religious identification should also be respected and correctly pronounced.

M ost of the discussions in South Africa focused on Christian misconceptions of Islam. Of the many stereotypes that were considered during these talks, five emerged as being the most obstructive to interfaith and cross-cultural harmony and cooperation. They link Islam with terrorism and fanaticism, subjugation of females, intolerance toward non-Muslims, hostility toward democracy, and worship of an alien, vengeful deity.

In the pages that follow, I illustrate these stereotypes—mostly from personal experiences—and provide a glimpse of what is being done to promote accurate comprehension. It is only a glimpse. In a sense, this book is a diary of my own exploratory journey, during which I corrected my own long-held stereotypes. But it is more than that. It is a record of the sustained endeavors of Muslims, as well as Christians and Jews—the valiant pioneers who form the vanguard of a worthy, long-neglected cause. There are, I am sure, thousands of others whose work is significant but has not come to my attention.

The followers of Islam are, of course, the people best equipped by knowledge, experience, and motivation to advance the correction process. Fortunately, the direct involvement of Muslims in this cause is significant and growing, but, regretfully, most Muslims do not participate. Their reluctance is understandable. Many immigrants are from countries where political activity is nonexistent or narrowly limited, and they hesitate to enter what must seem to them a foreboding free-for-all, often embroiling candidates in charges and counter-charges.

Another disheartening reality is the seamy, unappealing aspect of politics and politicians that dominates U.S. news reports. I know from long years in politics that most elected officials are honest and hardworking, but the media focuses on misdeeds, rare though they may be. Corruption seems always to be lurking at the edge of politics and sometimes at its center.

These somber realities should not discourage good people, especially those called to righteous living by their religious faith, from joining the pioneers. They should accept the responsibility to participate in the process that ultimately decides what government policies will be introduced and who will carry them out.

Engaging in political activity, in my opinion, carries a win-win assurance for all who participate. As Muslims take part, they will broaden interfaith acquaintance and respect. As non-Muslims join in these undertakings, their common cause and personal encounters with the adherents of Islam will dissipate the false notions that distort America's vision of that faith and ease the Muslim anguish that is the inevitable by-product of stereotyping. In time, these efforts will enhance the quality of life for Muslims, both at home and abroad, while strengthening America's record as a land of justice and tolerance.

My role as a catalyst in this process became a topic of conversation after I lectured to a Muslim gathering in

Pomona, California, in September 1999. After hearing my remarks, Dr. Naz Haque, a young professional who provides dental services in a nearby clinic she helped establish for needy children, came to me with a question. She said, "As a Muslim, I am curious to know what led you, a Christian, to become so concerned about the false images of Islam. Was it a particular person or event?"

No one had asked that question before. I paused to collect my thoughts, then told her that it was a cumulative process. Over the years I became convinced that correcting these misconceptions is an important step toward a just Middle East peace, in fact an essential one. Understandably, she responded to this sweeping declaration with a puzzled look.

Fortunately, she waited for me to explain that, in my view, the stereotypes of Islam are harmful to all Americans, not just Muslims. At the neighborhood level, they block interfaith tolerance and harmony. They cause discomfort, distrust, anxiety, even fear, and sometimes they lead to violence. In Washington, they create an unfortunate atmosphere in which legislation harmful to civil liberties is enacted. An example is the law that permits secret evidence to be considered in deportation hearings. At a still higher level, they promote a bias in foreign policy that tarnishes America's worldwide reputation and seriously impairs our nation's ability to provide effective international leadership for human rights, and not just for Muslims.

Before I left the assembly hall, I again caught Haque's attention so that I could add a few thoughts. I told her I was not satisfied with the answer I had provided. I failed to explain how stereotypes can be removed most rapidly. Removal requires political action, politics in the broadest sense. All Americans—Christians, like myself, as well as Muslims—have a responsibility to act. I recognized that her work helps needy children to achieve better health, but I urged her to take a major responsibility in the political arena. The Muslim stereotypes must be cleared away and cleared away promptly. Accepting a responsibility in this cause, I said, need not interfere with her professional service to young people. In fact, taking a constructive role in the political arena is a service to Americans of all ages.

With a smile, she said, "I'll give it some thought."
Perhaps the reader will too.

> PAUL FINDLEY
> 1040 West College Avenue
> Jacksonville, Illinois 62650
> March 20, 2001

Note:

1.   *They Dare to Speak Out,* pp 1–12.

Chapter 1: Hidden Kinship

False stereotypes can hide the truth from people of any age. At the age of six, my introduction to Islam got off to a bad start. While attending Presbyterian Sunday School in Jacksonville, Illinois, I was misled about Muslims and their religion and I harbored the misinformation until middle age.

Our teacher, a kindly volunteer who served faithfully for years, told us that uneducated, primitive, violent people lived in desert areas of the Holy Land and worshiped a "strange God." In one of my earliest childhood recollections, I remember that she called them Muhammadans and kept repeating, "They aren't like us." As she talked, we played in a large sandbox, moving into different positions miniature likenesses of palm trees, camels, tents and nomadic people.

Her comments stuck in my memory. For most of my life I held a vision of Muhammadans as alien, ignorant, threatening people. Like many Americans today, my teacher innocently repeated misinformation she had acquired from other poorly informed people. She recited to our class what she believed to be the truth, including the misnomer "Muhammadans." I do not believe she intended to instill misinformation or defame Islam. She simply lacked the facts, as did other teachers and the ordained minister who led our congregation. The national offices of the Presbyterian Church U.S.A have since issued informed documents about Islam and the need for interfaith understanding. But repairing the damage of earlier times has only begun.

Even a favorite hymn, "To the Knights in the Days of Old," perpetuated false images. Seventy years later, I remember its page number 219 in the hymnal, as well as the tune and the words.

Opening exercises always included group singing, and we sang Hymn 219 lustily. It is a rollicking song that celebrates the Christian Crusades in the Holy Land. "To the knights in the days of old, keeping watch on the mountain heights, came a vision of holy grail and a voice through the waiting night, calling, 'Follow, follow the gleam, banners unfurled, over all the world, follow, follow the gleam of the chalice that is the grail.'"

The hymn conveys a distorted view of Islam that is still widely accepted as accurate by many Christians, perhaps most of them. Its words give no hint that the knights, cast in the hymn as heroes, actually slaughtered thousands of innocent Muslims and rejoiced in the carnage. Calling themselves Christians, the Crusaders ignored their religion's commitment to tolerance, compassion, and justice. They acted instead like vengeful, bloodthirsty savages.

The hymn would have lost all appeal had I known what one of the Crusaders wrote on July 15, 1099, from the bloody scene in Jerusalem: "With drawn swords our people ran through the city; nor did they spare anyone, not even those pleading for mercy. The horses waded in blood up to their knees, nay, up to the bridle. It was a just and wonderful judgment of God."[1] The slaughter was not confined to Jerusalem. The Crusaders, seeking out "heathens and infidels," killed Muslims, Jews, and even other Christians throughout the Middle East, notably in Antioch and Constantinople. In contrast, on the three separate occasions when Muslims took control of Jerusalem, no blood was shed.

N ot until 1998, when I reached the age of seventy-seven, did I know why Muslims object strongly to the misnomer "Muhammadan." Andrew Patterson, an author and convert to Islam, explained: "It conveys a deep misunderstanding of Islam and suggests that Muslims worship the Prophet Muhammad as a deity. They revere and honor Muhammad as God's final messenger, but they do not worship him. In fact, belief in only one God ranks at the top of the five Islamic 'pillars' of faith and commitment." He said the other "pillars" are: engaging in prayer five times a day; giving generously to needy people; fasting during the month of Ramadan;

and, if health and funds permit, making a pilgrimage to Mecca at least once in a lifetime. Muslims who abide by these five obligations are considered observant, or practicing, Muslims.

The misleading term "Muhammadan" may survive, in part, because most Christians, although committed to a faith that is identified universally as monotheistic, believe in a trinitarian deity—God the Son, God the Father, and God the Holy Spirit. Some Christians may wrongly assume that a God in three persons exists in Islam. For others, the trinitarian faith may arise from childhood experiences similar to my own.

False images of Islam from childhood persisted for so long in my experience that it does not surprise me to find other Americans harboring similar misconceptions. It is sobering to reflect on the enormity of the misleading stereotypes of Islam that have flowed, unchallenged year after year, from Sunday School classes throughout America. Millions of impressionable young people may have accepted misinformation as the truth and, over the years, passed it on, uncorrected, to other millions of people.

M y knowledge of Islam began during my 1974 rescue mission in Aden, while conversing with Saleh Abdulla, a trim, handsome and energetic young protocol officer who served for five days as my escort and, unwittingly, as my instructor in Islam. Sight-seeing was limited, and radio broadcasts were in Arabic, a language I did not understand. Fortunately, Abdulla was fluent in English. Television was almost nonexistent. During the long hours we spent together, we reviewed Middle East politics, but our conversation seemed to gravitate regularly to Islam. Perhaps the subject attracted me because I felt the isolation of South Yemen, the lack of news from the outside world, the absence of crowds and heavy vehicular traffic, the tranquility of the desert, the emptiness of the glistening beaches, and the vastness of the Gulf of Aden. It was the first time I had discussed the faith of Muslims with anyone.

One day, as we toured the city, Abdulla identified a white-washed building as a mosque and said it was one of several in the city. This prompted me to ask if the Soviets, noted for both atheism and autocratic rule, had interfered with local religious traditions and closed the mosques.

"No. You must understand that our government is completely independent of foreign influence," he replied with understandable exaggeration. "We prize our independence very highly. I am positive that the Soviets, who have been helpful in many ways, have made no attempt to interfere with religion. It would do them no good if they tried."

I mentioned my Christian affiliation and asked if his government tolerated other religions. "Yes. Christians and others are welcome to practice their faith. Our government guarantees freedom of religion. In fact, just ahead on the left is a Christian church. It has few members now, but it used to be busy in the days when Aden was under British control. I believe all our people are deeply devoted to Islam. Young people are thoroughly instructed in the religion and are required to study the Quran, our holy book. All of us keep studying it, no matter how old we are. Many Yemenis, probably thousands here in Aden, have studied it so thoroughly that they can recite every word from memory."

I did not respond, but I found the last statement impressive. Some Christians of my acquaintance can recite portions of the Bible, but none the entire text or to my knowledge, even the text of one of its books. Only a small percentage of Muslims, I assumed, could recite the entire Quran, but all seem to have memorized large parts. Since then, as I question Muslims about Islam, a habit I developed during my time with Abdulla, their responses almost always include a suitable quotation from the Quran.

Abdulla said that our sightseeing that day was deliberately scheduled for Friday, a holiday. "Government officials are not available for appointments today, so this is the ideal time to look around Aden. Almost all offices and government services stay closed on Friday, the day of the week that Muslims observe as a special day of congregational prayer at the mosque."

When I said that Christians make Sunday the special day for prayer, he interjected, "For Muslims, every day is a day for prayers. Our faith calls us to pray five times a day, not just in the mosque on

Fridays." I couldn't resist offering this response: "I hope you will not be offended if I ask a personal question. We have been together long hours every day, and I haven't yet seen you kneel in prayer. Are you excused because you are with me?" Abdulla took no offense. "You just haven't noticed. The schedule allows me to pray at the required times while you are busy with other things, and prayer takes only a few minutes. As you know, we have rested separately during the heat of each day. I have maintained my prayer schedule. Islamic law does not permit us to skip prayers, and only when weather conditions are very bad, or when we are traveling, can we delay prayers."

A t that point, the driver, who spoke no English, brought our car, a well-worn Chevrolet, to a halt in front of a low, sprawling building. Abdulla explained: "This is the military museum. It is normally closed on Fridays, but it has been opened for you. We want you to see the military equipment our forces have captured during recent border fighting with Saudi Arabia and Oman. You will find that all of it is marked 'made in the United States.'"

Fareeda Daair, the museum guide, was eighteen, trim, attractively attired in western dress and like Abdulla, fluent in English. She was completing a year's required government service before studying pharmacy. In a short speech of welcome, she expressed pride in her country and enthusiasm about Islam. She added, "In our country, women have equal rights with men. All jobs are open to us, and we have the same political rights as men. This, as you probably know, is the Islamic way."

I didn't know. I later learned that in some Muslim countries, women do not have the same political and employment rights as men. Before arriving in Aden, I had assumed that Muslim women were kept at home and subjected to discrimination. As we left the museum, Abdulla said, "If we have time to visit villages in the desert, you will find that most women there follow ancient custom of dressing in black from head to toe, and wear veils over their faces. Many women in Aden, like Daair, wear western attire."

T he discussions of Islam with Abdulla were just the beginning of my education. It continued through the years that followed—unstructured, periodic, informal, and unplanned, with no classrooms, assignments, or examinations.

I have learned about Islam through correspondence and conversations stretching over twenty-five years with Muslims who live in Los Angeles, Chicago, Nashville, Washington, D.C., New York City, Houston, St. Louis, West Ontario, Cairo, Jeddah, Amman, and Penang, in Malaysia.

The information, as they say in court, is personally received, not hearsay.

While in a New Jersey mosque, I had an unforgettable experience. I observed for the first time Muslims at prayer, worshippers of different ethnicity and race going through the ritual, shoulder to shoulder. After the prayer, a blonde-haired visitor from London, told me, "I came to Islam at the age of forty and have found it very satisfying."

In Los Angeles, I gained a larger view of Muslims in America. Salam Al-Marayati, the son of Iraqi immigrants, and later to become director of the Muslim Affairs Council in Los Angeles, escorted me through the Los Angeles Islamic Center of Southern California. Like many other centers in America, this one provides a place for worship, a curriculum for elementary students, meeting rooms, and a large bookstore.

Al-Marayati has had his own journey of religious discovery. He recounted in the *Los Angeles Herald-Examiner* the religious awakening he experienced after entering college: "My heart felt empty. I had been preoccupied with self-gratification, a common American weakness. I concluded that my purpose on earth was not merely to establish a niche in the ecosystem, not merely to multiply, then die. My ambition led me to the Quran, which is a great resource of human understanding, where I learned more about our world, our history, ourselves, and our Creator."[2]

Al-Marayati gained a new appreciation of Islamic marriage and parenting when his wife, Laila, a physician and former president of the Muslim Women's League, attended an international conference on women held in Beijing, China. In her absence, he cared for their two young sons. He wrote that the experience helped him understand why "Islamic law says that women can keep their maiden names after marriage and that their personal income cannot be spent by their husbands, [and why] the husband also must share duties around the house or provide housekeepers for his wife." He said it led him to cite "harmony, compassion, justice, and liberty" as the "main social objectives of Islam."[3]

O ther glimpses of Islam followed in 1988 when I made my first trip to the Middle East after leaving Congress. One day, while riding in an automobile near Riyadh, Saudi Arabia, I noticed a shepherd kneeling alone, engaged in noontime prayer. Later, at a construction site inside the capital city, I observed a lonely figure in mid-afternoon prayer. Visiting later in a beach house near Jeddah, prayer again came to my attention. My host, Hamid Baghaffar, a prominent merchant, excused himself. As he stepped toward an adjoining room, he must have noticed a puzzled look on my face, because he paused to say, "It's prayer time. I will be gone only about ten minutes." Then he added, "Prayer reminds us of God." When I called on a businessman in Jeddah, I waited at his desk while, a few feet away, touching his forehead to a prayer rug, he completed noontime prayers.

Later that same year, back in America, I met two Muslims, Zainab Elberry, a Nashville financial services representative for MetLife, and her husband, Dr. Nour Naciri, an economist and lay scholar on Islam born in Morocco. After reading my book, *They Dare To Speak Out*, Elberry, born in Egypt, had arranged a local lecture date for me. Then, at my request, she became the first Muslim to serve as a member of the board of directors of the Council for the National Interest. Her commitment to human rights and enthusiasm for Islam, together with Naciri's willingness to share his detailed knowledge of Islam and its history, steadily advanced my Islamic education over the years that followed. Naciri's late father served Morocco's late King Hassan as Minister of Islamic Affairs.

Elberry is an effective ambassador of goodwill on behalf of Muslims and Arab-Americans in the Nashville area. She is a leader of the local International Committee and other civic groups, specializing in interfaith and interracial projects. The *Nashville Tennessean* once described her as a "one-person embassy." She also works in partisan campaigns, helping candidates for public office. She played a key role as a leader of Women for Gore in the 2000 presidential campaign of Vice-President Al Gore. In addition to raising funds, she supplied pastries to his national headquarters in Nashville so abundantly that she won recognition on national television as the "pie lady."

During several trips to Saudi Arabia and the United Arab Emirates, I broadened my acquaintance with Muslims. In 1988, I toured a high-tech museum sponsored by Aramco in the Eastern Province of Saudi Arabia, where computer terminals display reviews of Islamic contributions to civilization. I suggested to the museum director that installing a set of the terminals for public viewing in the Smithsonian Institution in Washington could help correct U.S. stereotypes of Islam.

Two years later, I had the first of several meetings with businessman Ahmad Salah Jamjoom, a former government official who leads several Islamic organizations and, at the time, served as director general of the Jeddah-based *Al Madina* daily newspaper. In Dubai, businessman Easa Salah Al Gurg became my close friend and counselor.

My most intensive exposure to public misconceptions of Islam came in September 1993 in Penang, Malaysia, when I participated in a week-long workshop that examined anti-Muslim stereotypes. The most sustained influence came from Andrew Patterson, a native of Illinois now teaching English at a university in China. We have corresponded for years.

In 1989, when Chicago Professor M. Cherif Bassiouni sent me a copy of his beautifully illuminated book, *Introduction to Islam,* I made rapid progress on my journey. I had first met Bassiouni in

1974, when he visited me on Capitol Hill after reading about my rescue mission in Aden. An expert in international law, he was then under consideration for appointment as legal adviser to the U.S. Secretary of State.

His book is one of the most concise and graphically attractive presentations of Islam that I have seen. He defines the Quran: "It is simply the last of the divine messages to reach humankind through the Prophet Muhammad, who was chosen by the Creator as the bearer of his last and all-encompassing revelations. This explains why there exists a strong link between Islam, Christianity, and Judaism."

He cites interfaith links: "Christians and Jews are referred to in the Quran as the 'people of the Book' because they are the recipients of the messages of the Creator through Moses and the Old Testament prophets and through Jesus who, in Islam, is believed to be the fruit of a miracle birth by the Blessed Virgin Mary."[4]

The Quran was revealed centuries after the Old and New Testaments came into being and contains frequent references to early biblical prophets, including Abraham, Noah, David, Isaac, Jacob, and Moses. It accords special esteem to Jesus, who is mentioned by name thirty-three times, and to the Virgin Mary, who is mentioned thirty-four times—the only woman mentioned by name in the Quran.[5]

Verse 3:84 in the Quran reads: "Say: We believe in God, and in what has been revealed to Abraham, Ismail, Isaac, Jacob, and the tribes, and in [the books] given to Moses, Jesus and the prophets from their Lord: We make no distinction between one and another among them, and to God do we submit in Islam."

One of the tributes to the mother of Christ Jesus is recorded in verse 3:45: "Behold! The angels said; 'O Mary! God giveth thee glad tiding of the word from Him: his name will be Christ Jesus, the son of Mary, held in honor in this world and the hereafter and of those nearest to God.'"

Bassiouni describes the Islamic links with Christianity as "fundamental," noting that Muslims, like Christians and Jews, worship the One God, the Creator of the Universe. He notes the importance of Arabic words that are used universally by Muslims, no matter what their native language may be. For example, Allah is the Arabic word for God and is used by both Muslim and Christian Arabs. In the front of the Gideon Bible, the word "Allah" appears where John 3:16 in the New Testament is repeated in several different languages. The word "hallelujah," used commonly in Christian hymns, is derived from the word Allah. In Arabic, Islam means peaceful submission to the will of God, and a Muslim is one who submits. In that sense, I believe, Christians can consider themselves "muslims" because they too pledge submission. Like Christians and Jews, Muslims are pledged to peace as the spiritual heirs of Abraham.

Bassiouni explains that *quran* is an Arabic word that means reading or recitation. The *Quran* is the recitation in Arabic of the Word of God as revealed over a period of twenty-three years to the Prophet Muhammad. The revelations began in Mecca in 610 A.D. and concluded in Madina in A.D. 632, the year of the Prophet's death. He dictated them to scribes who entered them on pieces of cloth, bones, or other durable surfaces. Just before his death, they were compiled in book form, an Arabic text of one hundred fourteen chapters that remains unchanged and its accuracy unchallenged by Muslims to this day.

Records of the Prophet's sayings and deeds, called the Hadith, explain and supplement the Quran. They provide guidance for Muslim daily life and specify ways to resolve conflicts among individuals and between the individual and the state. But Bassiouni offers a word of caution: "The influence of Islam must not be viewed in a narrowly legalistic light, but rather as providing a framework which guarantees basic fairness and justice to all. Repentance and mercy are among Islam's great themes."[6]

Although Christians and Muslims have much in common, there are differences, for example, in their relationship with God. For Muslims, it is always direct and personal. Islam has no equivalent of the formal clergy that guides Christianity and Judaism. Muslims have leaders, usually called imams, but none is granted or ordained to any religious authority over other Muslims. Bassiouni explains that the imam serves as the leader of Friday congregational prayer and is "usually either a person schooled in Islam or simply one among the group who is more knowledgeable, older, or recognized by the others as being especially pious." A mufti is a scholar who issues interpretations of the Quran.

Bassiouni writes that the Prophet, "drawing inspiration from the Quran," prescribed the frequency and manner of prayer: "Standing shoulder to shoulder, irrespective of status in life, symbolizes equality before God. At each kneeling, the Muslim places his forehead on the ground, a symbol of the equality of all men, humility, worship of the Creator, and the fact that from earth we come and to earth we return. All praying Muslims face Mecca, which provides unity and uniformity for all Muslims. Before prayers, Muslims are required to perform ablutions, which include washing face, hands, forearms, and feet in a ritual prescribed by the Quran and the Prophet. This is not only for purposes of cleanliness, but to provide a break from prior activity." During the Friday congregational prayers, there is never a distinction among worshippers on the basis of race, wealth, power or prestige.[7]

Through the prayer ritual, the Prophet Muhammad gave instructions on personal hygiene, as well as piety. Engaging in the rigors of prayer is an excellent program of physical exercise, and, as I learned from a Muslim neighbor, the requirement of cleanliness is precise and exacting.

Riding over dusty roads one day in rural Yemen, a professor who served as our escort, looked at his watch and said, "It's prayer time, but there is no place to wash up, so I will have to delay it. I am not clean enough to pray." When I recently mentioned his comment, Dr. Mohammed Bashardost, a friend since my days in Congress, said my escort could have prayed in the absence of water. He explained that, when necessary, Muslims can meet the cleanliness requirement by symbolically wiping their hands against clean sand, stone, or even by pressing their hands against a wall, then wiping them over the face and arms.

Bashardost and his family, refugees from Afghanistan, gave us glimpses of the Islamic religion when they became our neighbors in a Washington suburb late in my congressional career. Our family helped Bashardost, his wife, and their four children complete their adjustment to American life. In turn, they expanded our knowledge of Islam. Over a bountiful meal that marked Eid Al-Fitr, the holiday marking the end of the month of Ramadan, they explained the Islamic requirement of fasting—no food or drink during daylight hours throughout that month.

Later, on a hot afternoon, I learned about modesty in attire. Several neighborhood women were gathered together, engaged in backyard sunbathing. Chatting over the backyard fence with Dr. Bashardost, I assured him that his wife would be welcomed to join the scantily clad women. He explained that she would not, as public sunbathing violates the Islamic rule of modesty in attire, a rule that applies to both men and women.

I learned later that the fasting requirement led to embarrassment for a Los Angeles child. Salam Al-Marayati began observing the fasting requirement while in the fourth grade, but he found it difficult to explain to his non-Muslim playmates. Years later, he described his dilemma: "Since I could not explain this concept to my friends, I told them 'my parents are making me do it.' Of course, my peers developed a terrible feeling toward my mother and father. Later on, thank God, I gained the courage to explain the lesson of fasting—to learn will power and to nurture the spiritual aspect of our bodies. My high school friends learned and understood this aspect of my lifestyle. They came to respect my parents and me for fasting, and more important, they began to have respect for Islam."[8]

Few Christians observe religious obligations as rigorous as the ones that Muslims accept. Our family bowed heads for a brief prayer before meals and could always be found at church on Sunday mornings. Church attendance was an unspoken but firm obligation, as much a part of life as eating, sleeping, and breathing. Some self-denial was expected during the days before Easter Sunday, and Catholics abstained from eating meat on Fridays. Some of these practices have faded or disappeared, but even at their height they seem modest when compared with those of the Muslim faith.

Several Muslims who have met the obligation to visit Mecca describe it as one of life's greatest experiences. It is also a leveling one, as princes and paupers dress alike. One morning years ago, while waiting in the lobby of a hotel in Jeddah, Saudi Arabia, I watched as people boarded vehicles for nearby Mecca. All were garbed alike in simple white cloaks. I could not tell who was rich or poor, noble or commoner. In the summer of 1999, Daifallah Hindawi, a young Jordanian I had first met when he was attending a U.S. university, telephoned from his workplace in Dubai after returning from Mecca. Not usually given to exuberance, he offered a joyous report: "It was the most profound experience of my life. We prayed for everyone in the world, not just for ourselves, not just for Muslims."[9]

B eyond the fundamental requirements of prayer, abstinence, and charity, Muslims are enjoined to be restrained in critical language and to be tolerant and respectful of other religions.

Restraint in criticism surfaced when I was interviewing Nathaniel Ham, an African-American Muslim who is gaining prominence in Republican Party activity in New York City. I asked for his views of Louis Farrakhan, the controversial leader of the Nation of Islam, an organization of African-Americans whose interpretation of the Quran was, at the time, challenged by mainstream Muslims. Because my notes of the interview were incomplete, I telephoned Ham for clarification. I said, "When I talked to you at the Muslim Center in Queens, you criticized Louis Farrakhan. I made this call to make sure I quote your criticism correctly." Ham responded, "I am very glad you called, because my comment was not personal criticism of Mr. Farrakhan. I always make a point of avoiding personal criticism of anyone."

Muslims may be far ahead of Christians in their study of sacred literature. In my Sunday School experience, elementary age children memorized a few Bible verses and psalms. A high point of my youth was the moment during opening exercises when I stood before what seemed to be an enormous crowd and recited from memory the names of the books of the Bible. I raced through the names so rapidly that the recitation took only slightly more than a minute, but once finished I thought I had climbed a mountain. Compared to the achievements of Muslims, who commit to memory the entire Quran, my performance was modest indeed.

Muslims may also have an edge on some Christians in their literal acceptance of biblical text. At an interfaith meeting of religious leaders several years ago in Calcutta, Rev. Moncure D. Conway, a Christian of the Unitarian denomination, was asked to comment on the miraculous birth of Jesus, as reported in the Bible. In his response, Conway described it to the group as "a story of mythological and poetic interest but not to be regarded as historical." When the dozen or more high-ranking Muslims attending the meeting were asked for their view, they consulted together, then had a spokesman report that all of them felt "bound to accept the narrative just as it stands in the New Testament."

Conway wryly concluded that the Muslims were the only truly orthodox Christians present at the meeting. Later, he wrote: "Muslims are not Christians but [they are] the only ones in the East who maintain literally all of the miracles ascribed to Christ in the gospels or related passages in the Bible concerning His birth. It is very rare to find among them a skeptic."[10]

The Christian-Muslim kinship runs deep in history. Both Christianity and Islam exalt primary scriptures as the Word of God. For Christians, it is the Bible. For Muslims, it is the Quran. Both religions also have secondary literature that Inayat Lalani, a Texas physician, believes has waxed and waned in acceptance and have contributed at times to setbacks in both religious communities. In a letter, he states, "For Christians, this literature includes the works of Augustine, Aquinas, Dante, Luther, Calvin and Melanchthon. For Muslims, it includes: the Hadith, the reports of the sayings and actions of the Prophet Muhammad; the Sunnah, the customs and traditions of the Prophet; and the Shariah, the Islamic law derived from the Quran and the Sunnah."

Throughout history, Lalani notes an ebb and flow in the commitment of both Christianity and Islam to human rights, but he believes the steps forward in both communities have overcome periodic slippage: "Man surely progresses." He believes that, over time, both religious communities have made great strides advancing human rights but not in "lock-step" with each other. "Human rights were acknowledged and promoted by Muslims long before they became the norm in the West. Under the influence of Islam, the Arab-Muslim community pulled far ahead of Christendom during Islam's Golden Age, the period between the eighth and the fifteenth centuries. Christendom started its forward march in the thirteenth century, just before the Arab-Muslim community started sliding back. Religion played a very big part in all of this."

D r. Ralph Braibanti, a noted scholar and author, believes Islam is now experiencing a rise in acceptance worldwide at a time when Christianity seems, in some respects, to be losing ground. "The Muslim value system appears to be more pristine, more intact, than the doctrines of Christianity which are increasingly being rele-gated to the realm of myth or fanaticism.... Islam, on the other hand, is in a dynamic, effervescent stage of development."

Braibanti, an Episcopalian, cautions that Islam will rise to its full potential only if Muslims give close attention to the public image of Islam, as well as the behavior of individual Muslims. "At this moment in history, the dynamics and clearly defined values of Islam have the potential for resuscitating the western world's decline to morbidity. This can be done only if the image projected by Islam on the global screen and the actions of Muslims on the world stage are compatible with Islamic principles of peace, justice, and reverence for life."[11]

Lalani, in a somewhat contrasting view, notes a deepening problem. He is concerned that some Muslim leaders fail to recognize the flexibility and non-dogmatic character of the Quran, qualities that he believes nurtured the advances in Islam's early history. He writes,

"Compared to the canonic literature of Judeo-Christianity, the Quran is a remarkably non-dogmatic document. Over and over again, a verse in the Quran starts out pronouncing what sounds like a dogmatic, inflexible injunction and with equal frequency it stops in mid-sentence with startling abruptness, leaving one to ruminate about God's mercy, omniscience, and omnipotence to soften the harshness of His judgment.

"Since human affairs are too complex—with many factors that mitigate man's transgressions—and since man must have room to progress even beyond the highest standards of conduct appropriate for the age in which the revelation of the Quran occurred, such ambiguities are entirely appropriate for God, or so it appears to me. God did not want to stop man dead in his tracks as he marched toward ever greater heights of perfection."

Lalani continues, "Contrast that flexibility with the certitude of Paul and Augustine, whose positions now seem to be losing ground in Christendom's day-to-day life and are in danger of outright repudiation. Even the mainstream Protestant churches such as Lutheran and Reformed Calvinist politely put aside the doctrines of predestination and justification by faith alone and by grace. In my view, the Reformation's zeal for purity was simply the restatement of the dogmas of Paul and Augustine, inspired by the corruption of the Papacy and spurred on by taunting Muslims. But, with the exception of the writings of Thomas Aquinas and Erasmus, the sixteenth century Reformation missed the point of Christ's teaching.

"Today, however, the Arab-Muslim community appears to be in danger of missing the point with regards to the Quran, losing the commendable restraint demonstrated by Muslim leaders during Islam's Golden Age. I am referring to the ongoing trend toward elevating Islam's secondary scriptures to almost the same level as the Quran. The trend is unfortunate, because many of the secondary texts are clear attempts to undo the work of the Prophet Muhammad and resurrect the pre-Islamic darkness as it concerns the woman's position in the Islamic society.

"I am loath to compare religions. All religions are good, and God is benevolent. However, there appears to be more editing by human beings of Judeo-Christian scriptures than of Islamic scriptures by Muslims. The influence of what I call secondary texts on Christian thought until the eighteenth century was much greater than the influence Islam's secondary scriptures has had on Muslim society in recent times."[12]

R ev. John S. Kay, pastor of the First Presbyterian Church in Jacksonville, Illinois, where I am a member, makes this observation, "God has a high tolerance for ambiguity."

T he flexibility that Lalani finds in the Quran should encourage non-Muslims to reject the widely-held stereotypes that present Islam as a dogmatic, unyielding, vengeful, and harsh religion.

Tolerance is among the foremost doctrines of both Christianity and Islam, but there are times and places when it is missing and the kinship between the two religions goes unrecognized.

I believe that interfaith kinship is broadly recognized by Muslims, more so than by Christians. This is evident in the fact that Islam accepts both Christianity and Judaism as religions based on divine revelation. As Christians become more aware of this relationship, they will begin to speak of the Judeo-Christian-Islamic heritage, a term more accurate than the oft-used Judeo-Christian expression.[13]

The most astounding and gratifying revelation of my Islamic sojourn is the emergence of overwhelming evidence that a close kinship exists between Christianity and Islam, especially in primary literature. It is astonishing because it is the exact opposite of what most U.S. Christians believe. It is gratifying because of the assurance of great interfaith cooperation it offers, once Christians and Muslims learn the truth about each other. It challenges my Sunday School teacher's repeated declaration that Muslims, the people she mistakenly identified as "Muhammadans," are "not like us."

M ost Muslims of my acquaintance are strict in their observance of Islam's five pillars, a record that marks them as observant or practicing Muslims, but others have stated candidly and without hesitation that they do not always observe the prayer and charity pillars. In acknowledging their shortcomings, they nevertheless identify themselves as Muslim. This admission echoes a parallel practice of many Christians, who attend church services only on Easter and Christmas, if at all, but still consider themselves to be Christian. Attendance at church services does not necessarily establish piety or fidelity to Christian precepts, but it is noteworthy that about one-half of the people on the membership rolls of Christian churches are seldom in the pews for worship.

I am unable to cite published estimates of the number of Muslims who are considered non-observant, but several of my Muslim acquaintances believe that at least one-half of the people who consider themselves Muslim belong in that classification. Others place the estimate as high as 70 to 80 percent. Accurate information is illusive. Attendance at a mosque is not among the five pillars of the faith. Another factor is the Islamic tradition that prohibits one Muslim inquiring into another Muslim's sins or other personal shortcomings.

P rince Charles of Great Britain, heir to the British throne whose occupant is the titular head of the Church of England, believes Christians can learn a lot from Muslims. In a televised address in 1993 at Oxford University, he noted Islam's contributions to Western civilization and added, "Islam can teach us today a way of understanding and living in the world which Christianity is the poorer for having lost. At the heart of Islam is its preservation of an integral view of the universe. Islam refuses to separate man and nature, religion and science, mind and matter, and has preserved a metaphysical and unified view of ourselves and the world around us."[14]

Ibrahim Abu-Rabi, co-director of the Duncan Black MacDonald Center for the Study of Islam and Christian-Muslim Relations, expressed a parallel view while lecturing in April 1999 at Hartford Seminary in Connecticut. He observed that Islam strives to keep the "sense of the sacred" intact and added, "Ponder for a moment the great Hajj season when men and women from all strata of society, rich and poor, Arab and non-Arab, go to Mecca prostrating themselves before the Divine and begging for mercy and compassion."

Abu-Rabi pleaded for interfaith cooperation, "It is important to focus on building new theological and intellectual links among our three traditions, namely Judaism, Christianity and Islam—links that seem to have been lost in certain phases of human history.... It is only through rediscovering that immense reservoir of our spiritual underpinning that we can resurrect those links for our sake and the sake of our children."[15]

Notes:

1. Hassan Hathout, *Reading the Muslim Mind*, p. 38–39.
2. *LA Herald Examinder*, 2-26-1989, p. F–11.
3. *Los Angeles Times*, 3-8-1996 p. A15.
4. M. Cherif Bassiouni, *Introduction to Islam*, p. 28.
5. Bill Baker, *More in Common Than You Think*, p. 43.
6. Bassiouni, *An Introduction to Islam*, p. 42–44.
7. Ibid., p. 32.
8. *LA Herald Examiner*, 2-26-1989 p. F-1.
9. Letter, 8-1-00.
10. Ralph Braibanti, *The Nature and Structure of the Islamic World*, p. 76.
11. Ibid., p. 86.
12. Letter, 5-28-2000.
13. Ibid., p. 16.
14. Ibid., p. 38.
15. Hartford Seminary, *Praxis*, April 1999, p. 3.

Chapter 2: Strangers in Our Midst

66 You are doing what!" a startled neighbor exclaimed when I told him my latest project is writing a book about U.S. Muslims. Similar reactions came from other friends in Jacksonville, Illinois, a college town of 25,000 where we have made our home since 1984. They were puzzled and yet none pursued the subject, perhaps because they have no personal acquaintance with Muslims and preferred to talk about topics that they considered more relevant in their everyday lives.

They may not realize how close to home U.S. Muslims really are. Many Muslims live in nearby St. Louis, Chicago and Springfield, but only twelve reside in our home county. They are Attorney Allen Yow, his economist wife Rasha, and their young son; Saleem Mahmoud, M.D., his wife and two children; Shahnaz Rao, M.D., her husband Aleem and their young son; Jill Vorbeck, the wife of a farmer and orchardist; and Dan Clark, the owner of a filter service. Three of them—Allen Yow, Vorbeck, and Clark are converts. Mr. and Mrs. Yow have led discussions of Islam in several local churches.

America has been home to hundreds of thousands of Muslims for generations. The exact number is not known, but projections in recent statistical studies placed the total at over six million in 1999 and forecast seven million in the year 2000. Publications of the American Muslim Council placed the total at five million in 1992, seven million in 1996, and eight million in 1999.[1] An Associated Press report published in the *Chicago Tribune* on March 17, 2000, estimated the total at ten million.

A precise total is elusive for three main reasons: records are not kept at a single source;[2] the U.S. Census Bureau is not permitted to ask citizens to identify their religious affiliation; and officials at mosques do not customarily keep records of worshippers.

U.S. Muslims are hard to count because a large majority of them are not associated with any Islamic organizations. Abdurahman Alamoudi, director of the American Muslim Council Foundation in Washington, D.C., estimates that at least two-thirds are unaffiliated.[3] *The Oxford Encyclopedia of the Modern Islamic World,* edited by Dr. John L. Esposito and published in 1995, puts the estimate still higher, at 90 percent.[4]

Howard University Professor Sulayman Nyang, president of New York's Center for American Muslim Research and Information, explains: "American Muslims, like their religious counterparts in the larger society, are divided into two broad categories, namely, those who practice the faith and flock to the Masajid (mosques) and those who stay away from the religious centers and are therefore overlooked or missed by the head counters of the Muslim establishment."[5] He estimates that those who "stay away" are a substantial majority. Some scholars estimate that only 10 percent pray at mosques with any regularity.[6]

Leaders of Muslim organizations accepted six million as a conservative estimate for 1999, but Dr. Musa Qutub, president of Chicago's Islamic Information Center of America and a member of the faculty of Northeastern Illinois University, considers that figure far too low. He writes, "I believe the total could be as high as 16 million, a figure I have seen several times in the *Chicago Tribune* and on network television."[7] The 2000 edition of *World Almanac*[8] estimated the U.S. total at 5,500,000, up from 3,332,000 in 1999.[9] *The Oxford Encyclopedia,* published in 1995, ventured only a guess, "some three to four million adherents...."[10]

Scholars Ilyas Ba-Yunus of Cortland State University, New York, and M. Moin Siddiqui of East-West University in Chicago, after analyzing available data and using conservative projections, arrived at these rounded totals: five million in 1990; six million in 1995; and seven million in the year 2000. Their forecast for January 2000 was 6,712,960. They are the authors of *A Report on Muslim Population in the United States of America,* published in July 1998 by the Center for American Muslim Research and Information, New York City. *Muslims of Illinois: A Demographic Report* written by Ba-Yunus and published by Chicago's East-West University in 1997, provides data that support the estimate of seven million estimate.

Estimates in 1993 put the number of mosques at eight hundred. Six years later, the total had risen, by one estimate, to two thousand. Others believed the actual total is much higher. In Chicago alone, for example, a study by the Islamic Society of North America listed four hundred recognized places for congregational prayer, some of them small halls that are used for non-religious purposes the rest of the week. The Research Center at the Council for American Islamic Relations [CAIR] estimates the total number of Islamic organizations, including mosques, at 6,000.

A lthough there is a perceptible trend of U.S. Muslims moving to rural communities, most live in large cities in industrialized states. More than one million live in California, slightly less in New York. Other estimates: about 400,000 in Illinois; approximately 300,000 each in New Jersey, Michigan and Indiana; and smaller concentrations are found in Virginia, Texas, Ohio, and Maryland.[11] Among urban areas, New York City leads the nation with the largest Muslim population, followed, in order, by Los Angeles, Chicago, San Francisco, Detroit, Boston, St. Louis, Houston, and Miami. An August 2000 poll commissioned by the American Muslim Council and conducted by Zogby International showed a surprising dispersal of U.S. Muslims: 32.2 percent in the East; 25.3 percent in the South; 24.3 percent in the Central Great Lakes; and 18.2 percent in the West.

M ost of the early Muslim arrivals came to America in chains. They were Blacks who were sold into slavery, beginning in 1530, in West Africa to white traders and shipped across the Atlantic to Brazil, then into the Caribbean, and later to British colonies that would become the United States. Over the years, in one of the most shameful chapters in our history, an estimated ten million human beings, about 25 percent of them Muslim, were placed in permanent bondage in the United States and forced to forsake their religion. A provision of the U.S. Constitution required an end to the importation of slaves by 1808, but slavery itself did not end until 1865, twenty-six years after the British outlawed the practice.[12]

All other Muslims came to our shores voluntarily, and a few were among North America's earliest visitors. An ancient document suggests that Muslim sailors visited North America in 1178, three centuries before the first voyage here by Columbus. Several of these sailors were from China, others from West Africa.[13] In 1312, Muslims from the Mali region of Africa were the first to explore the interior of the future United States, using the Mississippi River as their access route. In 1492, Christopher Columbus had several Muslims in his crew on his successful voyage to the New World. He also carried with him a document in which the Arab scholar Al-Idrissi mentioned the discovery years earlier of a new continent by eight Muslim explorers.[14]

A mong later immigrants were Muslims from Spain and North Africa who had escaped the Catholic Inquisition by joining Spanish explorers. Some of them settled in Florida and the American Southwest, and Muslims were among the Chinese who helped build the transcontinental railroad system. The largest concentrated immigration of Muslims began in the late 1960s, mostly from South Asia and Arab states. Major Muslim immigrations began after the Civil War, and other increases coincided with wars and depressions.[15] By 1995, U.S. Muslims were divided evenly between immigrant and native born, with fifty different ethnic groups represented.

Among Muslims, African-Americans were, for long, the largest ethnic group, one-third of the total.[16] Ba-Yunus and Siddiqui concluded five years ago that those of Arab origin represented 32 percent of the total, while African-Americans and those of South Asian origin were 29 percent each. Those of Turkish and Iranian background were 5 and 3 percent, respectively. Other studies have shown a higher percentage of those of South Asian origin, with a lower percentage of both blacks and those of Arab ancestry.[17] A 1992 study reported the black component at 42 percent.[18] Eight years earlier, the nation's Muslim population was estimated as consisting of one million of African ancestry, 900,000 from Arab countries in the Middle East, 450,000 from Pakistan and India, and the remainder from the Balkans, Albania, Turkey, Iran, and North Africa.[19] A 1998 analysis of the one billion two hundred million Muslims worldwide concluded that Arabs and those of Arab ancestry constituted about 10 percent of the total, a contrast to their larger percentage in America. A Zogby International poll, taken in August 2000, showed the following percentages by origin: Middle East Arab 26.2; South Asia 24.7; African-American 23.8; Middle East Non-Arab 10.3; East Asia 6.4; other areas of origin 11.6.

Although African-Americans now constitute only 25 percent of the total U.S. Muslim population, they remain a vital part of the religious community. Among the numerous African-American Muslims rising to prominence through athletic achievement, two enlarged their stature by speaking out on non-sports issues.

M uhammad Ali is the best known and most admired of the world's living Muslims. The former boxing champion, named "Athlete of the Century" by *USA Today,* was high on the list of other centennial selections for athletic achievement. But he is even better known for his calm courage under political pummeling. Ali is widely revered for speaking out courageously on public issues and standing by his convictions at great cost to his athletic career.

He converted to Islam initially through the Nation of Islam organization but later became a mainstream Muslim, rejecting the racial separatist doctrines then embraced by the Nation of Islam. Long retired from the boxing ring, Ali spends most of his time and income supporting causes that promote human rights and world peace. He is rated as having the best name and face recognition worldwide of any American, past or present, and has unique standing as a cultural hero of people throughout the developing world, and especially among African-Americans.

Biographer Max Wallace, writing in *The New York Times,* declares that Ali "literally changed the world of sports forever" by ending the sporting world's "condescending tolerance toward Blacks," a racist practice that became popular during the career of Joe Louis, an earlier African-American boxing champion. Louis won praise from sports writers as "a credit to his race," because he maintained a public posture of uncomplaining docility and humility. Wallace writes, "Ali was also determined to be a credit to his race. But for him, those words had a very different meaning than they did for Joe Louis." Sports sociologist Harry Edwards writes, "Before Ali, Black athletes were merely twentieth-century gladiators in the service of white society."

In February 1964, the day after he won his first heavyweight title, Ali startled the sports world by announcing his conversion to Islam. At a news conference, he responded to hostile questions with an oft-quoted declaration: "I don't have to be what you want me to be." Soon after, he changed his name from Cassius Clay—he called it a "slave name"—to Muhammad Ali, but many sports writers, upset that a boxer would dare make a political statement, refused for months to acknowledge his name change.

In 1967, deeply opposed to the Vietnam War, Ali refused induction into the Army even though the Pentagon assured him that in uniform he, like Joe Louis in World War II, would never get near a battlefield. He could keep his heavyweight title and, like Louis in the earlier war, simply entertain troops with boxing demonstrations.

He refused and explained, "I'd be just as guilty as the ones doing the killing." Wallace notes that the New York Boxing Commission stripped Ali of his title, although it had granted licenses to more than two hundred convicted felons over the years. "Ali's most serious offense was a traffic violation two years earlier." He was convicted of draft evasion but never complained during a costly four-year legal battle that ended when the U.S. Supreme Court overturned the conviction. "My principles are more important than the money or my title….I knew I was right. I had to make a stand."

He proclaims his religious faith :"If I hadn't become a Muslim, I wouldn't be who I am today." He told *Playboy* magazine in 1975 that he would like to be remembered as "a man who tried to unite his people through the faith of Islam." Ramsey Clark, who served as U.S. Attorney-General when his staff prosecuted Ali for draft evasion, now views him as a worldwide beacon of hope. "To everyone, he means that you can be [both] gentle and strong.... For all his physical strength, he always evoked gentleness and love. The most important thing he communicates is his love and his desire to do good."

Except for the insulting remarks he routinely made about boxing opponents—comments that he dismisses as nothing more than "publicity hype" to sell tickets—Ali, responding to Muslim standards, avoids criticism of others. Sports reporter Jon Saraceno writes, "Over the years, many have taken advantage of Ali's loving nature. They have conned him, ripped him off, abused him—even to this day. Ali knows who they are, but never, ever will say a bad word about any of them."[20]

B asketball legend Kareem Abdul-Jabbar, another African-American Muslim, not to be confused with the football star of the same name, was elected to the Hall of Fame in 1995 as one of the greatest basketball players in history. While in high school, Abdul-Jabbar, seven feet two inches in height, led his teammates to ninety-five wins and only six losses. At the University of California, Los Angeles, he guided the Bruins to a three-year mark of eighty-eight victories against two losses.

During his twenty-year professional career, he was named most valuable player each of the six times his teams won national championships. On retirement in 1989, he had established new records in nine statistical categories in the National Basketball Association.

In 1996, Abdul-Jabbar added new luster to his name by writing *Black Profiles in Courage,* a bestseller that lifted the self-esteem of African-Americans by recognizing heroic achievements of Blacks beyond the world of sports. In September 2000, Shareef Abdur-Rahim, another African-American Muslim and one of the National Basketball Association's brightest stars, became a philanthropist when he contributed $100,000 to Muslim schools in Atlanta.[21]

L ouis Farrakhan leads the Nation of Islam, an organization of African-Americans that formerly espoused black separatism and, until recently, had other doctrinal differences with mainstream Islam. The organization has a following of more than fifty thousand people and operates one hundred and fifty mosques and fifty institutions called Sister Clara Muhammad Schools.[22]

Although the followers of Farrakhan constitute a relatively small fraction of the African-Americans who are professed Muslims, his national prominence and influence are significant. An eloquent television personality, Farrakhan is credited with inspiring self-confidence among African-American young people. He won praise in 1995 for organizing the Million Man March to Washington. It drew more than one million African-American males. In 2000, he sponsored the Family March that brought nearly a half-million people, including many non-Blacks, to the nation's capital.

Until recently, Farrakhan has opposed racial integration and has campaigned almost exclusively for African-American goals. At times, he expressed sweeping criticism of Jews and Christians, themes that mainline Muslims considered violations of the universality, tolerance, and interracial doctrines of Islam.

In February 2000, during the Nation of Islam's annual public prayer service in Chicago, Farrakhan and Imam W. Deen Mohammed, the widely respected leader of the mainstream Muslim American Society, joined hands. Leonard Muhammad, Farrakhan's chief of staff, announced to the congregation that all Nation of Islam followers now adhere to the Muslim creed: "There is no God but Allah and Muhammad is His messenger."

The prayer service marked the twenty-fifth anniversary of the death of Elijah Muhammad, who had led the Nation of Islam for many years. After his death, his son, W. Deen Mohammed, led an exodus from the organization and became a leader in the mainstream of Islam. His organization has about 70,000 members that are served by mosques located in major urban centers. He has a following that reaches beyond the formal membership. One estimate places its total at more than 200,000.[23] Among his attainments was being the first Muslim to offer prayer during a session of the U.S. Senate.

A prominent mainstream Muslim, Sayyid M. Syeed, secretary general of the Islamic Society of North America, saluted Farrakhan's statement at the Chicago meeting. He said, "This was an historic occasion. We have waited for seventy years for this moment to arrive. It is a great step toward Muslim unity." He believes that Farrakhan's decision will end a longstanding, confusing point of controversy among Muslims and at the same time expand the mainstream community, in which African-Americans already constitute a fourth of the total.[24]

S tudies assembled by Ba-Yunus and Siddiqui show that, in contrast to popular stereotypes, the U.S. Muslim community consists of people of many races and nationalities who are generally well educated, hardworking, successful, and law-abiding.

Muslims have remarkable attainments in higher education. Ba-Yunus summarizes an unpublished study showing that employed Muslims in the twenty-to-forty age group average three years of college—two years more than the national average. The average annual personal income of this group lies between the middle and upper brackets with a median of $39,700, strikingly high for a group that includes many recent immigrants. These estimates reflect, in part, the effect of U.S. policies that favor immigrants with college degrees. In contrast, the majority of Muslims outside the United States live in poverty.

Sample studies in 1994 showed Muslim unemployment only two percent, one-half the national average.[25] They also have a low crime rate. An unpublished study conducted in New York City in 1995 by Ba-Yunus shows that the rate of apprehension of local Muslim teenagers is a tiny .001 percent of all adolescents, far below the national average of 15 percent.

Ba-Yunus and Siddiqui conclude, "There is little doubt that Muslims in North America do not, in any way, resemble the conventional picture of a poverty-stricken, uneducated and unsettled minority that Americans have nightmares about."[26]

U.S. Muslims are prominent in engineering, business administration, medicine, finance, accounting, electronics, science, and education, as well as retail establishments.

Egyptian-born Ahmed Zewail, 53, a professor at the California Institute of Technology in Los Angeles, received the 1999 Nobel Prize in Chemistry for his development of a high-speed camera that can monitor chemical reactions at one-quadrillionth of a second and record the motion of atoms. His achievement has opened new vistas in technology.

Chief executive officers of major industries who are Muslim include Safi Qureshey of AST Computers, Ray Irani of Occidental Petroleum, and Farooq Kathwari of Ethan Allen Furniture Company.

Among Muslim notables are six professors: Kenya-born Ali A. Mazrui, an internationally acclaimed political scientist, Albert Schweitzer, Professor in Humanities and the Director of the Institute of Global Cultural studies at Binghamton University, State University of New York; Ibrahim Abu-Lugod, chairman of the political science department at Northwestern University, Evanston, Illinois; Cherif Bassiouni at DePaul University, Chicago; Rashid Khalidi, professor, University of Chicago; Hisham Sharabi, Georgetown University, who is also director of the Center for Policy Analysis, Washington, D.C.; and M. A. Q. Siddiqui, State University of New York Medical School.

Other Muslims who have attained national prominence include Mustafa Akkad and Assad Kelada, producers of motion pictures and television features; Imam W. Deen Mohammed; poet Amir Baraka, formerly Leroi Jones; and musicians Ahmed Jamal and Yusuf Lateef, not to mention the late Art Blakey and many others.

Muslims became prominent in the U.S. armed forces shortly after the 1991 Gulf War. Personal declarations of religious affiliation indicate that nearly two thousand Muslims served in the U.S. armed forces in 1992,[27] In 1999, Imam Yahya Hendi estimated the total at seven thousand.[28] In 2000, the first mosque at a Navy base opened at Norfolk, Virginia.

D ue to steady immigration and a 3.5 percent birthrate that is more than twice the national average, Muslims are America's fastest growing religious community. If current rates of immigration and birth continue, the U.S. Muslim population will double by 2027.[29]

The above-average birthrate is a major factor in this trend, because, for most people, religious affiliation is a happenstance of birth, not the result of the comparative study of religions. Like Christians, Jews, Hindus, Buddhists and people of other faiths, most Muslims inherit their religious identity. I became a Presbyterian and Lucille a Catholic during childhood because our parents had those affiliations. Few Americans make a deliberate choice, in which, after careful study, they select one religion in preference to others. When comparative study occurs, it is usually during post-high school years, long after the person involved has made an affiliation. It rarely leads to change. There are exceptions.

Conversions to Islam, which Muslims often refer to as "reversions," are numerous and rising. I have no totals, but my experience with Muslims during the past twenty-five years leads me to believe that the number is significant. Some African-Americans have left Christian affiliations, choosing to revert to the Islamic faith prominent among their West African forebears who were forced into slavery. In this process, some of them, like Muhammad Ali, chose Arabic names, discarding the slave names given their forebears by white masters. But these conversions, I believe, are only a small portion of the total.

Several years ago, Clinton Sipes made a 180-degree religious turn. He left a life of crime and active membership in the Ku Klux Klan and became a Muslim. "I was a full-fledged card-carrying hate-monger, heavily involved in Klan cross-burnings, media appearances, assaults, and property desecration." His conversion came during the last of several incarcerations. While an inmate in federal prison, Sipes befriended an African-American Muslim who assisted in his conversion.[30]

In my travels, I encounter U.S. Muslims with Anglo-Saxon ancestry or forebears from Eastern Europe, as well as Northern

Asia, the Middle East and Africa. When visiting college campuses, I frequently meet Muslim students, mostly males from South Asia or Arab countries, who have married recent converts to Islam, women of European ethnicity.

Interfaith romance that leads to matrimony does not always yield converts to Islam. Among my personal acquaintances, Naila Asali, board chairman of the American Arab Anti-Discrimination Committee, is a Christian, while her husband, Ziad Asali, M.D., chairman of the American Committee on Jerusalem and a leader in several Arab-American organizations, is a Muslim. Thomas Abercrombie converted from Christianity to Islam at the age of thirty, before he gained prominence on the editorial staff of the *National Geographic* magazine. His wife, Lynn, remains a Christian. Dr. Hisham Sharabi's late wife, Gayle, was a Christian.

R omance is not a factor in all conversions. April Szuchyt, thirty and single, is a Peace Corps volunteer in Jordan. I have not met her, but, thanks to e-mail, I have learned of her pilgrimage into Islam and how she has overcome the strains on family relationships caused by her change in religious affiliation. Our correspondence began when, after reading one of my articles about Islam, she asked me to speak at a fund-raising event to benefit a new Islamic school being built in a Maryland suburb of Washington, D.C. Due to previous commitments, I had to decline, but ensuing correspondence has helped in my understanding of Muslims and Islam.

Her experience may be typical of other converts. Asked if a particular episode was a religious turning point, she responded, "There wasn't a single pivotal event in my life. I was about twenty-two at the time and searching for something, but I can't say that it was religion. My family has always been somewhat neutral on the subject of religion. We believe in God for sure, but our practice of religion has always been limited to the occasional saying of grace before dinner or plea for help in times of difficulty. Despite the absence of organized religion in our lives, we were always taught to respect religion. I believe each of us maintained our own private relationship with God, which we rarely discussed. Even so, we were always very close. My parents worked very hard to instill in us honesty, fairness, and decency."

Why Islam, rather than another religion?

"About two years out of college, I worked as the finance manager for Toyota. The owner of the local franchise was Muslim, as were many of his employees. During that time, I befriended an Egyptian man who is Muslim. All of this led to long discussions of Islam. In the beginning, my reactions were typical of any liberated, educated Western woman with no knowledge of Islam. I accused Islam of being oppressive to women and obsessed with rules. I did not realize that I was missing the 'big picture,' that God is bigger than all other details.

"After months of discussion and reading, my perspective began to change, and I decided to convert. The only thing holding me back was the fear of being thrown into hell for denying that Jesus was the Son of God. I mean, I was pretty sure of my newfound beliefs, but what if I was wrong? Believe me when I tell you that I exhausted many hours of thought and introspection on this subject alone. What made it easier, I guess, was the knowledge that I wasn't giving up my belief in Jesus as a prophet. Islam holds him in that high regard."

Initially, April's parents said little about her conversion.

"I did not begin to wear the hijab [head-scarf] until two years ago. That was when my family became most concerned about my change in religion. I believe this outward display of religion, a religion they believed to be 'anti-American,' is what caused a rift to develop between us. Before my conversion, my family harbored misconceptions and bias with regard to Islam and Muslims. Today my family is very supportive of me. My parents respect my beliefs, although we do not openly discuss them as much as I'd like. I feel we have developed a mutual respect that has helped us build an even stronger relationship than the one we had before my conversion. I am certain, however, there are times they still mourn the loss of the old April."[31]

B eyond religious practices, Muslims are noted for hospitality, a pleasure that Lucille and I have experienced many times here and abroad. Especially memorable was our 1995 visit to Penang, Malaysia, for a week-long conference on Muslim stereotypes. On arrival at the airport, we were welcomed by Attorney John Mohideen, who took us directly to his home for a reception prepared by his wife, Muslimah. Her menu featured deep-fried bananas, a delicacy we found irresistible. A week later, the conference completed, we were ready to board an airliner for home when Mrs. Mohideen arrived at the airport departure gate and handed us a package of the steaming delicacies. Once airborne, we noticed envious glances from other passengers as we enjoyed the still-warm bananas.

Speaking engagements in Michigan and Iraq have provided insights into the community and family values held by Muslims. A visit to Dearborn, Michigan, in April 1998, was especially instructive. Before speaking at a local mosque, I visited the home of Ramze Bazzi, an importer of merchandise from the Middle East, and had a glimpse into how his extended family—consisting of his wife, Warde, four sons, three daughters, a son-in-law, and a sister-in-law—all live happily together. In practical terms, Bazzi's family also includes other people with whom he has no blood relationship. By unspoken consensus, Bazzi has become the personal counselor and leader of scores of neighbors. His residence is their regular gathering place. Sometimes the turnout exceeds fifty at a time, as it did on the afternoon of my visit. The welcome mat is out at almost every hour of the day and night for conversation, tea and coffee, with Arabic the favored language and the discussion topics varied.

The modest bungalow of the Bazzi family has been remodeled in order to accommodate the steady parade of visitors. By moving the kitchen and dining room to the basement, Bazzi tripled the main floor majlis [Arabic for reception room]. In the basement he established a backup majlis, which becomes a dining room when the table in the adjacent kitchen cannot accommodate all the diners.

Visitors became so numerous in 1997 that Bazzi had to convert his two-car garage into a third majlis. His wife, clad in traditional

Muslim head scarf and long dress, works closely with her husband in entertaining guests. Her daughters report that dishwashing and the brewing of coffee and tea never end. At the time of my visit, Bazzi had begun the construction of a much larger residence across the street, a dwelling designed with the expectation, he noted proudly, that both parts of his extended family will keep growing.

Bazzi's Dearborn home is a part of Greater Detroit, a city area area that is unique in having America's largest urban proportion of Muslims. They total over 280,000, about 15 percent of the area population. Most of them live in or near suburban Dearborn, a city whose public school population is also unique. Ninety percent of the students at Fordson High School in Dearborn are Muslim. The faculty percentage is the reverse, thirteen Muslims among one hundred twenty teachers. But, according to Tahsine Bazzi, the faculty director of student affairs and himself a Muslim, the school community is noted for harmonious relations, with no discord over religion. Organized prayers are not permitted on school property, but Muslim students are excused to attend congregational prayers on Fridays.

In 1995, for the first time, the school began the annual observance of the Muslim feast days that celebrate the conclusion of the Hajj pilgrimage [Eid ul Adha] and the ending of fast in Ramadan [Eid ul Fitr]. To advance statewide interfaith understanding among young people, Fordson recently hosted high school students from northern Michigan for a tour of the school and a subsequent discussion of religions in a local mosque. Muslims comprise about 25 percent of each student body in the other two public high schools in Dearborn.

Three years earlier, when Lucille and I were in Baghdad, we glimpsed another example of the Muslim tradition of extended families. The family, headed by Mohammed Al-Khafaji, provided generous hospitality during our first two visits to the Iraqi capital. Unmarried, he heads a busy three-generation household of sixteen that lives in a large residence built years ago by his late father. On our first visit, the family included Mohamed's mother,

Iftikhar, two unmarried sisters, two married brothers, Nashaat and Qassim, and their families, and Maha, an unmarried sister who was studying electrical engineering at a local university. Nashaat and his wife had two daughters and four sons. Qassim and his wife had three daughters and one son.

One evening, the family entertained us in their home for dinner. Like most Iraqi homes, Al-Khafaji residence is fully enclosed by a high wall. Inside, at one end, are beehives and a vegetable garden that are foremost among Mohammed's hobbies. At the other end is a large lawn, where the evening's hospitality began. We enjoyed tea and cakes while Mohammed grilled a large fish over a nearby open fire. The fish became the main course when dinner was served in the dining room of the residence. After dinner, we adjourned with the entire family for coffee and conversation in the main hall. Still later, Mohammed provided a guided tour of the home. Upstairs, on both sides of a long hall are many bedrooms. Mohammed's book-lined study is at one end. In the summer, the family prefers sleeping on the flat roof that opens from a small third floor. Mohammed holds a Ph.D. from a German university and only recently retired from an automotive business. He now devotes his full attention to the household.

Four of Mohammed's siblings live in America's Midwest. His brother, Amir, after reading my book, *They Dare to Speak Out,* provided my initial introduction to Al-Khafaji family when he invited me to speak to the Peoria, Illinois, Rotary Club. He too has a doctorate and heads the department of engineering at Bradley University. Another brother, Shakir, is a Detroit architect who arranged an appointment for me to lecture at the University of Michigan in nearby Ann Arbor. Ann, a sister, is a Detroit attorney, and Faris, a recent university graduate, is employed at the Ford Motor Company in Dearborn.

E xtended families, like the ones in Dearborn and Baghdad, are common wherever Muslims live. Mohammed Al-Khafaji told me that elderly Muslims are rarely obliged to live alone. They customarily live with one of their children or another close relative or friend. This tradition first came to our attention several years ago when a Kuwaiti student visited our home. When our conversation turned to the American trend under which elderly people live in retirement homes, our guest expressed deep concern. Perhaps exaggerating in order to emphasize his point, he said, "In Kuwait, anyone who put an aging parent away in a nursing home would be shunned. No respectable Kuwaiti would associate with such a person."

During my first visit to Dubai in 1988, Easa Al-Gurg, a businessman who later became a close friend, expressed a similar sentiment. He introduced me to his mother and said he insisted that she live with him during her remaining years. When I told him that my widowed mother, after living for several years with one of my sisters, announced that she planned to live in a retirement home near the families of a daughter and granddaughter, he remonstrated, "Don't let her do it. You will regret it all your life if you do. You should insist that she live out her life with one of her children." As he spoke, I remembered a comment made on an earlier occasion by Ovella Gemme, Lucille's father. Reflecting on the trend toward placing aging parents in retirement homes, he said, "A mother can take care of ten kids, but ten kids can't take care of one mother!" Despite my recommendation, my mother insisted on the retirement home. Ever since then, I have had feelings of guilt and have never forgotten the comments of Al-Gurg and my father-in-law.

The extended-family tradition was once common in America. Less than a century ago, it was the rule, not the exception. During my boyhood, my paternal grandmother lived with our family of seven in a small bungalow. In another city, one of my aunts cared for her parents until their death. In spite of the strong trend toward placing elderly people in retirement and nursing homes, many American children still accept the responsibility of home care for incapacitated or elderly parents.

Inayat Lalani, a Muslim physician, learned recently that one of his elderly non-Muslim patients insisted on living alone. "This sprightly seventy-four-year-old patient rejected my suggestion that it was her children's duty to invite her to stay with them. She bluntly told me that would cramp her social life, including her sexual freedom, and that she did not care for such indulgence from anyone." After reporting the experience, Lalani asked, rhetorically, "What is of greater value to a human being: security and support; or freedom, yes, even freedom to misbehave sometimes as long as no one is hurt?"

M uslims in Dearborn seem to be successful in keeping alive Islam's extended-family tradition, but they face nagging challenges. Despite the rapid rise in Muslim population, Ramze Bazzi's non-Muslim neighbors have little knowledge of Islam and little interfaith or inter-community discussion.

Several factors contribute to this lack of communication. Many Muslims, like the Bazzis, are first and second generation citizens. Following the tradition of other religious and ethnic groups that have come to America in recent decades, most of them group together in communities that are close-knit and substantially isolated from people of other faiths. The glue that keeps them together also tends to separate them from non-Muslims. It is a mixture of language, culture, attire, and religion.

Language is a substantial barrier, as many immigrants are not fluent in English and continue to use their native language. In Dearborn, Arabic is often the language of the neighborhoods, and the favorite newspapers for new and second-generation immigrants are *The Arab American,* a biweekly newspaper edited by Nouhad El-Hajj, and *Sada-Alwatan,* a weekly edited by Osama Siblani. In both, the news is routinely published in English in the first half of each issue, beginning on page one, and in Arabic in the other half, beginning on the back page.

Like other Americans, Muslims rarely mention their religion, even casually, in conversations with their non-Muslim neighbors or associates at work.

D espite the bleak fog of anti-Islamic stereotyping that hangs over America, almost all Muslim immigrants remain here and, like other immigrants, show no inclination to leave.

I can cite only one case in which immigrants chose to leave America. A Muslim family consisting of a physician, his wife, and three children, returned to Pakistan after enjoying five years in America. In a small city in the Midwest, they became friends with a Hindu family, also consisting of a physician, his wife and three children whose ages were similar to the children in the Muslim family.

In the sixth year, the relationship changed suddenly when the father, concerned that his family was losing Muslim and Pakistani traditions, decided that they should return to Pakistan. In the weeks before the move, the children of the two families continued to play together, but when the adults were together, the Muslim mother began following a cultural tradition popular in some Pakistani communities—not an Islamic requirement—by keeping her face fully veiled. The two families continued to share an occasional meal, but on those occasions, the mother ate alone in the kitchen, rather than show her face to the husband of the other family. Family problems did not end when the Muslim family arrived in Pakistan. The children were unhappy, and the father, unable to earn enough in Pakistan to maintain the family's accustomed standard of living, returned each year to work for several months in a U.S. hospital.

The American experience of other immigrants has been excellent. It is illustrated in an amusing experience that Vincent Checchi, my office landlord when I wrote *They Dare to Speak Out,* related several years ago. During a conversation with his mother, an immigrant from Italy, she complained about the drinking water, vegetables, fruit, and air being much better in Italy than in America. He finally protested, "Mother, if you like everything in Italy so much better than here, why don't you go back there to live." Her immediate response: "What? Leave America? Do you think I'm crazy?"

Dr. Mohammed Bashardost expressed a similar sentiment for his family of six—and no doubt, for many other Muslim immigrants—when he said, "My family is happy in America. We know there are some bad things here, but there are more things that are good."[32]

Notes:

1. AMC, *Our First Five Years,* p. 8.
2. Ibid., p. 12.
3. Abdurahman Alamoudi interview, 1-18-2000.
4. *The Oxford Encyclopedia of the Modern Islamic World,* vol.. 4, p. 278.
5. CAMRI, *Muslim Population in the U.S.A.,* 1998, p. 7–8.
6. Interview, Sulayman Nyang on 1-19-2000.
7. Dr. Musa Qutub e-mail, 3-22-1999.
8. Page 692.
9. Page 684.
10. *The Oxford Encyclopedia of the Modern Islamic World,* vol.. 4, p. 277.
11. CAMRI, *Muslim Population in the U.S.A.,* p. 19, and AMC, *Muslim Population in the United States,* p. 15.
12. CAMRI, *Muslim Population in the U.S.A.,* p. 16.
13. AMC, *The Muslim Population in the United States,* p. 19, 1992.
14. Amir Nashid Ali Muhammad, *Muslims in America* (Amana Publications), p. 3.
15. CAMRI, *Muslim Population in the U.S.A.,* p. 18.
16. AMC, *Our First Five Years,* p. 8.
17. CAMRI, *Muslim Population in the U.S.A.,* p. 33.
18. AMC, *Muslim Population in the United States,* p. 13.
19. *A Profile of Islam* (Melbourne: Islamic Publications), p 95.
20. *USA Today ,* 12-10-99, pp. A1-2 and C11, 13; and *New York Times,* 4-3-2000, p. 9.
21. *Muslim Journal,* 9-29-2000, p. 1.
22. Amber Haque, *Muslims and Islamization,* (Beltsville, Amana Publications), 274.
23. *USA Today,* 2-28-00, p. 3A; AP 2-28-2000, p. 5, *Journal-Courier,* Jacksonville, IL., and *Chicago Tribune,* 9-3-2000, p. 34.
24. Sayyid M. Syeed interview, 3-1-2000.
25. CAMRI, *Muslim Population in the U.S.A.,* p. 34.
26. Ibid., p. 35.
27. AMC, *Our First Five Years,* p. 17.
28. Interview, 5-19-1999.
29. CAMRI, *Muslim Population in the U.S.A.,* p. 35.

30. Muzaffar Haleem, *The Sun is Rising in the West* (Beltsville, Amana Publications), pp. 106–107,

31. E-mail interview, 2-21-1989.

32. Letter, 3-17-2000.

Chapter 3: Terrorism and Defamation

Years of correspondence with Muslims and discussions in many parts of the Islamic world have not made me an authority on Islam, but I believe the experience has given me a realistic understanding of the religion's image problem in America.

Some of the stereotypes about Muslims strike fear. A sobering example occurred in July 1999 in Newark, N.J., when Reginald Qurrie, wanting money for heroin and posing as a Muslim, handed a bank teller this note, "In the name of Allah, I have a bomb and I am willing to give my life for the cause of Islam. Put all the money in the bag, and don't be a hero." The frightened teller quickly complied. The hoax was exposed when Qurrie was arrested.[1]

On other occasions, false images prompt community-wide bigotry and other forms of religious intolerance, even destructive violence. In recent years, mosques were the target of arsonists in Yuba City, California, Springfield, Illinois, Greenville, South Carolina, and Minneapolis, and vandalism has occurred at mosques in Michigan, Indiana, Massachusetts, New Jersey, and Georgia.

During an early-morning patrol in May 1999, an alert policeman noticed a car "creeping into a parked position with headlights out" near the Colorado Islamic Center in Denver. As officer Terry Reibeling approached the car, the driver, later identified as Jack Merlyn Modig, drove off. After a pursuit across the city, police apprehended Modig as he tried to enter a residence. Resisting arrest, Modig shouted, "I am an enemy against the Islamic nation, and I was going to take care of business…. I was going to burn the place down." Officers discovered in his car a shotgun, a rifle, several revolvers, ammunition and bomb-making equipment.[2]

In June 2000, a gunman fired at a mosque in Memphis, Tennessee, wounding one Muslim and blasting holes in the mosque doors. Worshippers there were accustomed to vandalism and verbal confrontations. Danish Siddiqui, president of the University of Memphis Muslim Students Association, said, "We've had dirt thrown on us, and they've done everything from smoking marijuana and drinking in front of us to having their dogs chase us."[3]

T he same month, a community leader's misinformation about Islam sparked a controversy in a Chicago suburb that produced headlines and wide discord for several months. The dispute began when Karen Hayes, coordinator of the National Day of Prayer in Palos Heights, a village of twelve thousand near Chicago, described Islam as a "false religion," because it did not accept her concept of God.

She made the statement over a Chicago public television station to explain her opposition to the decision of Al Salaam Mosque Foundation, which had outgrown its facilities in Southwest Chicago, to buy a church building in her hometown and convert it into a mosque and Islamic school. Palos Heights is home to nearly four hundred Muslim families, a tiny fraction of the three hundred and fifty thousand Muslims who live in the Chicago area.

Mayor Dean Koldenhoven called Hayes' comment "disgraceful" and "not representative of the Christian faith." He asked, "How much do these [Muslim] people have to take?" However, confronted with a flood of protests against the mosque project, the city council voted to pay the Muslim foundation $200,000 if it dropped the plan.[4] Koldenhoven called the offer an insult to Muslims, but Rouhy Shalabi, attorney for the Muslim foundation, viewed it as "a gesture of goodwill." Ed Hussan, a Muslim who lives in Palos Heights expressed a conciliatory view: "I think people like [Hayes] have so much love for their religion that they just turn against other religions. We have fanatics in our religion too. But, in fact, God is one God for all religions...." He decried the local city council for acting "like a bunch of seventeen-year-old gang members trying to protect their turf." Rev. Edward Cronin, pastor of St. Alexander Catholic Church who coordinated an interfaith welcome for those sponsoring the mosque project, said, "We have to show that Christianity is not about closing the door."[5]

Mayor Koldenhoven vetoed the $200,000 buy-out, prompting the foundation to file a $3.5 million damage suit against the municipality. In late summer, the amount of the suit was increased to $6.2 million. Shalibi said, "This [law suit] is to send a message that the Muslim community will not be discriminated against and walk away." The Council of Islamic Organizations of Greater Chicago issued a statement thanking "those individuals within and outside Palos Heights who have spoken and stood up in support of the religious rights of Muslims...."[6]

Years earlier, area Muslims faced similar problems.

In 1981, more than two thousand angry residents signed a petition opposing the bid of the Islamic Foundation in Villa Park to purchase a school building for the purpose of converting it into a mosque. Local Muslims took the village authorities to court, and, after spending $51,000 in legal fees, they won the right to purchase the building but later opted to buy a different building in the community. Since then, according to foundation director Abdul Hameed Dogar, a steady improvement in community relations has occurred, despite a few incidents of vandalism.

In 1989, Morton Grove citizens protested when the Muslim Education Center wanted to buy land owned by the local public school district as the site for a Muslim school. With the help of Mohammed Kaiseruddin, the former chairman of the Chicago-based Council of Islamic Organizations, local Muslims prevailed over the protesters and established the school.

Early in the Palos Heights dispute, Kaiseruddin urged Muslims to stand firm in their plan for a local mosque. Stating that opposition comes mainly from people who fear the unknown, he recommended that Palos Heights Muslims open their homes and let their opponents see how they live. "They don't know what type of people will move in, and they fear property values will go down. These are baseless fears."[7]

Abdullah Mitchell, president of the Chicago-area Muslim Americans for Civil Rights and Legal Defense, said, "The fundamental problem is the lack of information the American community has about Muslims. Muslims are being characterized as terrorists or outsiders in the fear that they're going to disrupt [the American] way of life. The problem is ignorance. That was the problem in Morton Grove and that's the problem we're having in Palos Heights."[8]

By year's end, Chicago's suburbs were bustling with mosque construction. A $1.5 million mosque was being built in Schaumburg and a $3.5 million one in Des Plaines. Hinsdale is planning a new place of worship, and property in the Loop area of Chicago is being remodeled as a mosque.

S alam Al-Marayati, national director of the Los Angeles-based Muslim Public Affairs Council, personally experiences Islamic stereotypes: "When new acquaintances learn that I am a practicing Muslim, they are surprised that blood and smoke are not simultaneously seeping out of horns in my head. Later, they came to realize that I believe in and love God, wear a suit and tie, and at times talk about the Los Angeles Lakers, and not only because their greatest player is a Muslim."[9]

Misunderstanding sometimes provokes vandalism. During the violence that flared in Israel and the Occupied Territories beginning in October 2000, the Islamic Center of Southern California, which serves over one hundred and fifty students from preschool to the sixth grade, was vandalized on three separate occasions. On one, a rock was thrown through the glass entrance door while Muslims were gathered at prayer just inside. On another, a guard station at the center's parking lot was ransacked and smeared with paint and a nearby van was smeared with paint and graffiti. In the third incident, Jews seemed to be the target. Black swastikas were painted on the center's entrance pillars and the phrase "Jews get out," was scratched on the main door.

Mohammad J. N. Qureschi, administrator of the center, called the vandalism a "hate crime." He said, "We want the public to know who we are and accept us. These things always seem to happen immediately after conflicts arise in the Mideast. They trigger acts against us."

Joe R. Hicks, executive director of the Los Angeles Human Relations Commission, during a news conference at the center, denounced the vandalism and expressed support for the Muslim community: "The people who did this want their victims to be afraid. The community needs to step in and help in the healing." Howard Welinsky of the Jewish Federation was among those attending.

Al-Marayati found a silver lining in the vandalism. Noting the outpouring of support from police, the attorney-general, and Jewish leaders, he said, "If this had happened ten years ago, we would not have had those kinds of assurances." More than 250,000 Muslims, served by seventy-five mosques and Islamic centers, reside in Los Angeles County.[10]

S ome of the stereotypes of Islam are cultivated on Capitol Hill. In 1992, Ralph Braibanti, a prominent scholar and author on Islamic topics, found in a Capitol Hill office "the most comprehensive and frightening treatment of Islam as a potential enemy of the United States." He referred to the work of Yossef Bodansky, staff director of the Republican Task Force on Terrorism and Unconventional Warfare, a panel chaired by U.S. Rep. Bill McCollum of Florida. In a book on the 1993 bombing of the World Trade Building in New York City, Bodansky, former technical editor of the *Israeli Air Force* magazine, embarked on a remarkable flight of fancy. Bodansky wrote, "Islamic terrorism has embarked on a Holy War—Jihad—against the West, especially the United States, which is being waged primarily through international terrorism."[11]

Publicity of this nature inevitably leads some Americans to believe that an Islamic threat actually is taking shape in America. Alarmed by the steady growth of the U.S. Muslim population, they fear this trend will weaken America's longstanding, unconditional support of Israel. Another even larger group of citizens, led by television evangelist Pat Robertson, notwithstanding the constitutional separation of church and state, view America as a Christian nation and believe Muslims pose a threat to that concept.

In addition to people who indulge in stereotyping and exploit raw emotions for career or religious reasons, there are those who claim they are simply responding to reality. For example, American University Professor Amos Perlmutter warned in 1984 about "a general Islamic war being waged against the West, Christianity, modern capitalism, Zionism, and Communism all at once."[12] Perlmutter's assertion of fear is echoed by others in academic circles who ignore Islam's fundamental links with both Christianity and Judaism. They identify Islam as a major threat to the West, in which, in a remarkable geographical stretch of the imagination, they choose to depict Israel as a western nation and part of the West's culture.

Assaulting imaginary foreign villains is nothing new in America. Years ago, publicity-hungry politicians warned of the "Yellow Peril" in order to incite opposition to immigration from China. Later, when Governor Al Smith of New York became the first Roman Catholic candidate for the presidency, some warned— in whispers rather than shouts—that he would bring sinister papal influence directly into the White House. Still later, it was the "Red Peril," symbolized by the Soviet Union. Today, Islam is frequently called the new menace from beyond the horizon, replacing the defunct Soviet Union, but according to its detractors, retaining Soviet-like tentacles.

Edward W. Said, a professor at Columbia University, New York, and a Palestinian activist, explains: "What matters to 'experts' like Judith Miller, Samuel Huntington, Martin Kramer, Bernard Lewis, Daniel Pipes, Steven Emerson and Barry Rubin, plus a whole battery of Israeli academics, is to make sure that the 'threat' [of Islam] is kept before our eyes, the better to excoriate Islam for terror, despotism and violence, while assuring themselves profitable consultancies, frequent TV appearances and book contracts. The Islamic threat is made to seem disproportionately fearsome, lending support to the thesis [which is an interesting parallel to anti-Semitic paranoia] that there is a worldwide conspiracy behind every explosion."[13]

Al-Marayati laments the unfair, double standard in public references to Islam: "Islam teaches mankind decency, but it also acknowledges the reality of indecency. Islam means peace and attempts to establish peace throughout the world, [and] it proceeds with the greatest amount of tolerance. I am troubled by the publication of *The Satanic Verses* by Salman Rushdie for its distortion of Islam, but I also condemn the call to kill Rushdie.... Islam is a peaceful, tolerant religion, yet people associate it with violence and intolerance.

"There are many hypocrites among Christian leaders, but unlike other religions, Islam is routinely linked with violence in news reports and articles. Religious identification rarely occurs when awful deeds occur at the hands of people of other faiths. News accounts never identified the slaughter of Kosovar Albanians as killings by Eastern Orthodox Serbs, of Burmese as killings by Buddhists, or of Palestinians as killings by Jews. Perpetrators are routinely identified by nationality, not religious affiliation—except when they are Muslims. Violent Christians are not seen as discrediting Christianity. But if any Muslim does wrong, it is invariably reported as an element in an 'Islamic threat' to America. When we pause and reflect on the venom of the 'Jewish' state that invades Lebanon and kills thousands, that bombs Palestinian homes and transfers Palestinians from their homeland, we resist the temptation of thinking that Judaism has any violent or intolerant underpinning. Definitely a double standard applies here, in which Islam is blamed for international conflicts."[14]

This double standard reinforces the most widely held and virulent stereotype of Islam, the one that links Muslims with terrorism. It is imbedded in the consciousness of almost every general audience I address. When I ask what word comes to mind when Islam or Muslims are mentioned, the word terrorism is usually volunteered by several people in the audience without audible objection from others attending.

I do not believe the terrorism stereotype is the product of some giant anti-Islam international conspiracy, or even a national one, but I recognize that the promulgation of false stereotypes can serve narrow, bigoted interests.

S ometimes false images of Islam arise from malice, at other times, as William Shakespeare might write, from "vaulting ambition."

A desire for personal publicity and the income that it can attract are the motivations that most likely led Steven Emerson, a self-employed commentator on terrorism, to defame U.S. Muslims. He and other like-minded publicists play skillfully on religious prejudices and raw emotions.

In 1994, the year after radicals bombed the World Trade building in New York City, public television stations across the nation broadcast Emerson's principal triumph, a television documentary called "Jihad in America: An Investigation of Islamic Extremists' Activities in the United States." It was a patchwork of dark   predictions, innuendoes, and disturbing glimpses of frenzied, strange people chanting loudly in a foreign language. The film spread a cloud of fear across the nation and did more to create distrust of U.S. Muslims than any other event in my memory.

Using a false definition of jihad, the makers of the documentary wielded the term as if it were a ticking time bomb threatening innocent people everywhere. They created the impression that "fundamentalist" Muslims are dangerous, irrational people who have infiltrated the American countryside and established a sinister network whose goal is the destruction of the United States.

Jihad has only three objectives, two of which almost all Americans would enthusiastically applaud. The first is struggling within oneself for a life of virtue. The second is fighting against injustice. Both aims are listed in Islamic teachings—as well as in the doctrines of other religions—as supreme goals of human endeavor. A third objective is to defend Islam whenever it comes under attack. Contrary to the violent image portrayed in "Jihad in America," Islam denounces terrorism and fanaticism. "Violence in the name of Islam is un-Islamic," Andrew Patterson, writes. "It is the complete antithesis of Islam. Islam means peace, not violence." He cites "Jihad in America" as pure propaganda designed to inflame anti-Muslim passions. He believes it succeeded.

Because of the inflammatory themes reflected in the documentary, Emerson achieved national prominence for several months, notoriety that was reminiscent of the ill repute of Senator Joseph McCarthy in the 1950s. McCarthy used innuendo and hurled unfounded accusations of disloyalty against employees of the U.S. State Department, leaders in higher education, and people prominent in the entertainment industry. His accusations intimidated thousands of patriotic Americans. Ultimately, a new word, "McCarthyism," entered the dictionary as a synonym for character assassination.

I doubt that the term "Emersonism" will make its way into the dictionary, but through "Jihad in America," Emerson damaged American society more permanently than McCarthyism. The reputations of McCarthy's victims were restored when the U.S. Senate censured his misconduct, but Emerson's victims have not been as fortunate. Although Emerson has now largely discredited himself as a source of information and analysis, the damage he has done survives. Six years after "Jihad in America," his victims have scarcely begun to fight back, and much of the venom he spread still poisons the nation. *The Agent: The Truth Behind the Anti-Muslim Campaign in America,* co-authored by Ahmed Yousef and Caroline F. Keeble, chronicles Emerson's misbehavior, but no proposal to censure him has been introduced in the U.S. Congress.[15]

I have had two personal experiences with Emerson. The first occasion was a telephone conversation in 1984 when I was finishing work on my book, *They Dare to Speak Out.* He called to say that he was writing *The American House of Saud,* a book that tried—unsuccessfully—to smear the Saudi royal family as a major force in manipulating U.S. public opinion. He wanted to ask questions about congressional campaign contributions that I had received in 1982 from people with business interests in Saudi

Arabia. I told him that several had sent generous personal contributions, but these arrived too late to be useful in my failed attempt at re-election that year. Later, in 1986, I met Emerson personally when we made a joint appearance on CNN's television program, *Crossfire*. In the program's first segment, Emerson and I must have treated each other gently, because during the commercial break our hosts urged us to be more aggressive. I did my best to accommodate the request.

There was nothing gentle about the charges Emerson leveled against Islam in "Jihad in America," or in his subsequent televised appearances and articles published in prominent periodicals before and after the broadcast of the documentary. He sometimes delivered his assaults in a mild, almost apologetic manner, as if he were a kindly physician trying to soften the bad news to a patient on the verge of death. Sometimes, it became difficult to know whether Emerson was delivering cuffs or caresses. For example, before condemning U.S. Muslims in sweeping terms, Emerson's documentary stated that "the overwhelming majority of Muslims are not members of militant groups" and added that "Islam as a religion does not condone violence." But he obviously concluded that these disclaimers gave him a license to accuse Muslims in general of possessing the very militancy and violence he had just denied they espoused.

The documentary's text declared that "numerous command centers and communication posts" are scattered around the country, helping Muslims "establish an Islamic empire." It warned that "as the activities of Muslim radicals expand in the United States, future bombing attacks [like the one at the World Trade Center] seem inevitable," because "hampered by constitutional restraints, U.S. law enforcement agencies will have difficulty preventing the nation from becoming a war front."

In an article in *The Jewish Monthly,* Emerson smeared Muslims with a broad brush, asserting that "unfortunately, nearly all of the Islamic organizations in the United States that define themselves as religiously or culturally Muslim in character have today been totally captured or dominated by radical fundamentalist elements."[16] In the same vein, he warned a Senate subcommittee of the existence of "a vast interlocking network of activists and believers collaborating with one another from country to country. The nexus of Islamic fundamentalists stretches from Cairo to Brooklyn, from Khartoum to Brooklyn and from Gaza to Washington."[17]

I n *The Wall Street Journal,* Emerson contended that Islamic fundamentalists "use their mosques and their religious leaders to form the nucleus of their terrorist infrastructure."[18] In the *San Diego Union-Tribune* he declared: "The hatred of the West by militant Islamic fundamentalists is not tied to any particular act or event. Rather, fundamentalists equate the mere existence of the West—its economic, political and cultural system—as an intrinsic attack on Islam."[19]

Emerson hurled the term "Islamic fundamentalist" as if it were a grenade, launching the notion—however false but useful to his purposes—that there are two kinds of Muslims, those who are fundamentalist, and therefore bad, and those who are not. The term is almost unknown in Islam. Unlike Protestant Christianity, which is divided between denominations called fundamentalist and others that are known as mainline, the basic disagreements within Islam are few in number and small in consequence. The term "Islamic fundamentalist" is used widely as an instrument of stereotyping.

T he dreadful bombing in Oklahoma City on April 20, 1995, gave Emerson new opportunities for personal publicity. The debris had hardly settled at the horrible scene at the federal building when he appeared on national television networks, proclaiming that the bombing was likely the work of "Islamic" terrorists. On CNN, he declared that the bomb was like those used in the United States by "Islamic militant" groups.[20]

On CBS News, he said, "Oklahoma City, I can tell you, is probably considered one of the largest centers of Islamic radical activity outside the Middle East." For several days after the

Oklahoma City disaster, Emerson used loaded phrases and innuendo to link the bombing with Islam. On CNN's *Crossfire*, he said solemnly, "The bombing is not the type [of] activity that has been seen on American soil other than the Islamic militant ones."[21]

S ubsequent events proved that no Muslims or people of Arab ancestry were involved in any aspect of the bombing, but Emerson's media assault helped to create a general fear of Muslims. Public anxiety was greater than at any time since the immediate aftermath of the Japanese assault on Pearl Harbor in December 1941, when rumors of an impending Japanese invasion of the West Coast spread like wildfire.

On the day of the Oklahoma City bombing, I heard a major television network station announce that men in traditional Arab headdress had been spotted fleeing the scene. Within hours, President Bill Clinton appealed on television for calm and announced that it was not known who or what had caused the explosion, but this did not slacken the steady outpouring of rumors that pointed the finger of guilt at unnamed Muslims operating from an alleged terrorist base in Oklahoma.

A frightened America pondered somber questions. What would be the next target? The White House? The Capitol? Schools? Churches? Shopping malls? Everyone seemed ready—even eager—for strong, decisive action. Due process was nowhere on the public agenda. In the 1996 *World Almanac*, Jeffrey D. Simon, author of *The Terrorist Trip: America's Experience with Terrorism*, assessed the hysteria that followed the bombing. He wrote that it "struck a special nerve… as millions of Americans watched on television the heart-wrenching scenes of dead babies being pulled from the wreckage…." He continued: "This was not a major, world-famous metropolis that had been attacked, but rather a small city in the heartland of the country. Every town and city across the United States could now be considered a potential target for terrorism."

B efore the arrest of Timothy McVeigh, the man ultimately
convicted of the bombing, several "Middle Eastern looking"
people endured inconvenience, embarrassment, and humiliation at
the hands of law-enforcement officers. There were hostile
confrontations. Muslims and Arab-Americans across the country
experienced harassment and intimidation by law officers.

It was not one of America's finest hours. In Oklahoma City,
shots were fired at a mosque, and in one incident a frenzied mob
provoked a death. A few hours after Steven Emerson suggested on
a CBS network television broadcast that Muslims were involved,
an angry mob harassed a Muslim family—refugees from Iraq—
shouting anti-Muslim epithets and breaking windows of their
home. The protest was so threatening that it caused a pregnant
woman in the household to experience premature delivery. The
infant, a boy ironically named Salaam, the Arabic word for peace,
died soon after birth.[22]

An Oklahoma City citizen, Ibrahim Ahmad, traveling to visit
relatives in Jordan, was arrested at London's Heathrow Airport and
taken into custody because of his Arab name, his departure point
having been Oklahoma City, and the discovery of appliances,
wiring and tools in his suitcase. At the airport, he was handcuffed
and, at the request of the FBI, flown to Washington under police
custody for questioning. The items in his suitcase proved to be
harmless gifts that he had purchased for his relatives in Jordan. He
was later found innocent of any violation and released without
charge. But due to the harassment, inconvenience, and widely
publicized harassment, he filed suit against the U.S. government
and received an undisclosed financial settlement.

I n the tense moments following the explosion, most non-Muslim
Americans seemed to agree that the catastrophe was the work of
foreign fanatics who had infiltrated America's heartland. Stirred by
fresh memories of the costly bombing of the World Trade Center in
New York City and Steven Emerson's fabricated assessments, the
country seemed ready to assume that the guilty parties were Arabs,

Iranians, or Muslims—terms that were used interchangeably as if they were synonyms.

Some commentators viewed the bombing as the opening round of a titanic struggle against the West by sinister alien forces in the East. Others saw it as a monstrous act of retaliation for the U.S. government's longstanding complicity in Israel's repression of Palestinians. Attorney David McCurdy of Norman, Oklahoma, interviewed on television shortly after the explosion, said without hesitation that the explosion was "the work of Middle East terrorists." His assessment was given special credence, because, as a recent Member of Congress, he had served as chairman of the Permanent Select Committee on Intelligence in the U.S. House of Representatives.

It was widely assumed that no U.S. citizen would inflict such terrible destruction on innocent fellow citizens; it had to be the work of sinister forces—from abroad. Personally, I confess that I had an immediate, sinking feeling—one of the worst of my life—when I learned of the bombing. As one among many people who had been striving for years on behalf of interfaith cooperation in America and justice in the Middle East, I was heartsick. I mourned first of all, of course, for the families of those killed and injured, but I feared that the calamity would intensify animosity against Muslims and Arab-Americans.

As rumors flew, I pondered what, if anything, I could do to help avert a dreadful nationwide dragnet. I could imagine innocent citizens by the hundreds being arrested for questioning by the FBI—and being harassed in other ways—simply because of their religious affiliation, the spelling of their names, or the pigmentation of their skin. I felt immense relief when the man arrested and charged, Timothy McVeigh, had no Muslim or Arab connections.

The aftermath of the bombing is an instructive topic for reflection by everyone interested in interfaith understanding and cooperation. They should ponder what might have transpired if McVeigh had not been arrested. All citizens, especially Muslims, should be thankful for the alert, efficient work of Officer Charles

Hanger, a highway patrolman monitoring traffic eighty miles north of Oklahoma City shortly after the bomb exploded. He stopped a car driven by McVeigh, because it had no license plate and, on discovering a concealed weapon in the car, placed McVeigh under arrest, the first step in a journey that would take him to death row in prison.

McVeigh could easily have escaped. Hanger and his fellow officers might have been occupied with other traffic infractions as McVeigh drove north from Oklahoma City. Or, Hanger might not have discovered the concealed weapon. He might have decided to permit McVeigh to resume his journey, after giving him a ticket and a warning.

If McVeigh had not been arrested, Emerson and the other self-styled terrorism experts would likely have kept peddling anti-Muslim themes to news editors. The nation would have continued to echo with false rumors, and the "terrorist infrastructure" that Emerson had earlier accused Muslims of operating nationwide would have remained in news headlines. Fearful Americans would have kept Muslims under suspicion as arch villains who perpetrated the dreadful carnage at Oklahoma City.

Innocent citizens—many thousands of them—would have found themselves cowering helplessly on the defensive. Spurred by a frightened public, Congress might have enacted legislation even broader and more dangerous than the 1996 Anti-Terrorism and Effective Death Penalty Act, legislation that included a denial of due process to immigrants. Videotapes of Emerson's "Jihad in America" were distributed to congressional offices during the publicity campaign that preceded passage of the bill.

Public panic did not abate. Despite the swift arrest of McVeigh, during the year following the bombing, more than two hundred episodes of harassment of Muslims, including death threats, were reported in various parts of the country.[23]

F our years after the Oklahoma City bombing and five years after the broadcast of "Jihad in America," another televised documentary reinforced public concern about Muslims. This one demonstrated the damage to the reputation of Islam that just one professed Muslim can cause. In a production that seemed in some ways a sequel to "Jihad in America," the PBS network presented, "The Terrorist and the Superpower," a feature of the series called *Frontline*. It reported the fiery rhetoric of Osama bin Laden, a Saudi dissident who presented himself as a defender of Islam.

The broadcast alleged that bin Laden played a major role in the 1998 bombing of U.S. embassies in Kenya and Tanzania, explosions that were fatal to U.S. personnel, as well as to many local citizens. It also examined the retaliatory bombings of Sudan and Afghanistan later that year by U.S. military forces. The program cited as groundless Washington's claim that the assault on Sudan destroyed a plant engaged in producing chemicals of mass destruction.

In the documentary, bin Laden gave Islam a false, ugly, vicious image. In the name of Islam, he called on Muslims to "kill Americans where they can and when they can," an appeal that is a gross violation of the principles of justice that are hallmarks of Islam. He cited America as Islam's main enemy and said that all Muslims should make war on America.

This general call for the death of Americans, whether in military uniform or not, created an even greater uneasiness among U.S. Muslims, especially the thousands serving in the U.S. armed forces.

Whatever bin Laden's motivation for the outburst may have been, the producers of the documentary made him seem all the more maniacal by omitting from the documentary the impassioned statement of grievances against the U.S. government he made during a lengthy interview recorded by *Frontline* personnel who assembled material for the documentary.

In segments omitted by the producers, bin Laden attempted to modify his earlier call to kill Americans by limiting the threat to military personnel. He also condemned the U.S. government for its complicity in Israel's long history of sustained brutality against Palestinian civilians—men, women and children, most of whom are Muslim. Although he did not list it among his grievances, he could have mentioned that U.S. forces fired a massive barrage of cruise missiles against bin Laden's training camp in Afghanistan, an assault clearly aimed at bin Laden and his supporters.

The producers, to their credit, put the entire text of the interview on the Internet, enabling the curious to read bin Laden's grievances against the U.S. government and his modification of his call to kill Americans. But, to their discredit, by omitting all of these comments from the broadcast, they left television viewers to wonder what, if anything, triggered bin Laden's fiery verbal assault against Americans. Those who examined the full text of his interview on the Internet after watching the televised broadcast could not escape concluding that the producers of *Frontline* censored his statements in a way that shielded Israel from criticism.

In the last days of 1999, many Americans were braced for more violence. They had vivid memories of the carnage at Oklahoma City and were alarmed by announcements from the Clinton administration of a possible Muslim terrorist attack on New Year's Day or soon after. Fears deepened when an Algerian, a Muslim seeking entry into the United States, tried to slip what was described as bomb-making equipment past customs officials near Seattle on the Canadian border. His apprehension made headline news for several days on all networks and on the front pages of all major U.S. newspapers. Americans became even more anxious when two other Muslims were arrested in New York City and questioned about any possible connection they might have with the Algerian at Seattle or with bin Laden. At the time, bin Laden, wanted on charges of masterminding the 1998 bombing of two U.S. embassies in Africa, was living in Afghanistan. Although no prosecutions occurred, reports of the arrests, accompanied by photographs of a menacing bin Laden, strengthened nationwide fear of terrorism from abroad.

These developments prompted Mohamed El-Bendary, an MSNBC contributor and a Muslim leader in St. Louis, to write, "There is a rising sense of anguish among many of America's Muslims. As the nation braces for terrorism, [Muslims] fear that negative images of them and their religion are once again on the rise in the American media." He cited a survey that showed a 51 percent increase in December 1999. The increase, following immediately after news reports that linked Islam with terrorism, coincided with a warning by the U.S. State Department to American citizens traveling overseas. El-Bendary noted that stereotypes linking Islam with terrorism "hurt and cut deep."[24]

A few weeks earlier, after U.S. Muslims had suffered nearly four years of intense, false stereotyping in the wake of the Oklahoma City bombing and the television documentaries, the leadership of the U.S. House of Representatives decided to drop a resolution expressing goodwill to America's Islamic community by condemning "anti-Muslim intolerance and discrimination."

Drafted by a bipartisan group of Members of Congress, the resolution's original language noted "organizations that foster such intolerance create an atmosphere of hatred." It called upon government agencies and citizens to avoid a repetition of the "rush to judgment" against Muslims that occurred in the wake of the Oklahoma City bombing. One of the sponsors, Senator Joseph I. Lieberman, a Jew, said that it was time to bring to Muslims the "promise of our nation's ideals." Vice-President Al Gore later chose Lieberman as his running mate in his ill-fated 2000 presidential bid.

However, in the wake of complaints from fundamentalist Christians and a few Jewish organizations who objected to the original language, Republicans on the House Judiciary Committee severely amended the resolution. They eliminated

- the reference to Oklahoma City,
- a phrase appealing to legislators to "uphold a level of political discourse that does not involve making a scapegoat of an entire religion,"
- wording that condemned "organizations that foster intolerance,"
- a condemnation of "hate-inspired violence,"

- and a section deploring the fact that U.S. Muslims "have been portrayed in a negative light in some discussions" on terrorism.

James Zogby, a Christian who heads the Arab-American Institute, deplored the deletions as an offense against "already beleaguered" Muslims. He added, "Instead of becoming a salve to heal the wounds of the Muslim community, [the amendments to the resolution are] evidence of the problems that created the wounds in the first place." He dismissed the revised resolution as "meaningless."

Ali Abuzaakouk, executive director of the American Muslim Council, expressed shock at the amendments and said, "This should not have been a controversial resolution. It simply stated the facts."

In *The New York Times,* reporter Philip Shenon wrote that, through spokesmen, Republican Representatives Henry Hyde, chairman of the Judiciary Committee, and Thomas M. Davis III, a committee member, denied that the amendments were intended to water down the resolution. "Declining to identify the groups that wanted changes, they insisted that the contacts had no effect on the rewriting of the resolution. He said the reference to Oklahoma City was removed "because it might have led to detailed, time-consuming questions on the House floor about what sort of violent harassment followed the bombing."[25]

On the House floor, the resolution provoked no questions, time-consuming or otherwise. It did not reach the floor and received no further consideration. In the waning days of the congressional session, the amended resolution was quietly withdrawn from the legislative calendar.

Although the Washington staff of the National Council of the Churches of Christ in the U.S.A., an organization that represents mainline denominations, made no public protest, its governing board had adopted a constructive resolution in 1986. It deplored anti-Islam, anti-Muslim, and anti-Arab prejudice in the United States and called on Christians, churches, and church-related agencies to "advocate and defend the civil rights of Arabs and Muslims" and to "reject the religious and political demagoguery and manipulation manifest in the reporting of events related to the Middle East." Furthermore, it urged all parties to "seek an understanding of the underlying causes of the events labeled as 'terrorist.'"

In Hollywood, where most movies and many documentaries are produced, the image of Muslim "terrorism" keeps re-appearing. In early 2000, Paramount Pictures profited greatly from *Rules of Engagement,* a movie that maligned Muslims generally and Yemenis in particular and grossed over $43 million. Although the film company denied that it was an "indictment of any government, culture or people," the central episode depicted a mob of violent Yemeni Muslims firing on the U.S. Embassy in Sana'a, capital of the Republic of Yemen, and provoking a bloody counterattack by U.S. Marines who were rescuing embassy personnel. All this from the fertile imagination of a Hollywood scriptwriter.

The most misleading and inflammatory part of the film was a voice recording played during an imaginary U.S. court-martial trial of the Marine who ordered the counterattack. In the recording, the leader of the Yemeni mob exhorted his Muslim followers to "kill Americans," a call that he said came directly from Allah. While viewing the film, I wondered if bin Laden's fiery outburst for *Frontline* cameras had inspired the film writer to insert in the drama's script the voice recording that gave Islam the disturbing, false image. The film's closing captions misled viewers into believing the controversial drama was based on actual occurrences.

Yemen's ambassador to Washington, Abdul Wahab Alhajjri, told *People* magazine: "Nothing close to what happened in the movie has ever happened in Yemen, yet I have friends who know better call me up and ask me if this had actually happened." Ahmed Atef, a member of Yemen's embassy staff in Washington called it "without question the most anti-Arab film ever made." When an Arab-sponsored call for the public to boycott the film had little effect, Alhajjri invited the film's principal actors, Tommy Lee Jones and Samuel L. Jackson, together with the director and producer, to visit Yemen and see for themselves that the nation is peaceful and hospitable to Americans.[26]

A lmost every day I find new evidence of Muslim stereotyping, the most recent from Ronald Baker, an industry representative who was my seatmate on an airline flight to Chicago. Learning that I had served in Congress, he asked if I believed a major threat to U.S. security might arise in the near future. I answered in the negative, noting the dismemberment of the Soviet Union, America's chief post-World War II antagonist. He expressed strong disagreement, predicting that the greatest, most imminent threat would come from Muslim countries. "Just think what just one Muslim leader could do with a few nuclear bombs. I see a real danger from Muslim terrorists."

He related his experience on an airline flight the previous day. "Six of us were seated together in the cabin, three passengers facing three others. When the discussion got around to terrorism, all six agreed that Muslims would start the next general war. All agreed also that Americans, in general, believe that most terrorists are Muslims."

He said he first became concerned about Muslim terrorism in 1986 when he witnessed "the violent side of Muslims" during a visit in Singapore. Unruly crowds protested against Americans after U.S. aircraft bombed Libya, a Muslim country, punishment President Ronald Reagan had ordered for Libya's assertion of sovereignty over the Gulf of Sidra and its alleged involvement in a bombing that killed two Americans in a Berlin discotheque. The U.S. air attack killed several dozen civilians, including an infant, the adopted daughter of Libyan ruler Muammar Qadhafi.

Baker added, "The protests in Singapore were so threatening that, out of concern for my own safety, I pretended to be an Australian." I told him that my impression of Muslims over the past twenty-five years has been favorable, and I summarized my efforts to clear away anti-Islamic stereotypes. He was taken aback. "You are so outspoken about these controversial people and their religion. Aren't you worried about your own safety?" I assured him that I was not, explaining that I am simply trying to clear up public misunderstanding of Islam. When we parted, Baker showed anxiety when he said, "I don't mind if you put my name in your book, because there are probably a lot of Ronald Bakers in

America. But please don't publish my address. I don't want to get involved."

An example of anti-Muslim stereotyping appears in the 1999 State Department Report on Global Terrorism. Those responsible for the document—chief among them Secretary of State Madeleine Albright—need instruction in truth-in-packaging.

The report declares flatly that the "primary terrorist threats to the United States" emanate from Asia and the Middle East, where Muslims predominate, but the statistics and narrative presented elsewhere in the same document run counter to that conclusion. They identify Latin America as a far more active center of anti-U.S. terrorism than either the Middle East or Asia. The report lists ninety-six episodes in Latin America, thirty in Western Europe, nine in Eurasia, and sixteen in Africa. Six occurred in Asia and eleven in the Middle East. Several of the eleven were defensive in nature and therefore improperly classified as terrorism.[27]

The terrorism stereotype of Islam is bolstered by other factors. For example, the common linkage in the U.S. media of the words Islam and Muslim with anti-Israel violence in the Middle East helps keep false images alive. During my congressional years, the PLO was used widely on Capitol Hill as a code word for terrorism. It was hurled like a grenade by some of my colleagues. The word terrorist was used so frequently as a prefix to PLO that a stranger might mistake "Terrorist PLO" as the proper name of the organization. The adjective Islamic is now used in the same way. These days, the PLO is rarely used as a code word for terrorism, partly because the American people are better informed about the organization and PLO leader Arafat's efforts to achieve a just peace through negotiation.

The terrorist image has shifted from the PLO to Hezbollah and Hamas. In common parlance and in the American news media, the word Islamic is tied so often to Hezbollah and Hamas that most Americans view these organizations as naked terrorism under the banner of Islam. Largely because of the pro-Israel bias of government leaders, both groups are included in the State Department's list of terrorist organizations. Consequently, the mere mention of these organizations summons images of veiled terrorists firing automatic guns at defenseless civilians.

The linkage is strengthened by the identification of imams with both groups, and the occasions when individual members claim responsibility in the name of Islam for senseless acts of violence against civilians. To Palestinians, the violence is an extreme expression of anger against Israeli oppression, its continued occupation of their land and confiscation of their property. Many of them view these fanatics as freedom fighters—or martyrs—in the cause of justice and national liberation, but the violence is rarely reported in these terms in the U.S. media.

Most Americans would be surprised to learn that Hezbollah is a well-established, respected, major political organization. It came into being as a resistance movement, provoked by Israel's bloody and destructive invasions of Lebanon, its lethal bombardments of cities and villages, and the failure of the Lebanese government and the U.N. to rescue southern Lebanon from occupation by Israeli forces.

Hezbollah holds about twenty percent of the seats in the Lebanese parliament and maintains substantial medical, social, and educational services for its members. Its armed units have employed violence— sometimes fatal to civilians—-in resisting Israel's long military occupation of southern Lebanon, but its military assaults have been almost entirely defensive, confined to Lebanese soil.

N otwithstanding these facts, Israel and its U.S. supporters— both inside and outside government—have labeled Hezbollah a terrorist organization. The label arose originally from charges that the organization was complicit in the 1983 truck bombing that killed two hundred and forty U.S. Marines stationed near Beirut to protect Israeli interests in Lebanon. Despite the 1999 withdrawal of all Israeli forces from southern Lebanon, the label survives, partly because, over the years, the organization has received support from

Iran, a state that has long been listed by the U.S. State Department as a sponsor of international terrorism.

To many Palestinians, as well as Lebanese, Jordanians and other Arabs, Hezbollah consists of brave patriots who are willing to take great personal risk to keep Israeli forces from occupying any part of Lebanon. A U.S. Peace Corps volunteer in Amman reports that "almost 100 percent of my Jordanian friends consider Hezbollah and Hamas members as heroes." April Szuchyt, noting the heavy Palestinian casualties in Jerusalem and the Occupied Territories, asks: "Can you blame them for feeling this way, considering what's been happening?" [28]

H amas was founded inside the Occupied Territories a decade ago as opposition to Arafat, who, at the time, was based in Tunisia. From its beginning, Hamas has campaigned against Israel's occupation of all territory it seized in the June 1967 war. After Arafat signed the 1993 agreement, known as the Oslo Accords, with Israeli Prime Minister Yitzhak Rabin, the PLO leader moved his headquarters to the Gaza District and began negotiating for a staged withdrawal of Israeli forces. Under the Oslo agreement, the future of Jerusalem, Jewish settlements in the Occupied Territories, and the right-of-return for Palestinian refugees would not be settled until the last stage of negotiations. From the start, Hamas rejected the terms of the accords, opposed any compromise with Israel, and did not agree to the concessions that Arafat tentatively accepted.

Over the years, Arafat has sought Hamas' cooperation, with only intermittent success. In their struggle against Israeli occupation, Hamas members have confined their resistance operations to Palestine and Israel but at times have used extreme, suicidal measures against civilian targets—fanatical acts that clearly violate Islamic law.

Most Americans do not know that both Hezbollah and Hamas have important social and educational, as well as military, branches. Nor do they recognize the diversity of viewpoints within each group. Within both organizations are people with wide-ranging views and impulses. At one extreme, some members, disillusioned by decades of oppression and devoid of any hope for a decent future, have become despondent, fatalistic radicals who are bent on vengeance in almost any form. At the other extreme are those who—true to Islamic teachings—oppose any form of violence except in self-defense or to correct injustice.

A nother factor that keeps false images of Islam alive is the aggressive lobbying that occurs in Washington on behalf of U.S. aid to Israel. In its highly successful endeavors to promote enormous aid grants each year from Washington, lobbyists assert that Israel constantly faces serious threats to its security posed by "Muslim terrorist" groups, some of which unwittingly facilitate the campaign of the lobbyists by including the words Islamic, Islam, or Muslim in the proper names of their organizations.

Gene Bird, a former U.S. foreign service officer who heads the Washington-based Council on the National Interest and closely follows Middle-East related activities at both ends of Pennsylvania Avenue in Washington, calls the terrorist image of Islam a "hot button." He adds,

"It is used frequently, because it gets action. It plays on fears and stirs emotions. It is cultivated and propagated by lobbyists, because they know it wins support for multibillion dollar, unconditional grants to Israel year after year. In this lobbying, the specter of Muslim-sponsored terrorism is a frequent theme. It is used to rationalize the Jewish state's harsh treatment of Palestinians, most of whom are Muslim, and to justify Israel's periodic military assaults against Lebanon, where Muslims predominate. The terrorist image is the foundation of Israel's demand for regular U.S. grants of high-tech weaponry, as well as financial aid, to bolster its defenses against possible missile attacks from Syria, Iraq, and Iran, as well as other states where Islam is dominant."

The stereotype, Bird notes, prompts governmental decisions that are costly to the American people. In the past decade, the bias has facilitated annual U.S. grants to Israel that average $4.7 billion.

Besides this heavy load on taxpayers, America's unconditional political, diplomatic and military aid to Israel damages other U.S. national interests. It prompts reactions in most world capitals that range from disgust to amusement. Bird states, "It gets our diplomats into embarrassing positions at the United Nations. There, the U.S. representatives on the UN Security Council have vetoed, time and again, resolutions that condemn Israel's violations of Palestinian human rights, even though these condemnations are consistent with cherished American principles and enjoy the near-unanimous support of other governments." By providing unconditional aid, despite Israel's abuse of Palestinian rights, succeeding U.S. administrations have stained America's reputation as a champion of universal human rights.

B ird cites an imposing irony. "While warning against terrorism by Muslims, Israel employs its own state-sponsored terrorism in the guise of counter-terrorism." The Israeli government officially sanctions the employment of extreme physical measures—in plain language, torture—to elicit confessions from Muslims, even U.S. citizens, who are incarcerated on suspicion of security risk.[29]

This Israeli misbehavior is rarely noted in the U.S. media, but, in a notable exception, CNN broadcast during prime time one evening in September 2000 a report on Israel's arrest, detention and torture of U.S. citizen Anwar Mohamed, a Muslim who was visiting relatives in Jerusalem in 1998.

Although a U.S. citizen with a valid passport, Mohamed was held without charge for forty days in a dank prison. For long hours during his confinement, he was locked in painful positions on a chair with his head covered by an odorous sack, deprived of sleep and exposed to extremes of heat and cold.

This brutal treatment was a futile attempt to force him to sign a document confessing complicity in terrorism. Officials of the U.S. Consulate in Jerusalem, even though located only a few blocks from Mohamed's prison, provided no defense or assistance during his ordeal beyond handing Mohamed a list of lawyers he might hire. Ultimately, he was released without charge but forced to buy a Palestinian passport before he could leave Israel.

Investigating this example of torture, CNN interviewer Charles Glass learned from diplomats, past and present, that U.S. consular officials in Israel do not follow customary State Department procedures when the rights of U.S. citizens are violated. They do not insist that the Israeli government abide by the same humane rules that Washington insists be followed in other countries.

Glass asked Mohamed how he felt during his incarceration when he read "Made in the U.S." on the handcuffs that bound his wrists. He responded, "I felt betrayed."

I srael's state-sponsored oppression of Palestinians and other Arabs shows no sign of fading away. Nor does the false image of Islamic terrorism, which remains a vivid presence on Capitol Hill and a recurrent theme in Hollywood. From some of the highest offices in the land to conversations on airliners, anti-Muslim bias flows like destructive floodwater.

It is a phenomenon that cannot be blamed just on the general ignorance of U.S. journalists about Islam. Reporters are misinformed about other religions, peoples, cultures, and political currents, but none of these shortcomings provoke misconceptions and hatreds on a scale comparable to the anti-Muslim stereotypes that flood America. The impact of these images on Muslim community life is broad and deep. They afflict young and old, rich and poor, men and women, people on every level of occupation, education and income.

A few days into the twenty-first century, Laila Al-Marayati chose somber words to review the "tide of despondency" afflicting U.S. Muslims:

"Threats of millennial terrorism by Algerian extremist Muslims; a plane mysteriously plunging into the sea with the last recorded words from a well-known Muslim prayer; another plane hijacked by Kashmiri militants; weapons of mass destruction unleashed upon Chechen Muslims. The list is too well known. Surely this is a season of demoralization and depression in the

Muslim community, a community which is equally horrified by acts of violence against innocent civilians and fearful of irrational backlash that can follow such events."[30] Mohamed El-Bendary declares, "American Muslims are just as worried about the threat of terrorism as all their fellow Americans."[31]

Against this bleak scene, David Waters, a lonely but strong voice of reason as religion writer for the Memphis, Tennessee, *Commercial Appeal,* offers a comforting assessment: "In this country, when we think of Islam, we tend to visualize media-driven images of violence. In a recent poll, more than half of those surveyed mistakenly thought Islam supported terrorism. The heart of Christianity is peace, justice, and mercy. So is the heart of Islam. There's no such thing as a Muslim terrorist, nor a Christian terrorist, or a Jewish terrorist for that matter." [32]

Notes:

1. *USA Today,* 8-16-1999, p. 1.
2. *Rocky Mountain News,* 5-12-2000 (Denver).
3. CAIR e-mail, 6-22-2000.
4. *Chicago Tribune,* 6-29-2000, pp 1–2.
5. *Chicago Tribune,* 6-30-2000.
6. *State Journal-Register,* 9-29-2000 (Springfield, IL.), p. 10; and *Chicago Tribune,* 10-1-2000, p. 5P, sect. 16.
7. *Chicago Tribune,* 7-17-2000, pp. 1, 12.
8. Chicago Tribune, 7-17-2000, p. 12.
9. *Los Angeles Herald Examiner,* 2-26-1989, p. G-1.
10. *Los Angeles Times,* 11-9-2000
11. Ralph Braibanti, *The Nature and Structure of the Islamic World,* p. 7]
12. *Wall Street Journal,* 10-4-1984.
13. "A Devil Theory of Islam," *The Nation Magazine* 8-96.
14. *Los Angeles Herald-Examiner,* 2-26-1989, p. G-1.
15. UASR Publishing Group, 1999.
16. *The Jewish Monthly,* 3-95.
17. Senate Judiciary Committee report, 4-27-1995.
18. *WSJ,* 6-25-1993.
19. *San Diego Union Tribune,* 6-8-1993.

20. CNN, 4-20-1995.

21. Ahmed Yousef, *The Agent,* p. 56.

22. *New York Times,* 11-24-1999.

23. 1998 CAIR report on harassment.

24. MSNBC web page, 12-30-1999.

25. *New York Times,* 11-24-1999.

26. *People,* 5-8-2000, p. 28.

27. Department of State, *Patterns of Global Terrorism* (1999).

28. E-mail, 11-8-2000.

29. Interview, 7-20-2000.

30. *Religious News Service,* 1-6-2000.

31. MSNBC web page, 12-30-1999.

32. *Memphis Commercial Appeal,* 8-30-1996.

Chapter 4: The Taliban Factor

A mericans with little knowledge of Islam may mistakenly believe that the Taliban, the regime that controls most of Afghanistan and calls itself the Islamic Emirate of Afghanistan, is a foretaste of what future Islam-inspired governments would be like.

The Taliban government's misrepresentation of Islam arises from the following facts: The word 'Islamic' appears in its official name; the religious affiliation of almost all Afghans, including the Taliban leaders, is Islamic; and U.S. Muslim leaders rarely criticize the Taliban publicly for this misuse of the word Islam. In fact, until they destroyed Buddhist statues, they were seldom criticized publicly in any respect, and the comments of those who did speak out received no coverage in the major media.

These factors reinforce the misconception that a Taliban-like government in Afghanistan is the type that Muslims would like to see established elsewhere in the world. This image is especially disturbing to Americans who worry about how U.S. Muslims would change America if they gained political control.

The Taliban call themselves Islamic, but their abuse of human rights, especially those of women, and their failure to stop heroin-trafficking, are severe violations of Islamic teachings. In a little-noted 1999 report, UN Secretary-General Kofi Annan accused the Taliban of "massive and systematic violations of human rights," including the "summary execution of women and children."[1]

The Taliban's self-characterization of their government as an Islamic state casts a long shadow over U.S. Muslims, simply because the regime remains prominent in news broadcasts and newspaper headlines. Taliban governmental practices are inevitably identified with Islam by non-Muslims no matter how influential non-religious factors, like cultural practices and war zone reality, may be in shaping these policies.

The Taliban deserve the critical attention of U.S. Muslims, because their regime is not what they pretend it to be. They have not created a true Islamic state, nor has any other Muslim country, although several of them, like the Taliban regime, use the words Islam or Islamic in their official names.

The BBC's correspondent in Pakistan, Rahimullah Yousafzai, writes, "At present, there is no single government or country that is perfectly Islamic. The Taliban, the Saudis, the Iranians, Sudanese, Pakistanis, and so on, are all 'experimenting.'" He predicts that "the Taliban regime is not likely to be taken as a role model by Muslims elsewhere in the world," but his assurance is unlikely to relieve the anxiety of non-Muslims in the United States.[2] Few Americans hear BBC broadcasts with regularity, and many are already apprehensive about the growth of America's Muslim population.

Most Americans, I believe, are unaware of the common links between the governance by public consensus —the *Shura*—that is specified in the Quran and the U.S. constitutional system. They do not recognize that the two systems are compatible and complementary in their democratic structures. Lacking that knowledge, non-Muslims are easily misled into concluding that Afghanistan under the Taliban is truly Islamic. In important respects, the Republic of Yemen, a Muslim country, may come the closest because of its steady progress toward a democratic structure that is strikingly similar to the consensus government of, by, and for the people that is the clearly stated goal of Islam.

E xcept for the Republic of Yemen, Muslim countries are generally ruled by kings, generals or dictators. The Yemeni system is exceptional, because the president and parliament, both directly elected, are designed to provide checks and balances on each other. These advances toward consultative government, however, go largely unnoticed beyond Yemen's borders. My understanding of Yemen comes mainly from five trips there, the first two as a Member of Congress.

I have never visited Afghanistan, so my information and insights come from others. In my quest for a balanced view of the Taliban factor, I read several books and studies, talked directly and frequently with several Muslim men and women who are familiar with Afghan society, and consulted with people I have encountered at various times during my long journey through Islam.

My principal sources are five men. One of them is Andrew Patterson, who has recently completed a study of Afghanistan and its history. Another is Mohammed Bashardost, M.D., a refugee from Afghanistan and our next-door neighbor during my last years in Congress. In January 2000, responding to his holiday greeting, I informed him that my forthcoming book on U.S. Muslims would include a chapter on Afghanistan. He began supplying me with correspondence and documents. Although he assured me that he had no connection with the Taliban or other political entities inside Afghanistan, he wished to provide me with a correct understanding of the ordeal his native land has endured and the rebuilding endeavors it is now undertaking. He even offered to finance a trip so that I could gain firsthand knowledge of Afghan conditions, an invitation I declined for want of time. Another source is Saeed Ahmad Butt of Lahore, Pakistan, a retired foreign service official, who became an acquaintance when he sought my permission— readily granted—to arrange the translation and publication of my book, *They Dare to Speak Out*, in Urdu, the language of Pakistan. The extensive correspondence that followed made me recognize him as a qualified observer of Afghan issues and trends. He also helped by putting me in touch with two other valuable Pakistani sources on Afghanistan, BBC's Yousafzai and Tariq Majeed, an author and retired commodore in the Pakistani Navy.

Correspondence with these sources, along with my own research, convinced me that the Taliban regime, while responsible for a number of constructive achievements, is un-Islamic in significant ways.

Despite Islam's strong condemnation of drugs, the Taliban and Afghanistan's economy rely heavily on domestic production and foreign marketing of heroin and opium. Drugs constitute the country's largest source of export income.

The regime prohibits the local consumption of heroin but makes only superficial moves to halt production for export. The superior quality of Afghan heroin has long been legendary, and production is booming. In 1997, with the Taliban in control of most of the country, Afghanistan's production of poppies increased by 25 percent over the previous year.

The Taliban assert that poppy production is essential to the survival of poor farmers and, in keeping with that pronouncement, have not used their formidable police power to crack down on the drug trade. In his book, *The Taliban,* Peter Marsden disputes the official assertion. He reports, "Some of the most recent [Taliban] statements have indicated that, because of poverty, farmers in Afghanistan have no choice but to grow [poppies]." But he adds that, in reality, the poor benefit only when the large landowners need seasonal labor for cultivation or when they ask small-scale farmers to supplement their production to meet unexpected market demand.[3] Wealthy Afghans control the production of most of the poppies, as well as the processing and shipment of by-products to foreign markets.

D iscrimination against women, another violation of Islam, is pervasive and longstanding. Patterson reports that early in 1999 the Taliban began enforcing the following regulations on residents of Kabul and other regions under their control:

- Women cannot leave their homes except when accompanied by a male, even if an emergency merits the services of a physician or a hospital.
- Except in rare circumstances, male physicians cannot treat women, despite a severe shortage of female physicians.
- Women cannot be employed outside the home, except in limited job categories specified by the Taliban.

- When outside their home, women are required to wear veils over their faces.
- Government schools are for males only. Schools for females exist only in the planning stage.
- All men are required to wear beards and pray in mosques at prayer time.
- Television sets are outlawed.

None of these regulations, Patterson notes, are required or condoned by Islam. Most of them violate the principles of human rights that are exalted in the Quran. These violations arise mainly from the Taliban's determination to retain—and tighten—non-religious traditions that flourished in Afghanistan long before the present regime came to power.

The first of these traditions is the male domination of government, education, and private employment. While nothing can justify Taliban complicity in the drug trade, or the harsh regulations the regime imposed on women, it should be noted that the Taliban control most of a country where harshness typifies its present economic circumstances, as well as much of its history and geography. Patterson describes Afghanistan geographically as one of the most remote, isolated, mountainous countries in the world:

"Its people have had a rough ride through history, enduring difficult living conditions, wanton slaughter at times, and frequent military assaults as the political landscape kept shifting. In the thirteenth century, Haulage Khan, the grandson of Genghis Khan, raised an army and depopulated much of the area, slaughtering hundreds of thousands of its inhabitants and destroying entire cities and elaborate irrigation works.

"Land-locked and surrounded by neighbors that have different cultures and religions, Afghanistan has been a crossroads of repeated, violent military incursions. For years, it was under Persian, then British incursions. Soviet influence intensified during the 1970s.

"The Taliban consist of tough, dedicated young men, perhaps 20,000 at most, many of whom spent their boyhood as refugees in northern Pakistan during the years when Soviet forces occupied most of Afghanistan. They were educated in religious schools established in Peshawar by the British before Pakistan became an independent state. In these schools, the first six years of instruction were devoted to basic education, followed by two years of training that included ideological indoctrination which developed intolerance toward people of other religions or nationalities—harsh departures from Islamic standards. The two final years were devoted to military training."

Patterson sketches the "divide and rule" educational theme of that period: "The British intended the schools to foster interfaith hostilities. The purpose was to promote strife that would help justify overall British dominance of India, which then included present-day Pakistan. A major British goal was to nurture distrust and hostility between Muslims and Hindus. The British established schools in the future Pakistan where Muslim students were indoctrinated to be intolerant of Hindus, and they established schools in other areas where Hindu students were indoctrinated to distrust Muslims."

Patterson noted a change in focus that occurred when the Soviets invaded Afghanistan and young refugees from that country became dominant in the Peshawar schools:

"The indoctrination agenda dropped the anti-Hindu theme. It shifted instead to instruction that created hostility to the Soviet invaders and their Afghan collaborators."[4]

It was a timely change. Soviet forces carried out brutal attacks throughout Afghanistan including rural areas, especially against Muslim leaders and Islamic institutions. The West has little awareness of the enormous carnage and property destruction, partly because the CIA barred major news media from on-site coverage. Human slaughter was far greater in Afghanistan than the well-publicized massacres carried out in the early and late 1990s by Serb forces against Bosnian and Kosovar Muslims in Yugoslavia.

Journalist Bruce Richardson estimates that two million Afghans, mostly civilians in rural areas, were killed by the Soviets during the decade the Soviets occupied the country. Approximately

750,000 other civilians lost limbs to land mines. Nearly a million rural homes, including eleven thousand villages, were leveled, along with a similar number of mosques, and about three thousand primary schools. Over one hundred seventy thousand horses, fifteen million sheep and goats, and nearly two million cattle were killed.

Typically, a village and its inhabitants would be destroyed in one of two ways. In one, Soviet forces would first conduct an intensive air bombardment, then Soviet helicopter gun-ships would overfly the scene to kill any survivors trying to flee from the rubble. In the other way, Soviet artillery and rocket-launchers were positioned to destroy all structures. Then Soviet troops and those of the Democratic Republic of Afghanistan—the Soviet-controlled Afghan regime—would sweep through the wreckage and kill any villagers who were still alive. Then they poisoned wells, booby-trapped dead bodies, and placed land mines in grain storage facilities, assuring death or injury to anyone attempting to bury the dead or retrieve scarce grain.[5]

S aeed Ahmed Butt believes that religious faith played a major role in Afghan resistance:

"The American people are likely to give great credit to the military hardware their government supplied. They are forgetful of the fact that for two and a half years, the United States shipped no arms at all and did not even make a commitment that they would eventually help. The Afghans took on the Soviet tanks, gun ships, heavy guns, and millions of land mines, along with the forces of the entrenched Communist government in Kabul, on the basis of their sublime faith and confidence in God.

"It is next to impossible for Western journalists to capture their spirit. How can they? If the Afghan people had the same social norms and group behavior considered normal by Western observers, they would not have successfully borne the mighty Soviet onslaught for ten long years and finally been able to make the Soviet forces retreat. Something sustained and nurtured them throughout this dreadful ordeal."[6]

After remaining on the sidelines for nearly three years, the U.S. government decided to help fight the Soviet occupation by providing money, munitions, and training. By then, Osama bin Laden had assumed a prominent role, both as a construction engineer and a fighter. Once the Soviets were driven from Afghanistan, bin Laden took his heavy equipment and staff to Sudan, where he won gratitude by launching the construction of the vital 800-mile long Khartoum-Atbara-Port Sudan highway.

Later, after his departure from Sudan, he turned political fire against Israel and its close ally, the U.S. government. He criticized Israel for its sustained mistreatment of Palestinians and the U.S. government for its complicity in this injustice. He opposed the continuing presence in the Persian Gulf region of U.S. military forces and those of Britain—yesterday's imperial power in the region—especially the forces located in Saudi Arabia, whose territory includes Islam's holiest shrines at Mecca and Medina.

In response, Washington officials accused him of using the camps in Afghanistan to train terrorists for assignments around the world. They contended that some of the trainees, as well as bin Laden himself, were involved in the 1998 bombing of U.S. embassies in Kenya and Tanzania.

In light of bin Laden's substantial help in driving out the Soviet invaders, the Taliban gave him sanctuary. He is likely, however, to continue to be a hero in Afghanistan. Rahimullah Yousufzei's assessment is that "the United States has made Osama bin Laden the hero of the Muslim world. Every time the United States draws attention to him, he grows in stature."[7]

Bin Laden apparently played no significant role during the stormy period that followed the expulsion of the Soviet invaders. The country bin Laden helped to save fell into chaos. Bands of Muslim freedom fighters who had succeeded in expelling the Soviet invaders became independent warlords and fought among themselves for power.

With the support of the United States and Pakistan, a coalition of five of these factions was formed, but it quickly fell apart.

Touring Afghanistan at the time, author Bruce Richardson encountered "incredible corruption."

During this stormy period, the United States, Pakistan and Saudi Arabia supported the Taliban and helped them gain political control of urban areas and much of the countryside. Once in power, the Taliban established order by confiscating all privately held firearms and instituting harsh discipline.

Western journalists disagree on the aftermath. After traveling extensively throughout the country, Richardson noted "an absence of corruption and physical crime in the cities and, in rural regions, no abuse of the population, including women."[8] In contrast, during a tour during the early months of Taliban rule, British journalist Peter Marsden found Afghan passions divided over the behavior of the new government. "They [the Taliban] have emerged on the scene as holy warriors, overwhelming much of the country, through the onward march of young men willing to martyr themselves for the cause. They have also, from a Western point of view and from the point of view of most Muslims, behaved in an extreme, oppressive way toward women by enforcing their seclusion from society." Marsden expressed a "measure of sympathy and understanding" because of Afghan "weariness with continued fighting and disappointment with resistance leaders who failed to unite and form a stable government."[9]

Pamela Constable, a *Washington Post* correspondent, toured Afghanistan recently and found the Taliban had brought "positive changes." "After years of turbulence, there is now a sense of security in the region, whose fate once depended on the benevolence, might and shifting alliances of warlords...."[10]

Patterson noted that Afghan enthusiasm for the Taliban was short-lived. "At first, the Taliban was welcomed by the war-weary Afghans, but sentiment soured with the imposition of harsh, intolerant restrictions, a reflection of their indoctrination in Peshawar. The Taliban established a rigid autocracy, not the democratic principles which are ingrained in the Quran. They also reversed the rights of women that are guaranteed under Islamic law."

The major U.S. news media have given scant attention to Muslim criticism of the Taliban, but this lack of published or broadcast protest is not an indication of approval or disinterest by American Muslims. Some leaders have denounced the Taliban's repressive rules, human rights abuses, and the regime's posture as a true Islamic state.

L aila Al-Marayati, in a statement distributed in December 1998 by the Religion News Service, condemned the Taliban for "enforcing gender segregation at the expense of women's needs," and for prohibiting Afghan women from being cared for by male physicians, especially when female physicians are in short supply. She accused the Taliban of "controverting the Quran" by removing women from the workplace.

She wrote, "Any government that professes to enforce Sharia [Islamic law] must be aware that the essential purpose of Sharia is to guarantee for every citizen five broad rights encompassing all aspects of human endeavor. These are the rights to life, intellect, family, property and religion.... By obstructing Afghani women's enjoyment of these rights, the Taliban leadership exposes their own ignorance of Islam.... The repressive policies of the Taliban are doomed to persist until they and others who share their views can appreciate the spirit of egalitarianism expressed in the Quran."

Al-Marayati denounced Taliban policies as "an aberration in violation of the most basic tenets of the faith.... The Taliban have imposed harsh measures on all Afghanis, and particularly against women, in the name of Islam." Deploring the Taliban's use of corporal punishment without due process, she called upon the Afghan leaders and other Muslim leaders to "look within Islam itself," rather than through a distorting lens that is secular, not religious.

Hassan Hathout, M.D., a leader in the Islamic Center of Southern California, challenges the Taliban's self-proclaimed identification with Islam. "Obviously, the Taliban's military prowess far exceeds their knowledge of Islam. When they fought the Russians, they captured our hearts, and we invested so much hope in them. Our dreams were shattered as they emerged from their victory killing one another. Now the Taliban emerge victorious, but certainly Islam does not. Islam requires them to heal their enmities and build their country and clean it of hatred and prejudice. For this is the razor that, as the Prophet said, does not shave hair, but shaves off religion."

Hathout, whose latest book is *Reading the Muslim Mind,* adds, "Oppression of women is a clear violation of the teachings of the Quran, the model of the Prophet Muhammad and the authentic early practice of Islam.... Now, we witness [in Afghanistan] the gagging of the girl-child with the clubs and cloak of clerics.... We feel it is our duty to defend the religion and defend its reputation, often tarnished by the Western media, but in this case, regrettably, by ill-advised Muslims.... In some places in the Muslim world, women [and indeed men] are suppressed and denied their basic Islamic rights, but nothing to match the Taliban's recent decrees at the doorsteps of the twenty-first century."

Hathout adds this scathing assessment: "The one million Afghans who sacrificed their lives to deter Soviet aggression are now minimized. The story of their sacrifice has now been diminished and displaced with the fire of fratricidal warfare and the barks of humiliation by religious police."[11]

In a sermon, Imam Musa Qutub, head of Chicago's Islamic Information Center of America, described the Taliban as "deviating from the mainstream of Islam."[12]

The Taliban's regulations have generated other protests in the West. A report that the Taliban had issued an edict requiring all men to wear untrimmed beards—a report disputed by Dr. Mohammed Bashardost—infuriated Dr. Aslam Abdullah, editor of *The Minaret,* a monthly magazine for the Muslim community, and prompted him to shave his own neatly-cropped beard in protest. A few weeks later Abdullah reconsidered when Muslims in Kosova were under brutal assault. He grew back his beard as a demonstration of empathy with the Kosovars.

Patterson considers the Taliban practices an embarrassment to his Islamic faith. "I am so upset over the Taliban's interpretation of

Islam that I am inclined to end one of my books with this line from an old movie: 'God uses the good, and the bad use God.'"

Protests from the Feminist Majority, with the help of the widely syndicated column called "Dear Abby" and written by Abigail Van Buren, have received wide attention. A letter about the Taliban's repression of women published in the February 26, 1999, column brought more than 45,000 responses. Mavis Nicholson Leno, wife of NBC *Tonight Show* host Jay Leno, in addition to chairing the campaign against "gender apartheid in Afghanistan," contributed $100,000 to the cause.

In the "Dear Abby" column on July 12,1999, Leno reported results that extended beyond the torrent of phone calls. These included an endorsement by President Clinton, bipartisan support on Capitol Hill, and meetings with United Nations officials. In the column, she quoted a letter from a woman in Kabul: "I wish I could cover you with flowers to show how grateful I am. From this prison I can only send you a few drops of my tears as a gift." On September 10, 1999, the column published an unsigned letter from a New Jersey Muslim. "The suppression of women in Afghanistan or any other Muslim country is falsely attributed to the teachings of Islam. In fact, the acts of emancipation promoted by the Prophet gave women a place of honor and respect in seventh century Arabia. For instance, in the battles that were fought in the beginning of Islam, women worked in the field, nursing and comforting the wounded. They were neither sheltered nor shunned."

O bservers close to the Afghan scene offer contrasting assessments. Commodore Tariq Majeed writes, "Giving special protection and honor to women, escorting them when they go out especially after dark, encouraging them to seek medical treatment from lady doctors, affording them segregation from males in academic institutions—these are the norms in Muslim society and were also practiced in all Western countries, including the United States, before World War I. Can anyone say that society in the Western countries in those days was primitive or not progressive?"

Majeed finds that in past years, due to "geographical, historical, educational and tribal factors in some Muslim states or in parts of others, women were subjected to overprotection and were denied some of the basic rights granted to them by Islam." He writes, "Afghanistan was one such state. In recent times, Afghan leaders began to give them back their rights, such as education and employment. But the 'enforced rules' are not a peculiarity of the Taliban. The same rules, except for one or two concerning education, are also enforced in provinces of Afghanistan which remain under opposition control."

He is, however, sharply critical of the regime. "The Taliban are disgracing and ridiculing Islamic concepts, values and practices." As an example, he cites as "mischievous" the Taliban decision to name the government broadcasting unit "Radio Shariah." In his view, this is a desecration of the Shariah, the basic body of Islamic law. He objects to the Taliban leader calling himself "Amirul Momineen," a title historically reserved for the head of the entire Islamic community."[13]

Yousafzai notes that the Western media "very rarely report the achievements of the Taliban in disarming the population in a lawless country flooded with arms and ammunition, removal of roadblocks and checkpoints, and protecting the life and honor of people in areas under their control, and lastly reuniting almost 90 percent of Afghanistan under one authority which, until recently, was under many armed groups, commandos that established their own fiefdoms and loosed reigns of terror. These groups ruled by force alone, while the Taliban claim is not solely based on force."

He explains the Taliban's swift rise to power. "Their predecessors, the Afghan mujahideen had failed to bring peace or enforce Islamic law after having successfully fought the Soviet occupation and the pro-Moscow regime in Kabul. The Taliban were welcomed by the masses who were fed up with the mujahideen and wanted to get rid of them. This explains why most of the Taliban victories were gained without actual fighting."

He reports that some Taliban restrictions are now eased but, others viewed as normal, are maintained. "Women are increasingly going out of their homes, although they have to wear veils. They are taken to male doctors in case of need. Guarding female 'honor,' men wearing a turban and beard, the dominance of men folk, and the observance of religious rituals have been their tribal custom or tradition for centuries. These rules hardly need to be enforced in rural Afghanistan, because the people observe all these as a matter of routine. Only the Western-educated elite in Kabul feel the pinch of these Taliban regulations."[14]

On September 1999, Taliban spokesman Wakil Ahmed Mutwakkel announced that heavy military expenditures had left little money for education and health. Looking to the future, he said, "We intend to have an educational program for both genders." He stated, however, that none of the institutions will be co-educational.[15]

In late December 1999, the Taliban received good marks world-wide for their leadership in dealing with a crisis in which Kashmiri militants killed one passenger and held one hundred fifty-five others hostage on an Air India airliner for eight days at an Afghan airport. At first, the militants demanded that India pay a ransom of $200 million, release thirty-six fellow militants from prison, and exhume the body of another and return it to the custody of the Kashmiris.

When a Taliban negotiator notified the hijackers that "the whole process of hijacking and holding people for ransom and exhuming bodies is against Islamic teachings," the demands for money and the exhumed body were dropped.[16] After further negotiations with Taliban leaders, the hijackers ended the ordeal when the government of India agreed to release just one Muslim leader from prison. As a part of the deal, Taliban officers provided the hijackers with safe escort to an undisclosed mountainous region of Afghanistan where they were set free. In January 2000, the Afghan regime made another move toward improving its international image by inviting the CNN cable network to establish a permanent bureau in Kabul. It also gave BBC access for wider coverage of the countryside.

Mohammed Bashardost is optimistic about the future. "After decades of war, bloodshed, kidnappings and lootings, the men and women of Afghanistan were impatient for someone, some group, some institution to restore peace, security, and stability. They understand the value of unity, security, collecting weapons, and peace. They embraced the Taliban for these achievements, but they would have embraced any other group, nation, or international institution that would have done the same. They know a war-torn nation cannot be rebuilt and brought into the international mainstream overnight."

Bashardost hopes that the U.S. government will take the lead in "constructive dialogue" with the Taliban and urge an end to sanctions against Afghanistan. He defends the traditional protection of women in Afghan culture. "Namoos is a cherished term that signifies the extreme honor and respect that Afghan males have always extended to females."[17]

B ut honor and respect are difficult to discern in government policies toward female education and employment. In July 2000, the Taliban blocked a program for home-based employment of women and jailed its leaders. Sponsored by an organization called the Physiotherapy and Rehabilitation Support for Afghanistan, based in Arizona, the project was designed to enhance the earnings of homebound women. Its leader, Mary Mackmakin, and her staff were jailed for four days.[18]

The education of Afghan females has been long neglected. Male literacy is only 33 percent, but among women it is estimated at a pitiful 5 percent and may be even lower. This indicates that women, despite Namoos, have suffered discrimination in education long before the Taliban came to power.[19]

Bashardost recognizes the need for change. He writes that the Taliban have the potential "to be reformed from within." His prediction, "By the time your book is published, I am sure changes in government policy will occur that will create a better image of Afghanistan, including the status of women. Let me say that female education cannot be ignored forever. The same goes for other issues."[20] In early 2001, in partial fulfillment of Bashardost's prophecy, a United Nations inspection commission reported a sharp decline in Afghanistan's poppy production.[21]

Saeed Ahmed Butt writes from Pakistan, "Keep in mind that Afghans lost more than one million souls during this epic, unequal struggle against the Soviet Union. More than five million had to take refuge in neighboring countries and lived in miserable conditions for longer than ten years."[22] Other estimates put the death toll at two million. Butt notes that separation of the sexes in schools, hospitals, and physician services, the wearing of veils over female faces, the beard requirement, and the requirement of male escorts for females outside the home were traditions long before the Taliban came into power, and some of them long before the advent of Islam.[23]

B ut these practices, whether prompted by religion, secular custom, or civil strife, are mandated by government, not left to individual or family choice. On these issues, there is no freedom to choose in Afghanistan. The Islamic ideal of government by consensus that protects equally the rights and dignity of all people is nowhere to be found.

Afghan freedom fighters deserve unstinted praise for their extraordinary, sustained bravery in the fight to drive out the Soviet invaders and their Afghan accomplices. All Afghans deserve international empathy as they continue to grapple with numerous challenges in the chaotic aftermath of that decade-long struggle.

The struggle took on heightened intensity in late 2000 with the arrival of widespread famine. In March 2001, the United Nations warned that more than a million Afghans faced imminent starvation in the wake of three successive years of drought. Ironically, the same organization—the UN—intensified the agony by imposing concurrently, at U.S. behest, drastic economic sanctions on the entire nation because the Taliban refused to extradite Osama bin Laden from his safe haven in Afghanistan. He was wanted by U.S. justice officials on charges of terrorism. A Taliban leader in Herat commented: "We don't understand why the Americans are killing the Afghan people with these sanctions just to get one man— Osama bin Laden." [24]

Outsiders do not seem to recognize that bin Laden is one of the preeminent heroes of Afghans, occupying a role similar to the

Marquis de Lafayette, a Frenchman who fought at the side of the Colonials during America's Revolutionary War. Bin Laden was in the battle to drive out the Soviets long before the U.S. government took action.

The scene became all the more grotesque in February 2001 when, to worldwide consternation, the Taliban ordered the destruction of giant Buddhist statues carved into solid rock long before the advent of Islam. Afghanistan is one of the earliest sites of the Buddhist religion, and the statues were considered   priceless relics of antiquity by historians. Protests erupted worldwide. Muslim leaders in other countries lamented the Taliban   decision, contending that Islam, although opposed to images of its religious figures and to idolatry, does not condone the destruction of the symbols of other religions.

The tumult over the statues provided further evidence that the Taliban are not entitled to call their government an Islamic state, but the showdown over U.N. sanctions demonstrated gross insensitivity, hypocrisy, and ignorance by the world community. The destruction of two Buddhist statues elicited heavy, sustained international protest, far more than the impending obliteration of priceless relics at Kerma on the banks of the Nile in Sudan, all that remains of an ancient Nubian civilization. The relics will be engulfed and thousands of Nubians displaced from their ancestral homeland, when a third dam, as approved, is built below the High Dam at Kajbar on the Nile. Even more outrageous was the near-total indifference of world opinion to the death of multitudes of Afghans for want of food and medicine, misery magnified by the UN-imposed economic sanctions.

It is likely that the Taliban decision to destroy the statues, although a gross error, was to a great extent, a political act of defiance against the UN sanctions. A native of Sudan told me, "Saving people is no less important than saving their heritage. The two are inseparable; one is the reflection of the other. It seems to me that the Taliban action was a result of their isolation and the non-concern of the world community for their plight."

Notes:

1. *USA Today,* 12-29-1999.
2. Letter, 9-30-1999.
3. Peter Marsden, *The Taliban,* p 141.
4. Interview, 8-7-2000.
5. Ibid.
6. Saeed Ahmed Butt, letter, 8-31-1999.
7. Letter, 10-30-1999.
8. Interview, 7-6-1999.
9. Peter Marsden, *The Taliban, War, Religion and the New Order in Afghanistan,* pp. 57, 148.
10. *Washington Post,* 5-21-1999, p. A23.
11. News release, Muslim Public Affairs Council, 7-99.
12. Letter, 10-8-1999.
13. Letter, 9-24-1999.
14. Letter, 10-30-1999.
15. AFP news agency, 9-14-1999.
16. Amir Zia, Kandahar, Afghanistan, AP dispatch, 12-30-1999.
17. Letter, 4-16-1999.
18. *USA Today,* 7-13-2000, p. 8A.
19. Letter, 8-1-99; and *Afghanistan in Pictures* (Lerner Publications, 1990), p. 47.
20. Letter, 8-15-2000.
21. *Journal Courier,* 2-16-2000, Jacksonville, IL, AP dispatch, p. 10.
22. Letter, 8-31-1999.
23. Ibid.
24. *Time,* 3-7-2001, p. 47–48.

Chapter 5: "We Hold These Truths"

In assessing damage to the reputation of Islam, much of the blame must be placed on certain Muslims: Those who create inaccurate and unsettling visions of the type of government and society Muslims want to establish; those who commit acts of religious intolerance and other un-Islamic misdeeds in the name of their religion; and those who hear or see reports of such misbehavior by professed Muslims without speaking out in protest.

Religious tolerance is basic to the three great monotheistic religions, and it merits preeminent re-affirmation and dutiful application. It is often exalted in tenets of Christianity, Islam, and Judaism and in the laws and traditions of the United States. Nevertheless, religious intolerance remains a common occurrence in the behavior of many people who call themselves Christians, Muslims or Jews. Sometimes it is expressed in awful brutality. A horrible example occurred in Germany during World War II when the Nazi regime murdered an estimated six million human beings simply because they were Jews. Although not on the scale of the Nazi Holocaust, other awful examples of religious intolerance have occurred in recent years, notably the slaughter of Muslims in Bosnia and Kosova.

In January 2000 in Indonesia, where 90 percent of the country's two hundred ten million citizens are followers of Islam, Muslims were reported by U.S. media to have torched dozens of Christian churches, as well as shops and homes owned by Christians, and caused the death of three Christians, perhaps more. During 1998-9, Indonesia was the scene of even greater violence when more than one thousand people, some Muslim but mostly Christian, were reported killed.[1]

These episodes of violence may have been rooted in political issues, rather than religion, and Christians, not just Muslims, have also been aggressive and brutal. Christians may have torched mosques. Regardless of who struck first and why, however, the violence was portrayed in U.S. media as Muslims brutalizing Christians. The news reports, whether accurate or biased, dominated the headlines for days in America, reinforcing anti-Muslim stereotypes. The October 1999 issue of *The Message,* a magazine published monthly by the Islamic Circle of North America (ICNA), denounced the violence in Indonesia. Most other U.S. Muslim leaders, however, seemed to ignore these reports. None was quoted in the major media condemning this reported behavior as being un-Islamic.

At other times and places, religious intolerance is expressed in a non-violent manner, often through expressions of self-righteousness about one's own religion and a condescension toward non-believers.

The impulse toward religious intolerance may be especially strong in a country like America where one religion— Christianity—has been dominant since the birth of the nation.

I s religious intolerance a natural phenomenon, an inevitable by-product of intense but misdirected conviction? Most people establish their religious affiliation without first studying other religions. Perhaps this reality makes them prone to exhibitions of intolerance, some overbearing, others mild.

Attorney Allen Yow, a young neighbor and recent convert to Islam, reflects on his own experience: "Maybe it is partly human nature to slip into religious intolerance. In my case, a commitment to Islam was a very personal, soul-searching decision. In accepting Islam, I chose it over Christianity, the faith of my parents. Most people don't face a choice like that. Most Christians simply follow the religious path of their forebears. The same is true of most Muslims and Jews. For them, it really isn't a choice, a conscious selection of one faith over others. Unfortunately, most Christians are misinformed about Islam, and that misunderstanding, I find, breeds intolerance. It is easy to be intolerant of a religion you don't understand."[2]

Religion usually serves as the vehicle in one's quest for moral direction, a quest that is—or should be—intense and personal. No one should be surprised to find that the temptation to be self-righteous about one's religion is the breeding ground of intolerance. It comes from the depth of the human ego and is especially intense in people who have little or no knowledge of other religions.

F ixing the blame for religious intolerance emerged as the central theme of a recent conversation with a close friend of thirty years. A well-read professional, he is insightful and thoughtful, never inclined to impulsiveness or exaggeration. In his correspondence and conversation, he is concise, displaying what he calls an economy in language. His opinions and ideas are always engaging. As an elected official and a published commentator, he is experienced in partisan politics. Over the years our topics for discussion have ranged widely and have often dealt with religion. Reared an Episcopalian, his religious affiliation and interest recently shifted to the Unitarian Church.

On this occasion, once I mentioned my latest project, writing this book, religion dominated the rest of our conversation. At his request, I do not identify him by name. He explained that he does not feel qualified to discuss Muslims or Islam, and would not want anyone to think that he is. Still, his observations are pertinent to the theme of this book and add valuable insight into how a Christian politician reacts to the growing presence of Muslims in America.

Toward the end of our discussion, I told him that my personal experiences with individual Muslims have been pleasant, almost without exception. I have found them to be thoughtful, generous, hospitable, and good listeners. They have become an integral part of America. They are the second largest major religion; and if their birthrate continues at its present level, they will soon reach twelve million.

H is response was thoughtful and, for him, unusually long. "To my regret, I have never had what I could call a discussion about the Islamic faith with a Muslim or anyone else. I don't pretend to know the first thing about Islam. In fact, I cannot recall that I ever discussed anything with a person I knew to be a Muslim. But I am appalled at what Muslim leaders are doing to other Muslims. I'm troubled by a radical Saudi living in Afghanistan who calls himself a Muslim and is accused of masterminding terrorism. He was interviewed on television the other night. I don't recall his name, but he came through as a maniac."

I asked if his name is Osama bin Laden.

"That's the one. The newscast made both him and Islam look bad. Your Muslim friends may be wonderful people, but the images of Muslims I got from television this past week are far from attractive. In fact, I find them alarming and offensive."

I was not surprised at the force of his words, or the fact that he linked bin Laden with Afghanistan. Chilling reports about the Afghan government had dominated recent news reports. The images that reached us from television and newspaper headlines were shocking. They projected images of a draconian regime that took away the rights of its citizens, repressed women, and gave sanctuary to a wealthy Arab who had become a dangerous terrorist.

When he first arrived, my friend mentioned that he could not stay long. Now he looked at his watch, rose from his chair, started for the door, then stopped, turned, and spoke quietly but firmly:

"I am not worried about Muslims as individuals. I am sure they are as decent and hardworking as other people—maybe a bit more so. What troubles me is what is happening in Afghanistan in the name of Islam and why Muslim leaders in this country seem to accept these awful practices without protest. If Afghan leaders are violating the rules and principles of Islam, why don't leaders of the faith publicly denounce them for falsely identifying their government as Islamic?

"One would think they would be speaking out, but I hear no complaint. Are they, for some reason, afraid to speak? I can't imagine why they should be. Or, do they feel that the less said about it the better? Do they hope the American people won't notice, or if they have noticed, will soon forget?"

Here, of course, I understood that he referred to non-Muslim Americans, neglecting for the moment the six million or more Americans who follow Islam. He continued, "Or, does this mean, and this is what scares me, that U.S. Muslims are satisfied with what the Afghan government is doing?"

As he concluded his remarks, I noticed an uncharacteristic edge to his voice. "You say the number of U.S. Muslims will double in a few years. What does this mean for America's future as these Muslims gain influence in politics? What worries me most is what Muslims may want to change in America, in our own government, if they get the chance."

He glanced at his watch again. I wanted to pursue the discussion, but I knew that he would be uneasy if I delayed his departure. Moreover, I was somewhat taken aback by the intensity that I sensed in his last words. As I walked with him to the front door, I said simply: "You raise important questions. I will consider them carefully."

It was just as well that I did not respond at the time to the issues he had raised. I had not thought about them for years, but I, too, had been surprised and puzzled at the lack of Muslim protests against the excesses of bin Laden and the Taliban. From my own private discussions with U.S. Muslims, I had concluded that they were not "satisfied with what the Afghan government is doing." But neither had I heard nor seen evidence of Muslim protest against these abuses. At the time, I was unaware that several Muslim leaders in California, Illinois, and Texas had issued statements of protest that had been ignored by news media.

Clearly, my decent, high-minded friend was worried about how life in America might be changed if Muslims gained enough strength to influence America's political system. Moreover, I had to assume that many other Americans would share his concern, especially those who had seen the television reports and read the newspaper articles that disturbed him. Perhaps the audience of viewers and readers numbered in the millions. I needed time to study and reflect, and I knew that I should not neglect these unsettling issues. They needed to be addressed.

A s I watched my friend enter his car and drive away, my thoughts turned to a personal experience ten years earlier in South Africa, a country nearly as distant from America as Afghanistan. There, I discussed with Ahmad Deedat, an internationally prominent Muslim leader, the main topics raised by my unnamed friend. He was the founder and president of the Islamic Propagation Center International, based in Durban, South Africa.

A tall, stately man with a white beard, Deedat drew attention wherever he went. He projected an air of confidence that made him a natural leader. On this evening, he wore a traditional Muslim cap, a white flowing gown, and a Western suit jacket. He left his white shirt open at the neck with the collar flaps neatly covering the jacket lapels.

Opening our discussion that night, Deedat presented an image of Islamic governance that contrasted sharply with the one that emerged years later from the media reports about the Taliban in Afghanistan. He raised the subject in an unusual, roundabout way as we prepared to share the microphone before the immense crowd gathered in the Cape Town arena. Deedat told me that he had arranged to make two books available for the audience to purchase in the lobby of the building. He had selected his own edition of my book, *They Dare to Speak Out,* as one of them. The other he identified only as "the text of the constitution for world government."

This identification aroused my curiosity. I had long been interested in international organizations that would protect human rights and bring peace to the world. Who had written the book and what kind of government did it propose? I wondered what the proposed new government could accomplish that the United Nations and other international organizations had failed to attain. I was surprised when, just before the public meeting began, Deedat told me that the constitution of a world government was nothing more, nothing less, than the Quran. By then, it was time for the program to begin, and I had no time to question Deedat further. After the speeches ended and the audience had passed through the lobby that evening, I learned that book sales were astounding, over two thousand Qurans and nearly nine hundred of my book.

L ater that evening, after we had dined in the home of a local businessman, Deedat explained why he described the Quran as he did. "The Quran provides detailed regulations for everyday living, not just for prayer time. It is a framework to govern all relationships with members of the family, the neighborhood, and all the people of the world. It provides all the ingredients needed for proper government worldwide, a well-ordered, all-encompassing system in which justice and tolerance will prevail universally for all races, and for men and women alike."

At the time, I kept my feelings to myself, but his explanation left me puzzled and unsettled. I had never expected that a governmental system could come from a holy writ. Furthermore, all my life I had revered the U.S. Constitution as the best man-made system of government in human history. Did Deedat want to sink the U.S. Constitution without a trace? In my innocence, I considered the Quran vitally important to Muslims and inspirational to everyone who has read it, but I could not visualize it as a framework for an all-encompassing world government.

Returning to our hotel that night, I found myself pondering what this South African had meant. Was he forecasting an eventual world government, flying the banner of Islam, in which the text of the Quran would be its constitutional foundation? Or, was his statement akin to that of Christian clergymen who preach hopefully of the second coming of Christ but do not expect to live long enough to witness the event themselves? Had Deedat simply chosen this dramatic way to express his hope for a world in which Quranic principles would be in effect, no matter what flag was being saluted? How would these principles be implemented?

Would the world organization that he visualized be democratic or authoritarian? Deedat had traveled extensively and witnessed the diversity and strength of other religious traditions, and he must have realized that the prospect of establishing the text of the Quran as the framework for the government of the entire world would be a distant vision, far over the horizon.

A t breakfast the next morning, I learned that Deedat had left Cape Town for other appointments and would be unavailable for further discussions until the following day. Meanwhile, a senior member of his staff allayed my concerns. During a tour of the organization's headquarters in Durban, he said, "I want you to know that the opening phrases of your Declaration of Independence mean a lot to Muslims everywhere. In declaring that all people are equal in the eyes of God and endowed by God with inalienable rights, this document expresses sentiments that are deeply embedded in Islam and cherished by all Muslims."

I knew little about the Quran or the life and sayings of the Prophet Muhammad, and nothing about the Shariah, the legal system of Islam that has been derived over the centuries from the text of the Quran. And today, regrettably, I cannot ask Deedat to elaborate. In 1996, after a lecture tour in Australia, he suffered a massive, paralyzing stroke and can no longer speak or write.

In early 1999, I decided to ask Andrew Patterson to reflect on what the South African leader may have meant. He believes that Deedat found the U.S. governmental system generally consistent with the true Islamic state. "The Quran and the Shariah have important common threads with the U.S. Constitution. All three are dedicated to the equality of all people, the advancement of human rights, the sanctity of both person and property, government by the consent of the governed, and governmental decision-making through consultation with the people. The Quran calls for a democratic system of government in which the people are consulted broadly, regularly and thoroughly. Under this plan, the people choose their leadership and help leaders make policy decisions through a process of consensus."

A few days later, in a remarkable coincidence, Nour Naciri forwarded a reassuring statement by Raashid Alghanoushi, a respected leader of Al-Nahda, the Tunisian opposition party, and a commentator on public issues. "The contemporary revivalist movement has enabled Muslims to rediscover that Islam is capable of intelligent interaction with today's world. It neither rejects it in toto nor does it seek to melt into it. This development now allows Muslims to speak of a modern Islamic political system that derives its legitimacy from the people's will according to constitutional bases that limit government's absolute power." The statement added that these limitations protect the rights and dignity of everyone, "be they Muslim or non-Muslim, men or women."[3]

Further reassurance came from the pen of Dr. Ralph Braibanti, author of *The Nature and Structure of the Islamic World* and an authority on Islam: "There is a significant movement, scattered geographically, to reinterpret Islam to fit the present age.... Those bent on such reforms are in Jordan, Egypt, Turkey, Algeria, and Iran. They are typically professional people educated in the West. They do not repudiate Islam. On the contrary, they are devout, observing Muslims."[4]

D r. Agha Saeed, a university professor of political science and a proponent of political activism by Muslims, believes that followers of Islam are pleased with U.S. constitutional provisions. He reports that none of them support fundamental change in the principles or structure of the American governmental system. Indeed, the most prevalent Muslim criticism, Saeed reports, is the failure of U.S. leadership to apply rigorously and uniformly the principles expressed in the Constitution and the Declaration of Independence.

In a lengthy interview in a Los Angeles hotel room, he dismissed the idea that Muslims, or any other religious group, will some day control America:

"There is no chance of that happening, and if they did gain control, I believe they would want to keep the basic structure and principles now in place. But control? That's out of the question. The occasional warning that Muslims are an internal threat to America is ridiculous. It reminds me of the old cry that the

Russians are coming and that we must prevent a Communist takeover of America.

"At the very most, eight or ten Muslims might someday be elected to the U.S. House of Representatives. That's only about 2 percent of the total membership. Today, no Muslim serves as a Member of Congress. Muslims would like to be a part of the system, even a part that is numerically very small. They should have a presence. Being there is important, as it means that Muslims are seen as human beings, not as false stereotypes.

"Among U.S. Muslims, there is universal support for the American principles of human dignity, due process, equal access for all, equality of all persons before the law, equality of opportunity. I am fully in support of these principles. I would not like to change any of them, but I would like to see them faithfully applied.

"Many Muslims, like many non-Muslims, want these principles applied more broadly and uniformly to everyone. Only a few Muslims will say they want the structure and basic principles changed. A few might say they would like to have a Shariah council established that would apply Islamic law in America, but even these statements can be discounted. I don't know a single Muslim who seriously wants to change the basic framework and principles of the U.S. government."

Muslim scholars agree that any true Islamic state would provide full protection to the rights of non-Muslims as well as Muslims. Dr. John L. Esposito's *Encyclopedia of the Modern Islamic World* reports that "most constitutions of Muslim states now confirm the principle of equality of all citizens irrespective of religion, sex, and race.... [although] certain militant Islamic groups... advocate hostile suspicion toward non-Muslims." Islamic leaders, those called liberal or modernist, present a similar view. "Islam encourages Muslims to establish their government on the basis of modern reasoning, and on the basis of the rules of government that have been tested and proven by the experience of nations."[5]

The same section of the encyclopedia quotes the Quranic statement, "There is no compulsion in religion" (Quran 2:256), then adds, "This is interpreted to indicate the equality of Muslims and non-Muslims in civic rights and duties.... According to the liberals [or modernists], in dealing with worldly matters the challenge is to enter social transactions and relations on a basis that allows for adaptation to changing conditions.... This view and this way of life can be consistent with the religious doctrine of Islam."[6]

These references suggest that Islam has a fundamental resilience that enables it to adapt to changing times. Author Robin Wright predicts a rise in the influence of Islam—and individual freedom—in the Arab world during the first quarter of the twenty-first century. In a comment similar to one Ahmed Deedat made to me in South Africa, she cites Islam as "the most widespread alternative" to present regimes, because it "provides a legal forum and a legitimate format" and is "the only major monotheistic religion that offers a set of specific rules to govern society, as well as a set of spiritual beliefs." She predicts the growth of individual freedom during this process of transition: "To be a true believer, one must come to the faith freely."

She finds this doctrine popular among present-day Muslim reformers in Iran and writes, "Thus, freedom precedes faith—a quantum leap for a religion whose name literally means 'submission.' In the end, Islam is more likely to be a vehicle for the transition, not necessarily the finished product."[7]

I find in Wright's forecast a gleam of promise that Muslim countries will permit individuals greater freedom to select religious affiliation. If her forecast proves to be valid, these governments are likely to move somewhat closer to the U.S. system in the decades just ahead. Religious freedom and tolerance for the religion of others are a fundamental part of the American structure.

Texas Muslim leader Inayat Lalani, M.D., warns of an intra-Islamic doctrinal struggle between the modernists, with whom he identifies, and the traditionalists. He considers this contest to be more momentous than the one between Muslims and non-Muslims

and offers these specifics: "Some Muslims who present themselves
as scholars will, with a straight face, make statements such as
'democracy is un-Islamic' or 'there is no place for human rights in
Islam.' Of course, detractors of Islam seize upon such statements.

"There is a large segment in the Muslim community that is
inclined to reject any pragmatic approach to the problems facing
Muslims without offering any alternative solutions. They are
hypersensitive about religious dogma and are quick to call your
faith into question if you express an opinion that does not agree
with their pre-set notions. Most of them derive their 'knowledge'
from cultural traditions, not from the Quran. Many of these
traditions repress the rights of others and are outright anti-Islamic.
Some of these Islamic 'scholars' play into the hands of Islam's
enemies while honestly believing that they are being true
to Islam."[8]

Andrew Patterson sees a similar problem. "Not all Muslims are
enlightened. I will never be able to penetrate the minds of purists.
Some of them are attempting to isolate Muslims from the West."

Purists, he believes, should look to Charles Darwin for guidance: "I've never been fond of Charles Darwin's theories, but I
agree with him when he wrote, 'It is not the strongest of the species
that survives, nor the most intelligent, but the one most responsive
to change.' I believe his statement is applicable everywhere, and
before anyone jumps to oppose something, they should reflect
carefully. Darwin's statement reminds me of the Biblical assertion,
'The meek shall inherit the earth,' and that also brings to mind
Prophet Muhammad's counsel while he was walking with his
followers one day. He urged them to be cautious in what they say."

Ralph Braibanti writes, "It is a cruel irony that at the moment
when Islam is free of colonial domination and when some of its
segments are endowed with a degree of wealth, it is plagued and
fragmented by intra-Islamic conflict..."[9]

These concerns are central as I speculate on what changes, if
any, U.S. Muslims would make in the structure of the
American government if they gained political control.

My thoughts return to my discussions with Ahmad Deedat. I am convinced that he considered the principles set forth in the U.S. Declaration of Independence and the U.S. Constitution to be consistent and parallel with those set forth in the Quran. A similar inference can be drawn from the fact, as reported in Esposito's encyclopedia, that "most constitutions of Muslim states now confirm the principles of equality for all citizens irrespective of religion, sex, and race." From all that I have seen, read and heard, Islamic governmental principles reinforce the U.S. Constitution, rather than threaten it.

When Deedat spoke to me in 1989, apartheid was still the law that prevailed in South Africa. At the time, the fundamental structure of his nation's government directly undercut and violated the ideals and principles of both the Quran and the U.S. Constitution.

Ugly bigotry still dominated his country's government, and he was cautious in expressing his views. He avoided provocative statements about government policy, even in private conversation. Even though harsh, white supremacist policies had virtually isolated South Africa from the rest of the world at that time, he nevertheless expressed confidence that Islamic principles of equality and tolerance would ultimately prevail worldwide. That meant, by implication, that the policies of the white minority that had kept Deedat and the vast majority of other South African citizens from voting would eventually be overcome.

In light of Deedat's experience as a second-class citizen in South Africa under apartheid, I conclude that he could never support a system that imposes second-class status on any human being. I am confident that Deedat believes, as I do, that in the years ahead individual governments and international organizations will, step by step, promote and advance the principles of equality, justice, tolerance, and compassion that are expressed in both the Quran and the U.S. Constitution.

I slam, like Christianity, Judaism, Hinduism and other faiths, can continue to flourish within the American system of government. Secular governments need not, and should not, impinge on the practice of any religion. In reaching that conclusion, I am influenced by the views of scores of U.S. Muslims. I have heard many of them voluntarily express their pride in being American citizens. In spite of the anti-Islamic stereotypes they confront, they rejoice in the safeguards of human rights, due process, and individual liberty established in the U.S. Constitution.

When they take the oath of citizenship, U.S. Muslims pledge their allegiance to the U.S. Constitution, and I have encountered only a few Muslims who attained U.S. citizenship as a birthright who refused to join in the same pledge. After his conversion to Islam, Mahmood Abd al-Rauf, a basketball star with the Denver Nuggets, declined initially to show his allegiance to the flag but changed when Muslim leaders convinced him that making the pledge did not violate Islamic rules. In contrast, members of the Seventh Day Adventists, a Christian denomination, believe they should pledge allegiance only to God.

All the Muslims of my acquaintance, I believe, accept without reservation their obligation to respect and serve the American flag, laws, and Constitution, despite the fact that the U.S. system of criminal justice differs from the one developed in the "prophetic Tradition" inspired by the Quran.

Islam authorizes death for adultery and the severing of hands for theft, but demands testimony by several eyewitnesses or voluntary confession before these punishments can be carried out. As the crime is judged on the intention of the perpetrator, the Quran provides that these prescriptions can be softened with compassion, mercy, and forgiveness. For example, a person who steals food cannot be punished if he or she can prove that the theft was prompted by an urgent, humanitarian need.

In the case of murder, the aggrieved family can spare the guilty party from the death penalty—as the Quran clearly stipulates—by accepting compensation—"blood money"—instead. Persons accused of some lesser crimes can be spared corporal punishment if the victims accept similar arrangements.

Only a few Muslim countries—for example, Saudi Arabia, Pakistan, and Sudan—impose the most severe penalties that are ordained in the Quran. Other Muslim countries have legal systems that have been influenced by Western practices. In countries where Christian or other religions are established, those charged with crime are not tried by Islamic law, but Nour Naciri writes, "Everyone agrees that the deterrence impact of Islamic penalties is remarkably effective."

In other realms of policy and authority, Islam and U.S. governmental traditions share fundamental goals. Both are dedicated to peace, justice, and individual liberty for all people. Muslims are devoted to the proposition of the Declaration of Independence that all men are created equal. The Islamic tradition is anchored in the doctrine that a government must be accountable and responsive to the people, whom Islam sees as God's vice-regents on earth.[10]

April Szuchyt notes, "Most Muslims do not see the United States, or the Western world, as being the inventors or purveyors of democracy. To the contrary, they view Islam in this light. Nor do they see Muslims trying to emulate Western ideals. Instead, they often note with approval that the United States is implementing Islamic principles."

Curious to know what influence, if any, the Quran might have had during the drafting of the founding documents of the United States government, I asked the Library of Congress to search the papers of Thomas Jefferson, credited with drafting the Declaration of Independence, and James Madison, whose notes are the most complete record of the proceedings that produced the U.S. Constitution. Madison's notes contain no reference to Islam or the Quran, or to any other religion. Moreover, there is no evidence that his library included the Quran. Jefferson's personal library, one of the largest libraries of the period, included a copy of the Quran, the English translation by George Sale, printed in 1764, "commonly called the Alcoran of Mohammed."[11] There is no indication that Jefferson consulted its text in drafting the Declaration of Independence.

To those who may be troubled by a declaration that links the principles of governance set forth in the Quran with those expressed in the U.S. Constitution, I ask them to consider whether hundreds of thousands of Muslims in foreign countries would seek American citizenship if they believed the structure of the U.S. government to be in serious conflict with the basic principles of the ideal Islamic state. By undertaking the long, challenging journey to obtain U.S. citizenship, great numbers of Muslims have, in effect, voted for America. I conclude that many, perhaps most, of them believe America has a governmental structure that is closer to the idealism of Islam than other forms of government. The largest, most sustained flow of Muslim emigration is to American shores.

Why the attraction to the United States, a non-Muslim country whose governmental structure is among the most secular in the world and where Muslims number less than 3 percent of the total population? One might reasonably assume that they chose America as a place of economic opportunity, as well as a good place to rear their families and practice their religion. Before moving here, all must have received some indication of America's longstanding, rigorous efforts to protect freedom of religion, and its commitment to tolerance and human rights.

A Muslim leader who prefers to remain unidentified, reports: "Muslims often point out that they have more freedom to practice Islam here than in the land of their birth where political repression is rampant." He doubts that Muslims would be shocked or offended if they heard the U.S. government cited as providing the world's best available protection for people of the Islamic faith.

The United States, of course, cannot be called an Islamic state, and, if it were, that declaration would surely provoke sharp negative reactions from non-Muslims, as well as some Muslims. But, on reflection, all should recognize that the U.S. system contains elements that are fundamental to an Islamic state as contemplated in the Quran. Abraham Lincoln unwittingly expressed an essence of the true Islamic state in his famous Gettysburg Address when he spoke of "government of the people, by the people, and for the people."

Both Islam and the U.S. Constitution require leaders who: are chosen through consent of the governed; are required to function in collaboration with an assembly chosen by public consensus; recognize the equality of each person before God and the law, irrespective of race, religion, nationality or sex; and extend equal protection and justice to each person.

In offering that appraisal, I do not intend to leave the impression that I place the U.S. governmental system in the same realm as religion. Government is necessarily temporal and, to most people, less important than matters of faith. However, government can influence the practice of religion and either facilitate or restrict the individual liberties that are important in the development of religious affiliation. The Founding Fathers wisely provided for the separation of the state from the establishment of religion but, with equal wisdom, assured freedom of religious affiliation.

What sets America apart from most other nations is the determined, sustained quest by its government and the vast majority of its citizens for comprehensive and faithful application of basic principles. Of these, religious tolerance must be kept preeminent.

These heartening reflections have not led me to complacency about the false images of Islam that prevail in the United States. Most Americans, I fear, have been beguiled into the mistaken belief that Muslims would like to institute a form of government that would be abusive to non-Muslims and impair cherished principles of our society. Unfortunately, some of these who are beguiled are influential.

Nor do I conclude that all U.S. Muslims find perfection in the U.S. government, or even in the Constitution. Like other citizens, myself included, while rejoicing in the advantages of American life, many Muslims see ways to improve public law and its application, even with a constitutional amendment or two.

Agha Saeed cites an issue of towering importance, the need for comprehensive and faithful application of the principles of our society. He is right to note that our government falls short of applying these principles to all residents of the United States, but it is important to remember that religious tolerance deserves the same faithful application. Nevertheless, intolerance remains a common occurrence in the behavior of many professed Muslims, Christians, and Jews. It is not enough simply to declare our principles as goals in a constitution or religious text.

The fundamental test of a government or a religious faith is the rigorous application of basic principles in everyday life. Many autocratic governments, including the now defunct Soviet Union and others that still survive, have guarantees of freedom of speech, freedom of religion, free elections, and other liberties set forth in their laws but fail to enforce them. Under these regimes, fundamental rights are empty promises, and nothing more.

Notes:

1. *USA Today*, 1-18-2000 and 1-20-2000.
2. Interview, 12-1-1999.
3. *People's Daily,* 7-20-1999 (Cairo).
4. Ralph Braibanti, *The Nature and Structure of the Islamic World*, p. 83.
5. John L. Esposito, *Modern Islamic World*, vol.. 3, pp. 110–111.
6. Esposito, *Modern Islamic World*, vol.. 1, pp 358–359.
7. *Time,* 5-2-2000, p. 109.
8. Interview, 5-2-1999.
9. Braibanti, *The Nature and Structure of the Islamic World*, p. 85.
10. Interview with Inayat Lalani, 2-6-2000.
11. *Catalogue of the Library of Thomas Jefferson*, vol.. 2 (University Press of Virginia), p. 90.

Chapter 6: Equal as "Two Teeth in a Comb"

Notwithstanding the principles and requirements of Islam and other faiths that honor and protect the rights and dignity of all women, their abuse seems to flourish worldwide in every society, irrespective of race, nationality, economic status, or religion.

A report released in January 2000 by the Johns Hopkins School of Public Health in Baltimore, Maryland, offers the startling conclusion that "one of every three women worldwide has been beaten, raped, or somehow mistreated." Basing its conclusions on studies made in more than twenty countries, including the United States, the document reports that as many as 70 percent of the women had never told anyone about the abuse prior to their interview.[1]

Americans seem wont to cite severe discrimination in some Muslim countries as evidence that Islam condones mistreatment of women. Such discrimination—often harsh—exists, but Islamic leaders insist that any form of female oppression violates the doctrines and rules of Islam. Most discrimination arises from brutish customs and male chauvinism, not from the Quran or the Sunnah.

Islam may be the single most liberating influence on the status of women in recorded history, greater than Christianity and Judaism. Thomas W. Lippman, a Jewish journalist who served for three years as *The Washington Post* bureau chief in Cairo, writes, "In a society in which women were possessions, taken and put aside like trinkets, often held in conditions approaching bondage, the Quran imposed rules and prohibitions that curbed the worst abuses, ensured women's property rights, and encouraged men to treat women with kindness and generosity.... The Quran's dictates on women's legal status were quite advanced for their time, and Islamic law gives women some rights more liberating than those found in Western legal codes.... The Quran and the Hadith [sayings of the Prophet Muhammad] lay down rules ensuring for women the respectable and dignified status that had been denied them [in pre-Islamic society] and emphasize the stability of the family."[2] William Baker, a Christian leader, writes: "When we consider the status of women in the pre-Islamic societies, we learn that two-thirds were in some form of slavery....Women were nearly invisible in a male-dominated world in nearly every religion and every culture of the world."[3]

Not enough Americans read the messages of Lippman and Baker. When I address a general audience, I often begin my remarks by asking this question: In Islam, are women treated as being inferior to men? It always elicits a resounding affirmative. In America, the negative images of Muslim women remain deep, pervasive, and unsettling. They arise from varied influences: misunderstanding, differences in regulations that exist among Muslim countries, an occasional measure of malice, but, mainly, from ignorance.

After taking part in a dozen question-and-answer sessions with Muslim audiences and more than sixty discussions with general audiences in recent years, I have reached two conclusions: first, most Americans believe that Islam is biased, sometimes cruelly, against women, and second, U.S. Muslim women strongly disagree.

S ome of the misleading impressions of Islam arise from religion-related differences in attire, employment, marriage, and even handshakes. The apparel of many Muslim women is distinctive, often the only direct indication of Islamic presence that non-Muslim Americans encounter. It resembles somewhat the traditional attire of Catholic nuns—a long, loose-fitting gown and hair hidden by a tight-fitting head cover tucked under the chin, leaving only the face and hands exposed. Like the Roman Catholic nuns who lately have adopted less conservative attire, many

Muslim women cover their hair with loose-fitting scarves. Many, especially those of African heritage, wear head wraps or "turbans" and may not be recognized as Muslims by the public. Still others wear no head covering, except when in a mosque or at prayer.

Attire among Muslim men is less distinctive, although a few — particularly leaders in mosques and instructors in Islamic schools — wear a turban or a skull cap and a long, gown-like garment called a jallabieh. Some Muslims believe that beards are a religious requirement, but not all agree. Of the adult Muslim males in our hometown, two are clean-shaven, another wears a long untrimmed beard, and the third has a beard that is neatly trimmed.

Zainab Elberry assures me that the Islamic requirement for attire is modesty for both men and women. But she recognizes that women disagree on specifics. Most Muslim women would never think of wearing tank tops or shorts, but many reject the conservative attire that leaves only the face and hands uncovered. Muslim women rarely appear in public places with their forearms or calves of their legs bare. Nour Naciri, her husband, adds, "Islam has never decreed a certain 'traditional' type of dress. Of the costumes you have observed among Muslims worldwide, the common denominator is an absence of excessive, attention-baiting exposure of the body. The only valid adjective you can freely use to describe the dress of observant Muslim men and women is 'modest.'"

In Amman, Jordan, in October 1999, Lucille and I attended two dinner parties in residences. Most of the guests were Muslim, but none of the women wore headscarves. At a public dinner attended by more than 300 couples, almost all Muslim, only a few ladies wore headscarves. Many women wear modest attire as a matter of personal choice. Riding through the Jordanian countryside, I asked our driver, Army Sgt. Samih Majali, married and the father of three young children, if most of the young married women in Karak, his hometown and one of Jordan's largest cities, wear modest attire. He answered, "Yes, and my wife is one of them. She wears conservative dress, not because her father, mother or husband demands it, but because she wants to."

W hen I heard a similar sentiment expressed on an earlier occasion, a vigorous and enlightening discussion followed. After my remarks to a Muslim audience in Chicago in 1997, a woman dressed in a traditional headscarf and long dress came to me and said, "I chose this attire because I like it. If I wished, I could have chosen modest Western clothing and still be true to Islam. Muslim women are not abused or discriminated against. We have the right to education, the right to enter business or professional life. When we marry, we can keep our own name and maintain control of any fortune we may have. We also have the right of divorce."

I interjected, "I have heard that a man can secure a divorce much more easily than a woman." She responded, "That is true in some Muslim societies, but even there a woman can reserve the right of divorce at the time of marriage. In America and most other countries, Muslim women have the same divorce rights as non-Muslims. Speaking of divorce, there is a misunderstanding about the Islamic rules and traditions. The Prophet Muhammad said it is better for a couple to divorce than to live together in an atmosphere of rancor. And Christians should remember that the Roman Catholic Church outlawed divorce for centuries. It became one of the biggest rifts in Christianity."

I introduced another stereotype. "The other day during a Rotary Club meeting, I heard a woman say, perhaps as a joke, that Muslim women are required to walk a pace or two behind their husbands when the two are together in public. I am sure she is mistaken." The Muslim woman could hardly control her mirth. "That is totally false. A woman walks side by side with her husband, and they stand together as equals. The Prophet Muhammad said the equality of husband and wife is like 'two teeth in a comb.'" I had to wince when I heard her comment, because Lucille often reminds me that I routinely leave her several paces behind when we go for a walk. This results from my lifelong habit of pacing at full speed, not from any sense of superiority.

Did the Prophet Muhammad actually make the statement about teeth in a comb? It may be fact or legend. Seeking the answer discloses the enormity of published accounts of the sayings of the Prophet. There are thousands of statements attributed to him, some believed to be authentic and many that are not. Nour Naciri notes that there are four categories of compendia, starting with those that are accepted as verified by the best available authority and therefore considered the most reliable. Others are verified by lesser authority, still others are classified as acceptable or dubious. All were passed orally for a number of years before being recorded in writing.

Naciri recalls frequent references since boyhood days to the comb statement. Imam Mohamed Al-Hanooti, a Muslim religious scholar in Washington, D.C., says an historical record, not regarded by historians as authentic, reports only that the Prophet said, without making reference to gender, that "people are like the teeth on a comb." If he did, that statement could certainly and logically be interpreted as covering husband and wife.

Nour Naciri accepts the following as the orthodox Islamic consensus on what the Prophet said: "'The husband and the wife are as equal as two teeth in a comb.' It means that men and women, married or single, are equal in the rights their Creator gives them as human beings and in the obligations He entrusts them to discharge as His vice-regents on earth. Male and female must cooperate, each in his or her full capacity, just as the teeth of a comb, so to speak, must cooperate for any combing to be done. They must cooperate within the family unit and within society as a whole."

This discussion may strike the reader as nit-picking, but it illustrates the thoroughness—and intensity—of scholarly examination of what the Prophet Muhammad actually said and meant.

To outsiders, the equality of men and women in Islam is not always apparent. One of the reasons is that stereotypes, like the one about a Muslim woman being required to walk behind her husband, flourish widely uncorrected.

They are even kept alive in some college textbooks. *Marriage and the Family: A Brief Introduction,* written by David Knox and

Caroline Schacht and published by Wadsworth Publishing of Belmont, California, contains the following inaccurate, defamatory statements about Islamic beliefs and traditions:

> "A wife walking with her husband is expected to follow a few steps behind him."
> "At meals, a woman eats only after the men have been served."
> "In the presence of others, a wife must not speak to her husband or stare at him."

And this most outrageous statement of all—

> "In Islam, the most male-oriented of the modern religions, a woman is nothing but a vehicle for producing sons."

Wadsworth Publishing, a firm that supplies post-secondary texts in the humanities and social and behavioral sciences, has ceased distribution of the book and has sent to individual buyers and bookstores an "errata sheet" that corrects these false statements. The sheets are intended for insertion in books already distributed. Unfortunately, the damage is done. Loose-leaf sheets are often lost or fail to find their way to the correct spot within intended volumes.[4]

The attempt at corrective action by Wadsworth was in response to the protest lodged by Ibrahim Hooper, communications director of the Washington-based Council on American-Islamic Relations (CAIR). In a letter, Hooper wrote, "The fact that this anti-Muslim propaganda is targeted at impressionable students only makes the situation more disturbing.... More than 1,400 years ago Islam eliminated the chattel status of women, prohibited the pre-Islamic practice of female infanticide and gave women full control over their earnings and wealth. Other rights granted to women by Islam include the right of inheritance, the right to initiate divorce and the right to own a business."[5]

Similar stereotypes presented in a sixth grade classroom posed a dilemma recently to a twelve-year-old Muslim youth in Hastings Middle School in Upper Arlington, Ohio. Kareem and his classmates were instructed by their teacher, Scott Hall, to "compare [in a written test] the treatment of women in the Middle Eastern countries to the treatment of women in the USA." Kareem told his father, Taymour El-Hosseiny, how he met the problem. He said he wrote these words: "In the Middle East, men and women do not eat together, and, out of respect, women walk behind their husbands due to the Islamic religion." Astounded, his father asked, "Is this what you learned in school?" Kareem answered, "Yes. Mr. Hall showed a video at school that taught us that." His father remonstrated, "Surely you know that Islam does not require women to walk behind their husbands, nor does it prohibit men and women from eating meals together." Kareem said, "Yes, I know, but I wanted to get a good grade on the test, and, although the answer I gave was not correct, I knew Mr. Hall would believe it was."[6]

After El-Hosseiny sent a protest letter to the school, the offensive video was removed from the school library, and Kareem's teacher announced to the class that the information in the video about Islam was wrong. The school principal promised El-Hosseiny that other media material would be examined carefully for accuracy.

The Quran permits a Muslim man to have as many as four wives. This permission, while rejected as wrong by Salam Al-Marayati and other U.S. Muslims, is nevertheless as unsettling and well known to non-Muslims as the false images. There is, moreover, little awareness among non-Muslims of the strict rules that Muslim polygamists must meet. The Quran warns of severe punishment in the afterlife if polygamists fail to treat and support each wife with absolute equality, a requirement that is virtually impossible to meet.

From Jordan, April Szuchyt writes her personal view of Muslim polygamy: "When instituted, the verse in the Quran [on polygamy] served two purposes. The first was to limit to four the number of wives a man was permitted to have. At the time, some men had as many as twenty wives. Some of the kings mentioned in the Bible had as many as ten. Second, it helped solve the problem of women who had become widows and orphans as a result of a recent war in which many Muslim men were killed.

"At that time, plural marriage was considered a social obligation, not a privilege. I cannot imagine myself being so unselfish as to become one of several wives of the same man, but I have known women of plural marriages who are happy, well-adjusted individuals. I must add that I am also aware of cases where this 'obligation' is completely abused and women's rights are violated. "Andrew Patterson writes, "This was laid down long before Social Security. Polygamy exists in some Muslim countries but the percentage of people engaged in it is small."

Of the responses to inquiries I posed to a number of acquaintances in Egypt, Jordan, and Saudi Arabia, none could name from direct personal acquaintance anyone who practiced polygamy. Mazin Nashashibi, a retired Jordanian ambassador, tells me, "Polygamy arises mainly from ancient custom and will be found these days, if at all, mostly in remote desert regions." He says that polygamy predated Islam by many years and came into practice mainly because of circumstance peculiar to the nomadic, tribal life of that period.

Some Americans believe that polygamy is practiced widely among followers of Islam in the United States, as well as in Muslim countries, but U.S. Muslim leaders assure me that polygamy is not condoned where it violates public law, and is a rare occurrence among Muslims in America. In the few instances where it exists in America, it is best described as an aberration.

Abdurahman Alamoudi, director of the Washington-based American Muslim Council Foundation and for years a leader in Islamic affairs, agrees that polygamy is extremely rare among U.S. Muslims. "In fact, I have never heard even one U.S. Muslim identified as a polygamist. Where polygamy exists, the consequences can be serious, because public law in the United States will recognize only one woman as the wife of a man. Additional wives have no family rights whatever."[7]

Dr. Sulayman Nyang, a professor at Howard University in Washington, D.C. and an expert on Muslim demography, believes that only a few U.S. followers of Islam—not more than one thousand at the most—engage in polygamy. "They are mostly poor, uneducated African-Americans living in inner cities who may not be fully informed about the restrictions on polygamy in either the Quran or public law." The men, he states, quietly accept more than one "wife," not as a religious obligation but mainly to pool resources to the advantage of everyone in the family. He finds the arrangement much less formal and more secretive among the few U.S. polygamists who identify themselves as Muslim than among the polygamists who practice the tradition, with both legal and religious approval, in some Muslim countries.[8]

Salam Al-Marayati says, "Polygamy, of course, is against the law in America. But, given the fact that the U.S. Muslim community consists of at least six million people, I have to assume that polygamy may exist among a few Muslims. They are likely to be uneducated, poor and isolated from other Muslims."[9] Al-Marayati and Alamoudi agree that Islam strongly enjoins Muslims to obey public law wherever they live, and, accordingly, it is unlikely that many of them knowingly violate U.S. anti-polygamy laws.

All available data indicate that more Christians practice polygamy in the United States than Muslims, a fact that most adherents of Christianity will find surprising and disturbing.

At least 20,000 U.S. Christians—the actual total may be closer to 35,000—openly practice polygamy in Western states. Most of them call themselves fundamentalist Mormons because they have ancestral ties to the Church of Jesus Christ of Latter Day Saints, a denomination that permitted polygamy until a century ago when it was outlawed by the church, as well as by public law.

At least one thousand U.S. Christians who have no relationship to the Mormon heritage openly engage in polygamy. They cite passages in the Old Testament to justify the practice and sponsor several internet web sites that encourage polygamy.[10]

Little known to non-Muslims is the cultural objection of some Muslim women to shaking hands with any male who is beyond their immediate family circle. According to some Muslims, the

ımad encouraged this restraint, but other Muslims
ɩpretation. Imam Mohamed Al-Hanooti finds broad
ɩ, beyond the immediate family, shaking hands with
sex is not clearly against Islamic law but should be
much as possible."

During a recent visit to Saudi Arabia, I found that two female dermatologists, both Muslim, disagreed on handshakes. Both used their hands to examine my head and shoulders for signs of shingles. But when I left the office, only one responded when I offered a farewell handshake. The other physician declined, and, as I had encountered similar restraint by other Muslim women, I gave her refusal no further thought. But, before I left the hospital, the physician who had declined located me by telephone to make sure that I understood she was simply following a religious practice and did not wish to be considered discourteous.

Daifallah Hindawi, a recently married Jordanian who resides in Dubai and has been a friend ever since he visited my home in 1990, offers this explanation: "Muslim men shake hands with each other freely but, out of genuine respect and honor, they do not initiate handshakes with women. Many Muslim women consider it improper to touch a male who is not in their immediate family, but it is common for unrelated men to shake and hold hands." His comment reminded me of an experience during my first visit to South Yemen in 1974. I was surprised when the protocol officer guiding me on a tour of Aden, the capital city, reached over to hold my hand as we walked together.

The custom against female handshakes with unrelated males can embarrass women as well as men. While attending a ceremony in a Palestinian refugee camp in Jordan, I watched as Muhasen Muhasneh, a Muslim woman wearing Western attire, stood in a receiving line to greet an imam, a Muslim leader in the camp. When her turn came, the imam rejected her outstretched hand. Taken aback, she returned to her seat and remarked to her companions, "That's his loss."

Zainab Elberry does not consider the custom against hand-shakes an Islamic rule, but she adds, "Sometimes men or women will decline a handshake if they are about to pray. A handshake would spoil the ablutions. In the absence of actual or symbolic washing of hands, forearms, face and feet, prayers are not considered to be effective." The manner in which Muslim men and women greet each other varies widely from one region to another. In most countries a handshake is a normal way of greeting but some conservatives may consider that as inappropriate except among close family members. The most common form of verbal greeting is *Assalamu Alaikum* (Peace be upon you.)

One September evening in 1999, I addressed a large audience in a mosque lecture hall in California. Men and women were seated on opposite sides of the hall and visually separated by a wooden partition. After my remarks, a number of women, most of them in conservative attire, came forward for greetings and discussion. Some welcomed my handshake. Others, while declining, offered a warm verbal greeting. I habitually offer a handshake to almost everyone I meet, and I follow this practice when opening a conversation with Muslim women, even those in traditional attire.

One of the women said, "I don't understand the separation of men and women at this lecture. We mix freely on other occasions. Why can't we sit together when we attend a lecture?" When I asked one of the local Muslim leaders about the policy, he said, "We believe most women feel more comfortable this way." Then he added, "It is mostly tradition, arising partly from the requirement that women are separated from men while praying in a mosque."

Americans of other confessions may regard Islamic separation of the sexes in mosques as odd, but it was once commonplace among non-Muslims in the United States. To this day, women in some Christian denominations are seated separately from men during religious services, wear bonnets whenever they are outside the home, and are attired in long, modest dresses at all times, not just when they attend church events. Elberry believes some Islamic prayer forms have changed slightly since early times, "Men and women have not always been separated. In early days they would often stand in the same line with men—perhaps a group of women, then several men, and so on. But the Prophet Muhammad saw men were distracted by the women and directed the separation." She adds with a chuckle, "I guess he thought men were more distracted than the other way around."

Andrew Patterson comments on the separation issue: "Muslim congregational prayer is not a place for boys to meet girls and vice versa. There is a strict injunction against such an attitude. Prayer is for prayer only and for giving thanks to God." Patterson finds that women are not always situated behind the men during prayers: "In a mosque in Washington, D.C., women are separated, but they are stationed to the right of the men, not behind them. I have found similar policies in other mosques. In some of them, a curtain separates the women from the men. In the Iranian Cultural Foundation in Houston, women are grouped to the left of the men and behind, but not directly behind."

He reports that differences between Sunni and Shi'ite Muslims are mainly organizational, but prayer practices differ slightly. "Shi'ite Muslims touch their foreheads to little pieces of stone or baked clay during prayer. This is to remind them of their mortality, a sign that they won't live forever and their bodies return to the earth from which we come. Shi'ites also shake hands with those nearest them after each set of prayers. At one point in the prayer, they hold hands and raise their hands together in unison."[11] It is noteworthy that at a specified point during Roman Catholic mass and in some Protestant churches, worshippers shake hands with those seated near them.

When Lucille and I visited South Africa in 1989, we found that separation between men and women extended to the workplace and was intended to protect the honor and dignity of women. In the large building occupied by Ahmad Deedat's Islamic Propagation Center International, we found that male and female employees work on different floors. Deedat's son, Yousef, explained, "This keeps sexual distractions to a minimum." That afternoon, he instructed Lucille in a kindred rule. He politely declined to drive her a few blocks to a hairdresser, because the two would be alone in the car, a violation of Islamic propriety. He said the fact that she might be old enough to be his mother made no difference.

Later, when we visited the residence of his parents, Yousef expressed another Muslim tradition on division of responsibility within the Muslim family. "My father is president of the Islamic Center downtown, but in this house my mother is president at all times." Lucille smiled and applauded vigorously.

In Los Angeles recently, I interviewed a Muslim woman who objects to the separation of men and women at prayer. She considers it demeaning for women to be stationed behind men. "I have not entered a mosque for a long time. I refuse to be required to pray behind the men."

She gave another reason for staying away. "A couple of years ago, at the end of Ramadan, the annual month of daytime fasting, I went to the mosque to leave my zakat [the required annual contribution to the poor]. I was dressed as I am now," she said, pointing to her loose-fitting, modest Western attire. "When I approached the imam, he averted his eyes and offered a prayer in Arabic, which said, in effect, 'Forgive me, God, for the sin of looking upon this improperly clad woman.' I was furious. I turned around, went back to my car, drove away, and I've never entered a mosque since."

When I asked her if she still considers herself a Muslim, her response was immediate and emphatic, "Absolutely. I am a Muslim. I believe in God. I pray five times a day. I fast during Ramadan, and I give to the poor." Then she added, "Islam requires modesty, not long gowns and head scarves. I don't violate my faith by wearing Western attire, as long as it is modest." I asked her if Western attire is common among other Muslim women. "I have no way of knowing the numbers, but among my acquaintances the number who dress much as I do may be 40 percent, probably more."

O n August 3, 2000, the front page of the Living Section of *The Nashville Tennessean*, was devoted to a feature captioned, "Balancing Fashion and Faith: Show Brings Out the Beauty [and Modesty] of Islamic Fashions." In a first for Nashville, colorful Muslim fashions priced up to $325 were modeled from a banquet hall stage to an appreciative audience. The report by staff writer Tasneem Ansariyah-Grace, began: "For Muslim women, style is spiritual. The Quran encourages women to dress modestly, to shroud their sex appeal so the world values their character, not their curves…. The clothes are stunning. Purple, red, orange, and blue cloth is laced in gold. Matching headpieces slink to the shoulders or rise from the head in puffy halos. Skirts skim shoe tops." Khadija Majeed, a teacher and native of Morocco who attended the show, said, "A lot of people think Muslim women just wear black and white sheets. I love to dress up. I love bright colors."

M uslim women understandably do not take the initiative to explain what they are wearing, but I find that they are always glad to answer questions about any aspect of their faith. Unfortunately, most Americans shy away from asking, and Muslim women, like non-Muslim women, seldom initiate conversations with men.

In past years, I have often wondered why some Muslim women wear headscarves and veils over their faces, others wear only the scarves, while some wear neither. I admit that, despite ten years of close association with Muslims, I had never learned why, nor did I have the common sense to ask until I began writing this book.

Muslims disagree over whether female headscarves are required by their religion. Some insist that the mandate is explicit. The disagreement arises over differing interpretations of comments made centuries ago by the Prophet Muhammad. Salam Al-Marayati believes there is room for honest disagreement over the Prophet Muhammad's position. "The important point is that Muslims who consider a headscarf a religious mandate should be respected by those who disagree—and vice versa."

A Christian who serves as principal of a public school in Texas set a noteworthy example in early 2000 when he demanded that a Muslim girl be permitted to wear a headscarf during a soccer game. Two minutes before the game was scheduled to begin, the head referee, a member of the Texas Soccer Officials Association, notified the woman who coached the Sam Houston High School girls' team that one of the girls must either remove her headscarf or leave the field. He made no mention of the girl's other apparel. In keeping with the Muslim requirement of modesty in attire, she wore sweat pants and a long- sleeve shirt, in addition to the head-scarf. The garments left only her hands and face bare. The referee's ultimatum was especially surprising—and distressing—because the girl, a regular on the team, wore a headscarf during five previous games that year without objection by referees of the same association.

Informed of the ultimatum when he arrived at the field moments later, Principal Ricky Kempe demanded that the girl, scarf and all, be permitted to play. The referee refused. "A head-scarf is against the rules, and the rules will be enforced." The principal, a member of the Church of Christ, held his ground. "Soccer rules cannot violate federal law. The girl has the right to conform to religious requirements under the First Amendment to the Constitution and under public laws against religious discrimination." When Kempe threatened to file suit in federal court, the referee backed down and permitted the girl to play while wearing the scarf. The Texas University Intercollegiate League, the organization that sets statewide soccer rules, later announced its support for the principal's position. The Muslim Public Affairs Council, based in Los Angeles, issued a statement praising Kempe for taking a "stand for religious freedom" and "pluralism," and for demonstrating "courage for what is right."[12] Kempe later said, "The Islamic religion and Muslim attire are non-issues at Sam Houston High school. I've been principal here for four years, and during that time only once, to my knowledge, has a student even tried to make fun of the Muslim girls who regularly wear headscarves." He estimated that about one hundred of the school's two thousand five hundred students are Muslim. "The Muslims are good students, top shelf. About three or four of the Muslim girls always wear head-scarves, and they get along fine." His handling of the headscarf controversy produced no complaints. "I am glad to say that I received about thirty e-mails, all supportive. I received no objections," he said.

N our Naciri provides the historical background on the head-scarf issue:

"The veil over the female face is a longstanding cultural tradition in some Muslim countries, but it has nothing whatever to do with Islam. Nothing in the sacred literature of Islam requires or even recommends the veil. Women in pre-Islamic and early Islamic Arabia used to wear a head skullcap from which they suspended a cloth, or khimaar, the whole combination being usually referred to as a 'veil.' This so-called veil was allowed to flow down their backs to their waists or lower.

"Islam decreed [Quran 24:31] that women cover the upper part of their chest and the chest itself with this veil, unlike what they used to do before Islam, leaving their chests exposed. Muqaatil, a revered interpreter of the Quran, elucidates, 'Over their bosoms' means 'over their chests,' which was the location of their juyoob, or pockets. [At the time] the Arabs [men and women] placed their pockets on the chest of their garments [for added security]....A 'veil' is originally whatever is used to cover the head [not the face]. The Arabic jayb [singular of juyoob] means a pocket slit or a garment's neck slit. Sometimes it means a woman's shirt. What matters here is, as Muqaatil notes, the bosom must be covered, not the face.

"The wearing of a headscarf, usually called a hijab, is another matter. First of all, nothing in the Quran specifically requires women to cover their hair. See Chapter 24, verses 30-31. It calls only for modesty in attire for men as well as women, but many Muslims consider a headscarf for women to be religiously mandated. The source they cite for this requirement arises from a directive issued by the Prophet Muhammad in a conversation. He said, 'When a woman reaches puberty, it is not lawful that any [part] of her be seen, except this and this,' pointing to his face and hands. It remains unclear, as my late father Mohammed Makki Naciri, one of Morocco's foremost Islamic authorities, assured me, whether by pointing to his face, the Prophet meant just the face or the whole head. [Some Islamic scholars disagree with this interpretation.] Here lies the continuing controversy.

"Muslims in general believe that a command of the Prophet must be accepted as a religious mandate since the Quran tells them so. But since this was not a clear injunction, some Muslims find it open to interpretation. My wife [Zainab Elberry], for example, wears a headscarf only for her five daily prayers and when she enters a mosque."

Naciri's explanation reminded me of differences in attire that I observed in the extended families in both Dearborn and Baghdad. None of the women had veils over their faces. In the Bazzi family, the mother and one daughter wore headscarves and long dresses. The other two daughters, like the younger women in the Al-Khafaji family in Baghdad, wore Western dress and left their hair uncovered, a practice that did not appear to be exceptional for their age group either in the Iraqi capital or in Detroit.

One day, several young Muslim women discussed politics with me in a Dearborn hotel lobby, and I noticed that only one wore a headscarf. Later, at the mosque, I noted that they arrived as a group and, like all other females present, they wore headscarves. In my youth, women always covered their hair when in church, and some continue that custom. Most churches encourage worshippers to wear modest attire and some admit only those who do. While touring the Vatican City in Rome one day, I noticed that females in miniskirts were denied entry into St. Peter's Cathedral.

The attire of Muslim women in America reflects the variety of customs that prevail in Muslim countries. Not always apparent is the difference between apparel required by culture—veils over the face, for example—and Islam's requirement of modesty in attire for men as well as women. Many Muslim women customarily wear casual clothes at home. When they leave their residences, they wear loose-fitting, long overgarments to meet religious requirements.

In my travels, I found little uniformity, whether in Malaysia, South Africa, or the Middle East, although in Saudi Arabia, men and women wore traditional attire in both rural and urban regions, and all women wore head scarves and veiled their faces.

In a recent visit to Yemen, I noticed that female attire is mainly conservative in the North, while the men usually wear Western dress, especially in the cities. Most of the older women wear black while the long dresses of younger women are often in bright colors. No rule seems absolute. At a hotel in Taiz, a young woman clad in black with her face covered by an opaque veil served as desk clerk.

In other Muslim countries, dress customs vary greatly for both men and women. In rural areas they tend to be conservative, but in cities I found Western attire common among men. Female attire, while always modest, was sometimes Western. In Malaysia, the only Muslim country I have visited outside the Middle East and North Africa, most Muslim men wear Western dress, while the attire of women varies, some in colorful gowns and head scarves, others in Western dress with no scarf. In Africa, vibrant, bright colors are common in women's attire and in the turbans and robes that men typically wear. West African men typically wear caps called kufis, while women wear head wraps—all brightly colored.

Zainab Elberry explains the origin. "In the beginning of Islam, Muslim women were few in number and vulnerable to neighboring pagan tribesmen, and the identification in attire helped to assure protection. Since then, many Muslim women still like to be identified with Islam by their dress. This may serve as a protection to some extent, but it also reflects pride in their faith. It wasn't long ago that we called native Americans naked savages, even though they were not naked. Today, through the media, it seems that the more we show our bodies, the more civilized we are. Less is better! It seems that dress custom is driven by politics, economics and Parisian couture with its present focus on miniskirts. But in Islam, the rule that men and women must always be modest in attire has never changed."

Today, many Muslim women are "pro-choice" regarding hair covering, but others believe that they must wear a headscarf in public places, including places of employment. Dr. Musa Qutub, director of the Islamic Information Center in Des Plaines, Illinois, writes, "God legislated the hijab (headscarf) to protect the female and not to lower her status." He cites Chapter 33, verse 59, of the Quran, "O Prophet tell ... the women of the believers to draw their cloaks close to them. So it is likelier that they may be recognized and not harmed." He quotes Chapter 24, verse 31 of the Quran, which enjoins women to "draw their veils over their bosoms, and not reveal their adornment, except to their husband or to [close relatives]"

The government of Turkey, a predominately Muslim country, enforces a surprising policy prohibiting female hair covering in certain public settings. Continuing a tradition toward secularism started by Kemal Ataturk, founder of modern Turkey, the government prohibits women from wearing headscarves in public schools and government offices. In May 1999, officials enforced the regulation by refusing to seat a newly elected female Muslim member of the parliament because she refused to remove her headscarf for oath-taking ceremonies.[13]

Peer pressure can be a persuasive factor in women's choices. One evening in a marketplace in Sana'a, the capital of Yemen, a fully veiled woman with three teenage children stepped up to converse with our son, Craig. This was an initiative that a nearby storekeeper later described as unusual for Yemeni women. She introduced herself and children as residents of Stockton, California, and said that this was their first extended visit to a Muslim country.

When Diane, our daughter, joined the conversation, the lady, a Muslim, said she had planned to wear her customary Western clothes but quickly changed to headscarf, long dress, and a veil over her face. She gave this explanation: "No one scolded me or urged me to change, but the stares were so constant that I decided traditional attire would be best." She added that the experience in Yemen was a culture shock for her children, who, when at home in California, were used to playing with skateboards and going to movies, McDonald's restaurants, and shopping malls. Fast food restaurants are beginning to appear in Sana'a but, unlike Amman and Cairo, there are no movie theaters.

At Sana'a University, female students clustered around Diane, wishing to talk about Western culture. All were conservatively attired and wore veils, but Diane occasionally glimpsed high-heeled shoes and bright sweatshirts. In a thoughtful gesture of friendship and hospitality, one of the girls gave Diane a ring. Most of the male teachers, we noticed, wore Western attire.

Later, Diane reflected on female attire: "Veils were not a problem for me. It's easy to see beyond them, because one can tell a lot about people just by looking into their eyes." When I mentioned this to Andrew Patterson, he nodded, "The Prophet Muhammad said the eyes are a window into the soul."

Prayer customs are intertwined with female attire. As Elberry explains, "Female attire responds partly to the requirements of Islamic prayer. All Muslims are expected to practice their religion constantly, not just one morning a week. They are called to pray five times a day at specified hours. This means they are never more than a few hours from prayer time. Each prayer ritual requires the repetition of standing, kneeling, and bowing until the forehead touches the prayer rug, then reversal of the sequence. This routine helps to explain why women, out of modesty, traditionally station themselves behind men during prayer."

Muslims have retained customs that were once common among non-Muslims in America. To this day in some Christian denominations, women are seated separately from men in church and wear long modest dresses and hair covering whenever they are outside the home. Not long ago, modest attire was the rule for men and women alike, even when bathing in public or engaging in sports like tennis, track and swimming. I remember seeing pictures of tennis champion Ellsworth Vines, my boyhood hero, wearing long white trousers as he scurried around the court. Helen Wills Moody, the woman champion of that era, always wore a modest dress. Her skirt reached below her knees.

A generation ago, American women frequently wore veils over their faces, not because of religious mandate but, like many Muslim women today, in response to tradition. Black veils were considered proper at the funeral, and on other occasions light-colored ones were regarded as stylish. In the nineteenth century, American women routinely wore ankle-length dresses and bonnets.

Zainab Elberry explains the traditional division of labor in the Muslim family. "The Muslim husband has the primary responsibility to provide financial support of the household, while his wife has the main responsibility for rearing the children and managing the home." It is noteworthy that before World War II, most American families had the same division of responsibility. Since then, this tradition has weakened substantially. More women, both Muslim and non-Muslim, work outside the home and contribute to family income.

M ale chauvinism may be less apparent in Islam than in some Christian and Jewish places of worship. Rasha Yow, a young Muslim neighbor, reports that nothing in the Quran keeps a woman from serving as an imam. Women may lead congregational prayer or provide religious instruction for a mixed, all-female or all-male group—although they rarely take that responsibility. If they lead prayer for a mixed or all-male group, out of modesty they do so from the rear of the worshippers. These rules flow from long-standing custom and tradition, not from the Quran.

In contrast, conservative rabbis, as well as Catholic priests— Roman and Eastern Orthodox—are all male. For years, women have served as clergy in several Protestant denominations, but in others the leadership remains exclusively male. John F. Baugh of Houston, a prominent Baptist leader and author of *The Struggle for Baptist Integrity*, reports that in 1998 the new leadership of the Southern Baptist Convention, the largest of Protestant communities, declared that the denomination "wants all women subservient" to their husbands. It approved an amendment, now an article of denominational faith, stating that "a wife is to submit graciously to the servant leadership of her husband."[14]

S till, Islam has some patriarchal traditions that discriminate against women. A Muslim husband automatically has the right to divorce, but the wife must reserve the right at the time of marriage. Moreover, a Muslim man may marry a Christian or Jewish woman, but a Muslim female is enjoined against marrying a non-Muslim. According to one of my Muslim acquaintances, a Muslim woman is deemed guilty of illegal conduct, some call it adultery, if she marries a non-Muslim.

The rule against such marriages is so broadly supported in some Muslim countries that offending couples feel compelled to move to a non-Muslim country. A U.S. Muslim leader who prefers anonymity says, "On this point, I'm afraid the Muslim scholars are not up to speed with the modern era. This will be a problem for a long time to come." The problem seems minor in the United States, where, despite Muslim juristic injunctions, many U.S. Muslim women are married to non-Muslims.

I n the political realm, the achievements of women in Muslim countries should be the envy of U.S. female politicians. Zainab Elberry notes that every U.S. president and vice-president has been male, but women have served in the highest elective offices in the Muslim states of Pakistan, Bangladesh, and Turkey. In 1999, a Muslim woman, Megawati Sukarno, was elected vice-president of Indonesia, and in 2000 was accorded substantial authority by the man who was elected to the presidency. A woman served recently as a vice-president of Iran.

U.S. women, whether Muslim or not, had to wait one hundred thirty-two years to attain the right to vote. But in most Muslim countries where the democratic process exists, women achieved the right to vote simultaneously with men. Today, women have the right to vote in all Muslim countries in South Asia, as well as in a number of Muslim countries of the Middle East and Africa. In a notable exception, the all-male National Assembly, which has advisory powers in the government of Kuwait, a Muslim country, voted in December 1999 against extending the franchise to Kuwaiti women. Only men over twenty-one who have been citizens for at least twenty years can vote or seek office.[15]

In one respect, non-Muslim women are just now catching up with a longstanding Islamic tradition. Many non-Muslim brides are choosing to retain their maiden names in marriage, a practice almost unknown a generation ago. In Islam, it is a tradition protected by Islamic law and practiced for centuries.

Salam Al-Marayati finds that Islam promotes equality and therefore harmony and compassion between husband and wife. "Islam teaches us that Eve was not created from Adam's rib but was created equally. According to the Quran, she was not the one approached by the devil in trapping Adam into sinning, but the two fell together. And they were both forgiven by God after they asked for forgiveness. According to Islam, male and female were created from a single substance and a single spirit." He cites two Islamic legal requirements that are beneficial to women; the inheritance and personal income of a woman cannot be spent by her husband without her consent, and the husband must share duties around the house or provide a housekeeper for his wife. "Unfortunately," Al-Marayati adds, "many of these ideals fall short in the reality of our world today."[16]

In respect to ideals achieved and those unfulfilled, Christians and Jews need to reflect only briefly to realize that their own culture and religious traditions, past and present, have much in common with Muslims.

Notes:

1. Sheila Hotchkin, AP 1-21-2000.
2. Thomas W. Lippman, *Understanding Islam* (New York: Mentor Books, 1990).
3. William Baker, *More in Common Than You Think,* pp. 62–63.
4. Other publishers have defamed Islam. In 1997, Capstone Press of Minnesota and Simon and Schuster of New York, in response to demands by CAIR, recalled books with inaccurate material about Islam and Muslim culture.

5. CAIR Alert, 11-99.
6. Interview and written correspondence with Taymour El-Hosseiny, 1999.
7. Interview, 1-18-2000.
8. Interview with Sulayman Nyang, 1-19-2000.
9. Interview, 1-28-2000.
10. Hannah Wolfson, AP 1-14-2000.
11. Interview with Andrew Patterson, 4-23-1999.
12. Interview with Kempe, 2-11-00; and e-mail from MPACUSA 2-9-2000.
13. AP, 5-3-1999.
14. Grace Halsell, *Forcing God's Hand,* p. 108.
15. *USA Today,* 12-1-1999.
16. *Los Angeles Times,* p. A15, 3-8-1996.

Chapter 7: False Links to Islam

When I told a Muslim audience in California in 1997 that most Americans believe Muslim women are treated like property and are subjected to discrimination and abuse because of their sex, the women in the audience, obviously scornful of that conclusion, burst into laughter before I finished the sentence.

After my remarks, a woman came to the lectern and, with intense feeling, declared that Muslim women stand equally with men. She said, "It is wrong to believe that Islam oppresses women and treats them as being inferior to men. Some are oppressed, of course, but never because of the rules of our religion."

Her comments suggest a massive gap in communication between Muslim women in the United States and their non-Muslim neighbors. The false image of Muslim women that Americans accept as accurate is not a laughing matter, nor is the status of women in many African countries, several of which are identified as Muslim.

The women who laughed at my assessment would not be amused if they knew that many Americans, perhaps millions of them, blame Islam for two customs that deserve to be described as brutal assaults on females—the "honor" killing of women accused of promiscuous sexual conduct and the circumcision of young girls that is accurately called female genital mutilation (FGM) in the West

The murder of women suspected of promiscuity occurs in a number of countries —some of them Muslim—such as Pakistan, Jordan, part of the Arabian peninsula, and in India. In non-Muslim Latin America, they are called "crimes of passion."

Since both "honor" killings and FGM occur in some countries where Muslims predominate or are prominent, many people in the West wrongly assume that these practices are condoned by Islam.

The surgery varies in extent and effect, but in some cases could deny the subject the pleasure of sexuality and in some cases makes sexual intercourse impossible until further surgery is performed. It is a tribal practice that dates back to pre-Islamic times and is performed on girls in their teens or younger.

One estimate concludes that two million females in Africa are subject to various types of female circumcision.[1] Among them are the majority of females in Somalia and rural Egypt. In February 1999, the Population Council reported on the survey conducted in 1997 of more than nine thousand Egyptian children and their parents. It disclosed that 84 percent of the girls between ten and nineteen years of age were subjected to the surgery. Although noting some decline in the practice, the report added: "More than 90 percent of Egyptian girls are circumcised around the age of five or six. Around 70 percent of the operations are performed in the home in unhygenic conditions, sometimes resulting in death from bleeding or infection.... The practice persists due to religious and cultural beliefs that [it] is necessary to moderate female sexuality and make girls more feminine and marriageable."[2]

A year earlier, in February 1998, Ismail Sallam, Egypt's minister of health, criticized Muslim "fundamentalists" for opposing Egypt's ban on female circumcision and defying the position of a senior Muslim authority in Egypt who says female circumcision is not a religious duty. Sallam added: "We know that wealthy people, officials, and senior clerics don't circumcise their own."[3]

The surgery is common in several other African countries, some of them Muslim, and is found, only rarely, in southern Europe, Latin America, and according to Dr. Cherie Thibodeaux, president of Physicians Management Systems, in some U.S. neighborhoods.[4]

Although outlawed in the United States in October 1996, thanks to a twenty-year campaign led by U.S. Rep. Patricia Schroeder [D-CO], the surgery is still inflicted on some females of recent

African origin. The Centers for Disease Control and Prevention estimate that more than 150,000 women and girls of African origin living in the United States have had or are at risk of being mutilated. The Centers stated: "The practice is performed to keep women faithful and can lead to severe complications, infection, and death."[5]

A parent—usually the father—decides if and when the surgery is to occur. In Egypt, where FGM has been a strong tradition for centuries, it is done so secretly that some well-educated Egyptians mistakenly believe it is nearly extinct. In most countries, it is performed clandestinely and usually without anesthesia in crude, unsanitary circumstances by an unlicensed woman traveling from village to village. Occasionally, it is performed in sanitary conditions by a licensed physician but even then in secrecy.

FGM is often likened to male circumcision, but this is an incorrect and misleading characterization. The procedures and consequences differ radically. Male circumcision removes only the foreskin of the penis. It is common worldwide, widely approved by Christianity, required by Islam and Judaism, and for years recommended widely as a health measure. Male circumcision is a rite that is considered an important event in Islamic, as well as Jewish, family life. It does not impair men's health, fertility or sexuality. In contrast, FGM has drastic consequences for women. The Population Council lists the following risks that FGM poses: injury and infection of vagina, rectum, bladder and urethra, leading to lifelong disabilities; infertility; tetanus; debilitating menstrual pain; malformation of the genital area; painful urination and urinary retention; painful sexual intercourse; childbirth difficulties, endangering baby's and mother's health and life; death from uncontrollable bleeding or from shock. Whether minor or extensive, the surgery is usually treated as an embarrassment that must be kept from the light of day.

In Kenya, the surgery that is routinely performed on female genitalia is intended to remove only the hood, or cover, of the clitoris. In this respect, it is similar to male circumcision, but it is not considered a healthful measure. To the contrary, it too risks grave consequences. A slip of the knife may permanently harm female sexuality.

Far from being secret, the surgery in Kenya is usually the occasion for lengthy public celebration. It is the climax of festivities lasting for several days that celebrate the young woman's coming of age. It is closely linked to tribal and ethic customs and has nothing to do with Islam. A detailed description of the festivities and the surgical procedure is presented in *Facing Mt. Kenya,* a book by Jomo Kenyatta, the founder of modern Kenya and for many years the nation's leader. In it, he describes the preparations for the rite made by the family and community, as well as anesthetic and health precautions that are taken before and after the surgery.

In August 1996, Kenya's National Women's Group began promoting a new non-surgical ritual to replace the "dangerous and painful" traditional practice. It is called "Circumcision Through Words" and involves a week of seclusion and education for young girls. One hundred and fifty families participated in the new ritual during the first year.[6]

The surgery is often brutal and extensive, largely the product of ignorance, poverty and the chauvinistic notion of male superiority. In some regions, men consider females who are not circumcised to be unsuitable for marriage. The practice is rarely found among educated people. In rural Egypt, Somalia, and other African countries where FGM occurs widely, education is limited, and living conditions are primitive. For example, in rural Egypt, the rate of illiteracy keeps rising despite the government's long, vigorous efforts to extend education to all citizens. On an average, a new classroom is put into service every day, but this pace has not matched population growth. Egypt's population, currently sixty-four million, increases by more than a million each year.[7]

Contrary to the stereotype that links FGM to Islam alone, it is widely practiced in several non-Muslim countries in Central and West Africa.

The false linkage to Islam results partly from the fact that U.S. news media provide little coverage of life in Africa and are misinformed in many ways. As a consequence, the American people are unaware that FGM is widely practiced in several African countries where Muslims are only a minority such as Kenya, Ghana, Benin and Liberia. Nor do most Americans know that a large number of Christian, Jewish, as well as other non-Muslim females in African countries are among the victims. In Ethiopia, for example, it is practiced by the Christian and Jewish populations.

Most of the world's 1.2 billion Muslims were unaware of FGM until recently, when magazines, books, and documentaries made it the center of worldwide controversy. Until then, it was common knowledge only in certain regions of Africa.

Alice Walker, author of the Pulitzer Prize-winning book, *The Color Purple,* provided the first breakthrough with the publication in 1992 of her book, *Possessing the Secret of Joy,* a fictional narrative that attacks the FGM custom and the mythologies that various cultures use to sustain it. It tells the story of an African woman who submits to the surgery, then spends the rest of her life trying to understand its meaning and live with its consequences.

D espite the popularity of Walker's book, FGM remained little known until the June 1999 issue of the *Readers Digest* featured an article, "Silent no More," in which Waris Dirie, a brave and beautiful young woman from Somalia, recounted her own ordeal with FGM. Her article, featured on the cover of the world's most widely circulated magazine, brought awareness of the brutal practice to millions of people worldwide.

Until Dirie's article, FGM was rarely mentioned in newspapers and seldom in private conversation. Perhaps because of the intimate nature of the surgery and feelings of embarrassment and shame, the victims, whether followers of Islam, Christianity or other religions, hesitate to mention their ordeal even to close friends. Except in a few countries like Kenya, where the surgery is very limited in extent, the custom is rarely discussed even within the immediate family. As a result, those circumcised like Dirie, usually do not learn in advance what will be done and why.

Because of the article, Dirie, whose portrait appeared on the *Digest* cover, has become the world's best-known victim. Her health problems began at the age of five when her father, a goat herder in Somalia, arranged for her mutilation to be performed outdoors in a desert area without anesthesia. It was done by an itinerant woman who used a broken, blood-stained razor blade.

After the surgery, the wound was stitched tightly, leaving an opening so small that for years Dirie could pass urine and, after puberty, blood only a few drops at a time. Her menstrual periods were prolonged agony. Years later in London, surgery enabled her to relieve herself normally. She rose rapidly to international fame as a model. She is married, the mother of a four-year-old son, and resides with her family in New York City.

In the magazine, Dirie describes the physical price she has paid. "Besides the health problems that I still struggle with, I will never know the pleasures of sex. I feel incomplete, crippled.... I've got to speak ... for the millions of girls living with FGM and those dying from it."

The linkage of FGM with Islam led Lillian Bete, a New Englander I have known and respected for years, to strong resentment against the religion. When she read *Do They Hear You When You Cry?*, a book by Fauziya Kassindja, a Muslim girl who escaped female genital mutilation in Togo, then viewed a late-night television program on the same subject, Bete was outraged.[8]

The broadcast featured two Muslims, a victim of female genital mutilation and a man. The woman, her face shielded from view, recalled the "great pain and shame" she experienced when forced to undergo the surgery at the age of eight. The man defended the surgery, citing "moral" reasons. Bete remembered his defense. "He said in so many words that the surgery cuts out the part of the female anatomy that stimulates sexual desire. Therefore, it keeps a woman from being promiscuous before marriage and promotes fidelity to her husband after marriage."

The broadcast had a lasting impact. "Few things in my life have disturbed me so deeply. I was greatly offended. When I heard his defense, I rebelled totally. I was convinced that this barbaric surgery was condoned by Islam, and I decided I wanted nothing to do with Muslims. Up to that point I had tried to be understanding and tolerant of Islam, but this was too much."[9]

The exact words expressed on television in defense of the surgery are less important than the impression that the broadcast left with viewers. It gave no hint, for example, that Christian and other non-Muslim females are often victims of mutilation in a number of African countries. The televised finger seemed to point the blame only at Islam and convinced Bete that mutilation is central in Islamic teachings and practices.

She now realizes that it is not approved in Islam, but her experience is instructive. She is well educated, an avid reader, a thoughtful observer of public issues, and, through the years, sympathetic to my efforts for human rights. The television program that prompted her resentment against Islam undoubtedly led other uninformed viewers to a similar reaction. If a televised discussion of genital mutilation could turn her against Islam, I conclude that the stereotype of Islam that it has fostered represents a major obstacle to those who seek understanding of Islam and fairness to Muslims.

B y publicizing the surgery and accepting a special ambassadorship in a United Nations campaign for its eradication, Waris Dirie believes she is exposing herself to personal risk. "Friends have expressed concern that a fanatic will try to kill me, since many fundamentalists consider FGM a holy practice demanded by the Quran." Fear was in Dirie's mind as she prepared to lead the campaign. "I'm sure my work will be dangerous. I admit to being scared. But I might as well take a chance. It's what I've done all my life."

F ear is one of the major factors that unfairly burden Islam—a religion devoted to justice, equality, and dignity for women— with blame for FGM. Fear and its handmaiden, secrecy, tend to spawn unfounded rumors and nurture false images. As reflected in Dirie's statement and personal experience, the possibility of retribution, even violent, meted out by religious radicals who wrongly proclaim FGM as a Quranic mandate, may account for much of the silence of Muslim leaders.

In areas where FGM is widely practiced, most people—rich and poor, young and old—seem to have an excuse for ignoring, in public at least, this towering violation of human rights.

I was not surprised when a U.S. Muslim mother requested anonymity when she explained to me the role of ignorance in this unfortunate, although ancient, practice. She did not want the following words traced to her doorstep: "The men who order the mutilation in rural areas of Egypt, Somalia, and other African states, as well as the females, are often poorly educated. They cannot read holy literature and are apt to be heavily intimidated by the popularity of tribal customs and legend. Even some of the imams and other Muslim leaders are similarly handicapped."

Today, despite this fear, FGM has become a major, international scandal, arousing worldwide public concern because it victimizes women on a massive scale. It is frequently in the headlines of newspapers and magazines and mentioned on television and radio programming. And, because it relates to sex and clandestine surgery on female genitalia, prolonged news media attention is almost certain to occur. It is surely the ultimate in injustice, inequality, and indignity -practices that Islam thoroughly deplores.

The media play a major role in linking FGM with Islam. The linkage is usually expressed in reports written by people who assume it is valid simply because the surgery is routinely inflicted annually upon hundreds of thousands of Muslim women. It is widespread in some countries—like Egypt and Somalia—where Muslims predominate, and it is not common in countries where Christians or Jews are in the majority.

Reporters may be further confused by the attitude of the professed Muslims, including some imams and other community leaders, who give their assent—silently, if not openly—to limited surgery like that done in Kenya. The reason for this assent may be the intimidation prompted by long-observed tribal custom or ignorance, a combination of both, or opinions expressed in the on going debate about the position of Islamic law on varying degrees of genital surgery.

Faulty and incomplete news coverage is often a major culprit, according to Nihad Awad, national director of the Council on American Islamic Relations (CAIR): "There is nothing in Islamic references that supports it. It is reported by non-Muslim sources as Islamic practice because some Muslims engage in it. Unfortunately, Muslims do not have the same media access as those sources have to dispel the stereotype."[10]

Part of the confusion arises when radicals who say they are Muslims make the unfounded assertion that FGM is required by the Quran. Nowhere is FGM mentioned in the Quran, but it was widely practiced on the Arabian peninsula where the revelations to the Prophet Muhammad occurred.

Some Muslims who are recognized as authorities in Islamic law add to the confusion. They tiptoe around the practice, issuing comments that seem at times to be contradictory, citing statements attributed to the Prophet Muhammad that suggest he gave tacit approval, for example, to limited female circumcision. Other scholars question the authenticity of these citations.

The unqualified denunciation of genital surgery that I hear from ordinary Muslims is more precise than criticism expressed in some scholarly quarters. Even Islamic law, while prohibiting most forms of FGM, seems, ever so cautiously, to approve "minor" cutting. Of the four classical schools of Islamic jurisprudence, one even takes the position that the surgical removal of the hood of the clitoris is obligatory, and two others called its removal a recommended "noble deed." All four schools agreed that cutting beyond the hood of the clitoris is "not allowed."[11]

Attempts by Islamic scholars to clear up public confusion and dismay have been only partially successful. Dr. Imad-ad-Dean Ahmad writes that Islamic law prohibits three procedures: cliterodectomy, that is, complete or partial removal of the clitoris; infibulation, excision of part or all of the external genitalia and stitching or narrowing of the vaginal opening; or any genital mutilation which impairs the woman's ability to enjoy sexual relations. He adds that Islamic law permits "only the mildest form of circumcision (of females) and that only if it produces no adverse effects on the child." This qualified language comes close to a sweeping denunciation of all forms of female genital mutilation, as does his summation: "Since it has neither hygienic nor religious value, there is no justification for Muslims to engage in this painful and potentially harmful practice, and it would be best to avoid it completely.... As to the mildest form of female circumcision, the risk to the girl's future ability to enjoy sexual relations with her husband must place it at best in the category of disliked practices."[12]

Dr. Taha Jabir al Alwani, chairman of the High Council of the Islamic Society of North America, writes: "There is no text in the Quran or authentic Sunnah (interpretation) that commands female circumcision. This was a tradition from pre-Islamic days, to which Islam brought moderation." Other Muslims who are prominent in Islam's legal hierarchy, leave the issue untouched. Al Alwani reports: "Three of the four major Islamic [classical] schools of thought have not considered this to be an issue requiring a religious ruling, indicating that it is only a cultural practice with little Islamic standing."[13]

In some circles, Islamic law, while prohibiting most forms of female genital surgery, seems to leave moderate cutting on the approved list. Some experts seem cautious, even guarded, in expressing opposition to this practice. Their caution may be prompted by a principle in Islamic law which holds that "what is not prohibited is allowed." Because the revealed literature of Islam contains no explicit prohibition against female genital surgery, this silence leaves open the possible inference that the surgery is not disallowed.

The Prophet Muhammad is believed by a few Muslim scholars to have called for "moderation"—not prohibition—in what is accepted by some scholars as a hadith referring to the surgery. They believe he said to a woman performing the surgery, "Do not cut severely as that is better for a woman and more desirable for a husband." But the authenticity of this implied approval of limited surgery by the Prophet Muhammad is challenged by a number of authorities on Islamic law, including Abu Dawud in his *Sunan*, a compilation that records the episode. He calls its standing "weak."

Even in the United States, where the surgery is performed in some communities of immigrants, the public outrage has prompted little response from Muslim leaders. Those who speak out on the subject are, without exception, strongly opposed. In fact, I have discussed the surgery with a number of U.S. Muslims, and all have privately expressed opposition to it, even in the limited form performed in Kenya.

Dr. Muzammil Siddiqi, president of the Islamic Society of North America and a member of the Islamic Law Council of North America, cites "the need for a review of the rulings of the different schools of Islamic thought in the light of present-day realities confronting Muslims." He adds, "This is delicate ground and one needs to tread on it with exceptional care.... There is debate among Islamic scholars over whether something that may, for instance, appear only once in the Quran is to be taken occasion-specific or can be generalized."[14]

Whether silenced by this confusion or other factors, U.S. Muslim leaders have generally ignored the genital surgery question, bloodstained as it is. Their silence suggests that the constituency for male primacy remains aggressive and successful. I have yet to meet a Muslim female anywhere who endorses even the limited surgery.

The few public protests, although notable, have been largely ignored by the media. Public statements against the practice by the Muslim Public Affairs Council of Los Angeles, and Maher Hathout, M.D., a gynecologist, author and lecturer on Islam, have received little news coverage.

The Muslim Women's League, a California-based organization, condemns it and denies it has any linkage with Islam: "Clearly, mutilating a woman's genitalia in the name of Islam violates the most sacred tenets of our faith. Therefore, we must oppose this practice and join efforts with others who are working to educate women and men about its harmful effects." The league notes among Muslims, a strong, negative resentment against the publicity about female genital mutilation: "Many Muslims responded with disgust, easily dismissing any possible connection between this practice and the religion of Islam." The surprise and disgust are understandable, but dismissal of the mutilation as an anti-Islamic stereotype will be neither easy nor swift.

Zainab Elberry is explicit in her denunciation. "Genital surgery is an affront to Islam. There is absolutely nothing whatever in the Quran or the teachings of the Prophet Muhammad to justify it or condone it. In fact, the Quran has dozens of verses that say, in effect, don't try to change what God has created. The female body is God's creation, and this means that removal of a clitoris defiles and desecrates a holy vessel."

She declares, with fervor: "If God disapproved of the clitoris, He would not have made it a part of the female body." Then, she adds: "But I am sorry to have to admit, it is still performed in my native land [Egypt] by people who call themselves Muslim and ordered by fathers and sometimes mothers and neighbors who call themselves Muslim. It is in direct conflict with the Quran, and yet some leaders of Islamic organizations remain silent."

Abdurahman Alamoudi, one of the founders of the American Muslim Council (AMC), is among the prominent U.S. Muslims who declare unequivocally that any degree of female genital surgery is un-Islamic. He says, "There is no Islamic authority for cutting away even the hood of the clitoris. This surgery is offensive to Islam and to the dignity and well-being of women." Alamoudi's interpretation is, I believe, the prevailing view of all Muslims of my acquaintance and likely shared by almost all Muslims worldwide.

In response to Dirie's *Digest* article, more than 3,000 readers requested information on female genital mutilation from the UN's World Health Organization. Congress responded to testimony presented personally by Dirie by dedicating $25 million for women's issues, such as genital mutilation, to the UN Population Fund. Her campaign in Africa is bearing fruit. Senegal, where 20 percent of females are customarily subjected to the surgery, has joined other African nations in passing laws that prohibit the practice. Senegal banned the surgery in January 1999, following the example of Burkino Faso, Central African Republic, Djibouti, Ghana, Ivory Coast, Guinea and Togo.

Ghana outlawed the practice in 1994 but few people have been prosecuted and the surgery continues.[15] Ivory Coast, a country where 60 percent of the population is Muslim and over 40 percent of all females have been subjected to the surgery, outlawed the practice in 1998.[16] In March 1998, Albertine Gnanazan Hepie, the minister for women and family welfare, said, "There are three arguments used to promote the practice of female circumcision—religion, mutilation as a form of purification, and mutilation as a way of integrating young girls into adult society. All of these arguments have no religious [or] moral justification."[17]

UNICEF director Carol Bellamy comments that the ban "reflects the resolve of women to end a cruel and unacceptable practice which violates the right of all girls to free, safe, and healthy lives."[18]

The campaign for the eradication of mutilation is made more challenging by the fact that the surgery is an easy target for critics of Islam. The Muslim silence that largely surrounds the practice, in effect, relinquishes its discussion largely to the people who enjoy transmitting to others unfounded rumors, especially those related to human sexuality. The false linkage to Islam is particularly appealing to bigoted people who are eager to give Muslims a bad name, as well as to the millions of Americans who have already been conditioned to accept negative images.

Missing so far—and badly needed, in my opinion—is a unanimous denunciation of FGM by the authorities on Islamic jurisprudence.

Another reprehensible custom that is frequently and wrongfully linked to Islam is called "honor" killing. It occurs in Jordan, Pakistan, Egypt and India, and in regions of the Arabian peninsula. Under it, a male is considered free to kill a female accused of dishonoring the family through sexual misconduct.

Although the killing is plain murder, it is defended as necessary to restore "honor" to the woman's family, and government authorities routinely ignore the crime or, at the most, mete out light punishment.[19]

"Honor" killing is wrongly identified with Islam by non-Muslims in America, partly because U.S. television coverage focuses on its practice in Muslim countries, mainly Pakistan and Jordan, while largely ignoring similar practices where Christianity predominates. In Latin America, some professed Christians commit such killings with the same impunity as professed Muslims elsewhere, but these murders receive little attention in the United States.

Dr. Riffat Hassan, a Muslim who is a professor of theology at the University of Louisville, campaigns against "honor" killings in her native Pakistan, where more than three hundred women were victims in 1997. The BBC recently chronicled the death of a sixteen-year-old Pakistani woman who suffered fatal burns when her husband's family accused her of infidelity, doused her with kerosene, and set her aflame. Mufti Ziauddin, a Pakistani lawyer specializing in human rights cases, chronicled the "Status of Court Cases for Murdered Women," a compilation of "honor killings" in his home region in Pakistan. The killers are routinely acquitted. Speaking recently before a United Nations commission, he said, "Suppose I kill my wife. I walk like a king to the jail. People come and hold a march for me. And I go free."

In the *Los Angeles Times,* Margaret Ramirez writes, "Some Muslim fundamentalists see 'honor' killings as just punishment recognized by Islam. Others avoid discussion of the subject, fearing that publicity about it will only lead to discrimination against Muslims in Western nations." Hassan's conclusion: "We need a radical revision of how the Quran is interpreted. If we were to construct a society on the true basis of Islam, we would find men and women are equal in the sight of God. These killings are not happening because they're following Islam. People are distorting Islam."

Hassan puts part of the blame on "erroneous theological concepts common in traditional Muslim societies" and warns that discrimination under the guise of Islam will continue until these concepts are rejected. Ramirez explains the professor's position: "Some Muslim theologians and Pakistani judges have employed one verse of the Quran to establish men as the custodians of women. On the basis of custodianship, a man who kills another for defiling the honor of his wife or daughter is deemed to be protecting his property and acting in self-defense. Hassan, who has analyzed the Quran for thirty years, provides a contrary interpretation. She denies that the Quranic verse gives men authority over women; instead, it ensures that, while women are bearing children, they cannot be required to be breadwinners as well." Gossip, denounced in the Quran, is the usual basis for "honor" killings. Zainab Elberry adds this somber note: "The Quran specifically forbids gossip and equates it to 'eating the flesh of your dead brother'" (Quran 5:32 and 49:12).

Hassan reports varied reactions among U.S. Muslims. "A lot of young people are really horrified and embarrassed.... They have a gut feeling that ["honor" killing] is not Islam. Yet they don't have guidance on why." In traveling across America, she senses substantial opposition to her eradication campaign. After she requested financial assistance during an address to a convention of the Association of Pakistani Physicians in America, she reports being shunned by the audience. One Pakistani woman told her the "fuss about honor killings" was unnecessary.

"I was extremely discouraged," she recalls. "They were in a state of denial. But I can't give up on this. In a way, God has brought me to this. It's the journey of my life."[20] She senses the need for a broad, worldwide educational program and is encouraged by a United Nations initiative. In June 2000, a UN Special Session on Women's Rights called for strong measures against "honor" killings.[21]

Zainab Elberry sees the combination of female mutilation and "honor killings" as a vicious cycle. "For social and economic reasons, most of the victims have no way to escape. These customs overshadow religious teachings. Even educated women are afraid to speak for fear that they will be ostracized and treated as outcasts.

But women must take the lead in ending these terrible customs and breaking this vicious cycle. As Muslims, we have to do better for the benefit of future generations. Muslim women have to take a more aggressive role. Many of them raise their children with two standards, one for boys and another for girls. They must teach the same morality to both sexes."[22]

In an informal survey of the literature of the U.S. Muslim organizations, I found to my astonishment, only two references to FGM or"honor" killings. Moreover, I have detected a general reluctance on the part of leading Muslims to say anything about the practice.

This suggests that, in general, U.S. Muslims do not fully grasp the misfortune to Muslims posed by the false images that link Islam with FGM and "honor" killings, not to mention the agony inflicted on the females. It must be noted that similar measures are rarely taken to discourage sexual misbehavior by males.

FGM and"honor" killings are the ultimate expression of male chauvinism, ugly relics of tribal practices that for centuries have kept males dominant.

Notes:

1. *Readers Digest,* 5-00, p. 222.
2. Population Council, February 1999.
3. Agence France Press, 2-13-1998.
4. Interview, 6-26-1999.
5. *New York Times,* 10-12-1996.
6. *Africa News Online,* 11-1997.
7. Interview with Ford Foundation representatives in Egypt.
8. Fauziya Kassindja, *Do They Hear You When You Cry?* (Delacore Press, 1998).
9. Interview, 11-8-1999.
10. Letter, 3-1-2000.
11. Jamal Zarabozo, "Female Circumcision," *Al-Jumah* 8, no. 12.
12. *Female Genital Mutilation: An Islamic Perspective, Pamphlet No. 1,* (Bethesda: Minaret of Freedom Institute).
13. E-mail, Sayyid M. Syeed, ISNA secretary-general, 5-19-2000.

14. Pakistan Link, p. 1, 9-1-2000.

15. Associated Press, 7-14-1999.

16. Agence France Press, 6-4-1998.

17. InterPress Service, 3-27-1998.

18. CNN, 1-15-1999.

19. Personal interview with citizens.

20. Ellen Goodman, *Boston Globe,* 3-12-2000 and *Los Angeles Times,* 3-11-2000, p. B-2.

21. *Washington Times, 6-12-2000*

22. Interview, 7-8-1999 and letter, 8-23-1999.

Chapter 8: "Bridging the Gap"

A breakdown in interfaith communication jolted me from complacency and led me to focus more than ever before on America's distorted vision of Islam. The breakdown was especially unsettling, because it occurred near our hometown.

Muslim students at Sangamon State University in Springfield, Illinois, an institution which is now the University of Illinois at Springfield, scheduled a campus lecture on Islam for the evening of February 16, 1990. They hoped to improve understanding of their religion among members of the Christian and Jewish communities in the area.

To promote attendance, they bought advertising in local newspapers and on local television and radio stations. They mailed notices of the event to more than three hundred Christian churches and the two local synagogues. Expecting a large crowd, they rented a hall seating five hundred people and prepared ample refreshments. One of the student sponsors, aware of our interest in Islam, telephoned and urged Lucille and me to attend.

The publicity brought only seventy-five people to the hall, and all but five were Muslims. The non-Muslims were four Christians and one Jew. The scant turnout reflected several factors. For one, the negative image of Muslims is as deeply rooted in Illinois' capital city as in most other U.S. cities. Then too, pastors and rabbis are usually committed to a heavy schedule within their own communities and are reluctant to include outside events. But the main reason for the poor turnout was the failure of the sponsors to back up the advertising with personal telephone calls to people they wanted to attend. Additionally, they scheduled the event on a cold February evening. We probably would not have driven thirty-five miles to attend if a student we knew had not telephoned a warm invitation the night before.

T he sponsors were disappointed at the small crowd, but the evening proved to be a major milestone in my life, an important episode in a series of events that would lead me, step by step, into a challenging new career.

The lecturer, David Zwink, a member of the staff of the Islamic Society of North America in Plainfield, Indiana, and the son of a Methodist minister, presented an outline of Islam, listing the principles and practices that Islam has in common with Christianity and Judaism. He also discussed the misconceptions of Islam that are widely held in America. I left the hall convinced that the stereotypes he had identified must be corrected, not only for the well-being of American Muslims but for all Americans. For the first time, I recognized that these misconceptions are a source of discomfort and uneasiness for U.S. Muslims, but, more important, they form a major barrier to the formulation of wise U.S. policy in the Middle East. These misleading images blind the American people to important realities of that region and lure the U.S. government into biased policies.

I did not realize it at the time, but I was hooked. There would be no turning back. From that day forward, I would give priority to correcting the false images. A week after the lecture, in an article published in the *Jacksonville Journal-Courier*,[1] our hometown daily newspaper, I summarized Zwink's lecture and lamented the poor turnout. I concluded with an appeal:

"Every religious movement has radical elements—but the Muslims with whom I have dealt are kind, respectful, hospitable and considerate of others. I have chanced upon Muslims at prayer in offices, on farms and, of course, in mosques. Islam calls them to prayer five times daily. Not all Muslims live up to Islam's standards, of course, nor do Christians and Jews always behave as they should.

"My plea is not for Islam but for understanding. Christians and Jews should get acquainted with Islam and see Muslims as human beings, not in ugly, false stereotypes. For our own sake, as we strive to live happily on this ever-shrinking globe, we should demolish the false images that flaw our vision and sometimes misdirect our government's policies." I could have easily included a quotation from poet Robert Burns, who wrote, "Like it or not, we are all on this planet and there's no place else to go."

My article, reprinted in a Presbyterian Church newsletter, came to the attention of Dr. Malcolm Stewart, a retired college professor who had been my instructor in logic and religion in 1941-42. He was sincere, thoughtful, and meticulous. Years later, we established a friendship when I became a member of the college's board of trustees. After reading my article at his winter home in Arizona, he sent me a supportive letter which included an observation so profound that it has remained close in my thoughts ever since:

"There will not be peace in our world until there is peace among the religions. And there will not be peace among the religions until the adherents come to understand one another. The beginning point is to emphasize the similarities, the likenesses, the agreements — not the differences. The expressed purpose of each religion is peace, unity, harmony. It is interesting to speculate what might be accomplished if the religions could cooperate to achieve these expressed goals." He cited several journals on world religion that he had found helpful in reaching these conclusions.

In December 1990, I spoke during the World Day banquet sponsored in New York City by the Muslim Foundation of America. There I quoted Stewart's words, and in a late night discussion with five of the foundation's officers, I urged Muslims to become politically active. The evening also brought sobering evidence of Muslim security concerns. Our hosts kept guards outside the banquet room during the program and outside our sleeping quarters throughout the night.

Back in Illinois, I was surprised and delighted to receive in the next postal delivery a small book, entitled *Neighbors: Muslims in North America,* the first brief, easy-to-read document in my experience that puts a friendly, human face on Muslims. Written by Rev. Elias Mallon, a Roman Catholic priest, and published by

Friendship Press, the book presents fascinating interviews with nine Muslims in various occupations and from different regions of North America. In his introduction, Mallon offers this observation: "We begin truly to understand a religion when we have a friend who is a follower of that religion."

Years later, Luther Warren, one of my African-American neighbors, expressed a parallel sentiment when he said: "It's hard to hate someone you know." A Jewish actress from Israel brought a welcome note of interfaith conciliation when she moved to the United States in 1993. Mili Avital rose to stardom in Israel and now is acclaimed as the fabled Scheherazade in the ABC production of "Arabian Nights." Asked how she feels, given the Arab-Jewish conflict in Israel, as a Jew playing the role of an Arab, she responds: "I'm part of the new generation that doesn't believe in that stuff. The more cultures there are in the world, the better. And if I get to represent my [Palestinian] neighbors, great. They have a beautiful culture."[2]

In lectures and conversations that followed the New York City experience, I repeated Malcolm Stewart's theme and cited *Neighbors* as must reading. One opportunity came in April 1991 in Tampa, Florida, when I spoke at a dinner meeting of the local Islamic Society. Earlier in the day I visited an elementary school built for Muslim children and toured once-blighted neighborhoods that had been cleaned up and made attractive by civic-minded Muslim volunteers. My host explained: "Our cleanup program is not intended to help Muslims. In fact, I do not believe that any Muslim owns any property here or benefits financially in any direct way. We simply want to be good neighbors and show that Muslims are glad to help make Tampa a better place to live."

The next February, I urged Muslims in New Jersey to engage in partisan politics, first in a lecture at a public middle school in Teaneck, then before a gathering in a nearby mosque. Before leaving the mosque, I learned for the first time that I had represented at least one Muslim during my congressional years. Mohammed Shakir was among those who greeted me after my remarks. As a college student working part-time as a hotel desk clerk, he had occasionally checked me in as a guest in a hotel in Alton, Illinois, a part of my district.

In September 1993, Rafeeq Jabr, a tireless champion of Palestinian rights who frequently opened Muslim doors for me in the years that followed, arranged a meeting in Chicago where I again summoned Muslims to political action.

The next stop was San Jose, California, where the Council on American-Islamic Relations [CAIR] organized a day-long "Call to Muslim Activism." I had long admired the organization's success in championing the civil rights of U.S. Muslims, especially in the work place, but this conference was the first time, to my knowledge, that an Islamic group had urged Muslims to become active in politics.

An audience of one hundred-fifty people, mainly Muslims, participated in a long afternoon of vigorous discussion. It included a surprise, at least for me. One speaker, an African-American imam, sharply criticized the activities of both the Republican and the Democratic parties and announced that he considered the U.S. political system so corrupt that Muslims should avoid any involvement. "I tell my people to stay away from politics and politicians." Other speakers, myself included, urged Muslims to take the opposite course, active leadership in elections and participation in campaigns for party slates or individual candidates.

These experiences led me to write an article on the political potential of U.S. Muslims. It appeared in the October 1992 issue of the *Washington Report on Middle East Affairs*.[3] a bimonthly magazine that is widely read by people interested in the Arab-Israeli dispute. In it, I listed popular misconceptions about Islam and noted the rapid growth of the Muslim population in America. Calling on Muslims to awaken to the full opportunities and responsibilities of American citizenship, I predicted that they could help correct these false images about Islam and, at the same time, exert a powerful, constructive influence on U.S. policy at home and abroad. I noted that most Muslims live in industrialized states where their influence could be especially crucial in presidential elections. I also urged vigilant monitoring of news media. Muslims, I wrote, should demand correction of any media expressions of anti-Muslim bias as an essential step in dismissing false stereotypes. All that is needed, I said, is for Muslims to do their duty as U.S citizens.

My article found its way to a Muslim leader abroad, prompting an invitation to take part in a workshop on Muslim stereotypes. Scheduled for September 1996, it would be held in Malaysia under the sponsorship of the International Movement for a Just World. I accepted, welcoming the opportunity to learn more about Islam and test my ideas on steps that should be undertaken in America to correct misconceptions of Muslims.

The conference brought together forty-four delegates from twenty-three countries. I was one of six from the United States. Each presented a prepared statement, and all participated vigorously in the discussions that followed. When my turn to speak came, I presented a grim image of Islam that most Americans accept as truthful: "Most Americans view Muslims with concern, if not fear. They see Muslims as a source of senseless violence and religious strife—a threat to Christianity, to our system of government, and to our basic liberties. They believe that Muslim men abuse women and treat them as property. They see Islam as intolerant of other religions. The time has come for U.S. Muslims to shed their shyness and engage in an aggressive program to erase these false images. They must take the lead in spreading the truth about Islam."

At the final session, the organization's director, Dr. Chandra Muzaffar, a Muslim reared in India as a Hindu, asked each participant to state specific follow-up actions that he or she would undertake on returning home. I pledged to write a short statement about Islam that U.S. Muslims could comfortably hand to non-Muslim neighbors. In explaining my decision, I reported that U.S. Muslims, for whatever reason, seem reluctant even to mention their faith to their neighbors, much less try to explain it. I added that Christians who are unaware of the faith of their neighbors cannot be expected to take the initiative to seek understanding. I promised to emphasize in my statement the goals that Muslims share with Christians and Jews, along with facts that would help correct the false stereotypes.

O ver the next six months, back home in Illinois, I used the telephone and postal service to consult with Muslim leaders, as well as a number of Christian scholars, and drafted a concise statement on Islam that I believed any reader could easily grasp.

More than thirty people cooperated, among them Thomas J. Abercrombie, a retired senior editor for *National Geographic* magazine whom I first met in 1983 while writing *They Dare to Speak Out*. A convert to Islam at the age of thirty, he provided detailed recommendations. Others came from Inayat Lalani, a physician in Fort Worth, Texas; two Muslim leaders in Nashville, Dr. Nour Naciri and his wife, Zainab Elberry; Dr. Chandra Muzaffar, president of the Malaysia-based International Movement for a Just World; and Al-Haaj Ghazi Y. Khankan, director at the Islamic Center of Long Island.

When the final text, captioned "A Friendly Note From Your Muslim Neighbor," emerged from more than twenty drafts, I felt I had reached an important milestone in answering the ultimate question: What is Islam?[4] [see Appendix A]

The document has good potential, I believe, because it provides an easy means of person-to-person presentation, the ideal level of communication. I have distributed copies while lecturing to Muslim gatherings in Chicago, St. Louis, Detroit, Los Angeles, Ann Arbor, Philadelphia, Pittsburgh, Toronto, Dallas, San Francisco, and Athens, Georgia, and have provided other copies by mail.

B ut I have to be realistic. While there is no substitute for the human touch, the "Friendly Note..." has limitations. Most Americans do not have a Muslim neighbor next door, nor down the street or around the corner.

It became apparent that a concise book that focuses on the threads common to both Christianity and Islam would help. Books have a definite immortality. They live on from one household to another, from one generation to the next. That was on my mind when I made plans for this book.

Books, too, have limitations. Relatively few Americans take the time for extensive reading, so the impact of books on public opinion—and public policy—is seldom immediate. As I pondered what measures should be considered, I turned to television, the medium that I consider to be the best way to influence millions of people in a short period of time. Television advertising is effective in marketing a variety of commodities, causes, and ideas, and I concluded that it has the potential of quickly defusing, softening and dismissing stereotypes about Islam.

Our son, Craig, who owns Findley Associates, a public relations firm, agreed to organize an experiment. In 1997, he secured funding that led to the production of a thirty-second television message about U.S. Muslims. The process that he arranged brought me into renewed acquaintance with three impressive men I had met years before, the Zogby brothers, James and John, and William Baker. They are engaged in different vocations, but they are united in their lifelong commitment to human rights. Each is a Christian but well known and respected by Muslims. I became acquainted with all three during the writing and marketing of my book, *They Dare to Speak Out.*

Dr. James Zogby is the founder and director of the Arab-American Institute and former executive director of the American Arab Anti-Discrimination Committee, the organization that sponsored my nationwide book tour in 1985. He is a frequent guest on television when Middle East issues are discussed and is known as an aggressive insider in Democratic Party politics.

John, founder and owner of the Zogby International polling firm, lived in his brother's shadow for several years but is now prominent in his own right. He is frequently quoted by political commentators and interviewed on television in connection with his public opinion surveys. I first met John Zogby in 1985 when he was employed by the American Arab Anti-Discrimination Committee. We shared podiums, often in mosques, on a tour that promoted his employer as well as my book. We heard each other speak so often that I jokingly assured him that I could prompt him if he lost his train of thought while addressing an audience, and I knew that he could provide the same service to me when it was my turn to speak.

After a decade of infrequent communication with John Zogby and Baker, they both came back into my life during Craig's experiment in televised promotion of Islam. Before designing a television message, Craig sought data on public attitudes toward Islam. At my suggestion, he hired Zogby to find the answers.

In order to measure the level of misconceptions about Islam among non-Muslims, the Zogby team telephoned more than four hundred people in each of four markets: Tacoma, Washington; Wilkes-Barre, Pennsylvania; Charleston, West Virginia; and Wichita, Kansas. Each person was asked two sets of questions.

In the first set, the pollsters sought reactions to the mention of nine different religions, without first providing background about any of them.

The results confirmed the prevalence of negative stereotypes. Among the people surveyed, the mention of Islam or Muslim, Buddhism, and Hinduism, elicited more unfavorable reactions than favorable.

	Favorable	**Unfavorable**
	Percent	Percent
Presbyterian	84	9
Judaism or Jewish	74	14
Roman Catholic	72	16
Lutheran	70	10
Fundamentalist Christian	51	20
Mormon	45	35
Islam or Muslim	37	40
Buddhism	37	40
Hinduism	34	39

Next, the Zogy team asked for reactions to statements that mention Islam or Muslim. Only 33 percent of the respondents made a favorable response to the word Islam, but one-half said that they have sensed a "tendency to discriminate" against Muslims. Twenty percent felt that "the Muslim population in the United States is growing too rapidly"; 33 percent favored restrictions on the number of Muslims permitted to immigrate to the United States; 40 percent said that school cafeterias should not recognize Muslim dietary needs; 33 percent opposed permitting Muslims time off to pray each Friday; 46 percent opposed giving Muslims days off with pay on Muslim holidays; 46 percent said that Muslims tend to be religious fanatics; 33 percent believed that Muslims are intolerant of other religions; 50 percent believed that Muslims lead clean, respectable lives, but 16 percent disagreed.

In a surprising departure from the trend of earlier responses, 75 percent said Muslim women should be permitted to wear head-scarves at work.

The final set of questions asked for reactions to a series of factual statements about Islam. The results were remarkable.

Statement	Percent Expressing Positive Reaction
Muslims are pledged to peace with justice, family responsibility, and tolerance	54
Muslims respect the traditions of Abraham, Moses, and Jesus and have identical ethical values with Jews and Christians	51
Muslim women have a right to own property, engage in business, professions and public life, and have the right to divorce	46
Muslims abhor terrorism and oppression	43
Muslims believe in the same God as Christians and Jews	83

The survey[5] disclosed a slight improvement in religious tolerance when compared with a similar one conducted by Zogby International for the American Muslim Council in 1993.[6]

T he survey results were so promising that Craig hired a professional firm to proceed with the preparation of a thirty-second television message. In a series of words and images, it makes the point that U.S. Muslims have much in common with their non-Muslim neighbors. Its text: "American Muslims. This we believe... that all people are free to pray for peace... to worship God in their own way... to raise their families... to honor Jesus... to hope for a future that respects all people... celebrates their differences... and endures forever. American Muslims. More in common than you may think."

The message was broadcast during the summer of 1998 in a limited test campaign in the Washington, D.C., area during days that Congress was in session. In pretest telephone interviews, the Zogby firm asked three hundred and eight people a set of twenty-six questions. The target audience consisted of adults between the ages of twenty-five and fifty-four who tend to be opinion-makers, a group expected to be above average in their knowledge of Islam. The broadcasts were scheduled during news programming, such as "Meet the Press" and "Face the Nation," and scattered over an eight-week period in early summer. In late July, three hundred and eight people who had seen the television advertisement were asked the same questions.

Statement	Percentage Who Agree Before Campaign/After Campaign
The vast majority of Muslims hate terrorism	51 / 61
Muslims do not tend to be religious fanatics	45 / 55
Muslims are tolerant of others	37 / 42
Muslims tend to lead clean and respectable lives	62 / 69
Muslim women should be allowed to wear traditional head covering to work if they desire	76 / 79
Muslims respect the teachings of Jesus	34 / 34
Muslims should be allowed to take time off for Friday prayers	53 / 62
Muslims should be allowed days off with pay for major Muslim holidays	45 / 52
My overall impression of Muslims is favorable	49 / 55
Overall impression of Muslims by frequent CNN viewers	42 / 65

The survey disclosed positive movement in viewpoints, the size depending on the age, education, gender, and television viewing habits of those interviewed.

Young people were more tolerant of Muslims than those who were over sixty-five years of age. Females were more tolerant than males. Negative feelings toward Muslims tended to drop among people who had attained higher levels of education.

The most dramatic improvement occurred among people who are frequent viewers of CNN. Before the television campaign, 42 percent reported an overall favorable impression of Muslims. After the campaign, the percentage jumped to 65, an increase of 23 percent. Among all of those polled, the overall favorable impression increased from 48 percent to 55, an improvement of 7 percent.

The analysis showed that in six weeks the campaign had created an improved understanding of Islam over a broad range of topics. John Zogby described the improvement as "truly exceptional." He added, "This may seem like a minor improvement, but, given the brevity of the campaign, it is excellent. Positive results may be expected from a more extensive campaign."[7]

The survey results suggest that many Americans are open-minded about Muslims and Islam and will respond favorably when supplied with even a few nuggets of truth. If funds become available, the broadcast of this thirty-second commercial and similar television messages could quickly lead millions of non-Muslims to dismiss false images of Islam.

On the day that Zogby's analysis of the television experiment reached my desk, a remarkable coincidence occurred. The postal service delivered a copy of a new book by William Baker, *More in Common Than You Think: The Bridge Between Islam and Christianity*. Its title alone demonstrated that it developed in book form the same theme that Craig's television message presented. Baker is a former archeologist in the Middle East and professor of ancient history. He is an ordained minister with a wide personal acquaintance among Islamic leaders worldwide.

In this concise, readable, instructive, and compelling new volume, Baker presents the common principles and beliefs that should summon Christians and Muslims to work together. He supports his theme with direct quotations—always complementary and often parallel—from the Quran and the Bible. Reading it will be an edifying experience for anyone willing to cross the bridge that links Islam and Christianity.

He appeals for fairness: "If Muslims and the religion of Islam are to be judged by the actions and policies of a miniscule few who preach violence, hatred, and death, then Christians and Christianity, Jews and Judaism, Buddhists and Buddhism, all must likewise be judged on those exact same standards."[8]

He adds: "The [Islamic] concept of sin is at once similar yet distinct from the biblical account in that man is a free moral agent capable of choosing to do right or wrong, obedience or disobedience to God's commandments, yet born into this life without original sin. Islam teaches that man can no more be born with original sin than he can be born an original saint. The Quran sets forth the proposition that all are born innocent, pure, true, free, and disposed towards worshiping God and doing good."[9]

His book will have great interest within the Christian community—a broad and diverse group—partly because of the favorable review provided by the Rev. Robert H. Schuller, one of America's best-known Christian clergymen. He is the founder of the Crystal Cathedral in Los Angeles and pastor of the Hour of Power program that is televised worldwide each week. Baker serves as his adviser on Islamic affairs.

Schuller recognizes the importance of Christian-Muslim understanding: "I am convinced this book by Dr. Baker will prove to be a significant contribution to bringing Christians and Muslims together to live in peace and mutual respect."[10] Schuller has told associates that he has decided to focus his ministry on bringing about Christianity-Muslim understanding.[11]

Muslims will be impressed by the assessment of Dr. Muzammil H. Siddiqi, president of the Islamic Society of North America and one of the most respected Muslim leaders. In applauding Baker's book, Siddiqi writes, "We Muslims and Christians together make up more than half of the world population today. Better understanding, communication, and peaceful relations between our communities are not only good, but they are essential. We have much more in common than we think or accept."[12]

More in Common Than You Think provides chapter-and-verse evidence of the common roots and branches shared by Islam, Christianity, and Judaism. In Chapter 4, Baker writes, "Few Christians are aware that the Prophet Muhammad, the messenger of Islam, believed Jesus and Moses were the most important bearers of God's revelation to mankind, the message that is enshrined in the Torah and the New Testament. Islam embraces both books.... Both the Torah and the New Testament are viewed by Islam as inspired revelation of God to mankind.... Muslims are asked to follow the good examples of the earlier Prophets of the Bible.... As Christians believe the New Testament was the completion of the Old Testament of Judaism, so Muslims believe that Islam and the Quran serve as the final completion of both books, and Muhammad as the last Prophet or Messenger of God."[13]

Baker acknowledges that "many battles were fought down through the centuries between Muslims and Christians" and "numerous wrongs and acts of barbarity were committed in the name of God and church as men, both Muslim and Christian, often failed to practice the very heart and soul of their own religion."[14]

During the rapid expansion of Islam, he writes, conquered people were guaranteed tolerance—religious and otherwise—by Islamic law: "Perhaps the best illustration of tolerance and peaceful co-existence envisaged by Muhammad is the Charter of Medina... a covenant between the Jews, Muslims and other inhabitants of the city which guaranteed religious liberty and determined the rights and duties of members of all religions." At the time, only a few Christians lived in the region.[15]

In a 1987 interview with Baker, Sheikh Ahmad Kuftaro, the Grand Mufti of Syria, said, "My dear brother, you cannot be a true Muslim unless you love, respect and honor Jesus." Kuftaro added that both Islam and Christianity teach that God is in control of all things, including the destiny of humankind, collectively and individually, and concluded that "the sovereignty of God in both the Quran and the Bible is remarkably similar."[16]

In quest of interfaith understanding and peace, Baker and John Wallach, an author and former Washington bureau chief for Hearts publications, lead separate projects that focus on intercultural and interfaith harmony among young people.

Baker is founder-president of Christians and Muslims for Peace [CAMP], an organization with chapters in several countries. Each chapter sponsors a summer camp that brings Christian and Muslim young people together for interfaith fellowship.

Wallach, the son of Holocaust survivors, left a successful career in journalism to found and manage summer camps in Maine where Jewish youths from Israel and young people, mostly Muslim, from Arab countries learn about each other's culture and religion. The project is called Seeds of Peace International. Three camps, each three weeks in length, are held each summer. Wallach opens each camp with this challenge: "This is the only place in the world where Israelis and Arabs can come together on neutral ground and try to be friends. No matter what else you do in your time here, I want each of you to make one friend from the other side." Wallach explains why he left a career dealing directly with the country's political leaders to manage the camp project: "I've learned that the answer to life is not the poobahs. It's the basics."[17]

On the national scene, several Christians play important roles in bringing Islam out of the political shadows.

Professor John L. Esposito is the director of the Center for Muslim-Christian Understanding in the School of Foreign Service at Georgetown University in Washington, D.C. The Center promotes interfaith dialogue at the international level. Esposito edited the four-volume *Oxford Encyclopedia of the Modern Islamic World,* a comprehensive source of Muslim information published in 1995. He serves as a professor of religion and international affairs at Georgetown, writes extensively, and directs international seminars. He is the author of twenty books, including *Islam: The Straight Path,* a volume that has become a standard text for theology students, and *The Islamic Threat: Myth or Reality?*

Two other Christians, retired diplomats Richard T. Curtiss and Andrew I. Killgore, publish a magazine that, among other things, enlightens Americans about Muslim politics at home and abroad. If a just peace agreement is achieved, their contributions deserve a major commemoration.

Curtiss and Killgore entered magazine journalism after long careers in the U.S. Foreign Service, and by 2000 were well into their second decade as editor and publisher, respectively, of the *Washington Report on Middle East Affairs,* a bimonthly magazine. Instead of spending retirement sitting in the sun and playing golf, they work long hours every day in the magazine's offices and do so without compensation. Moreover, they dig deeply into their own pockets to keep the magazine solvent. Curtiss explains, "Publishing our magazine gives us a good reason to get up in the morning. Andy and I feel that we are helping the American people gain a correct understanding of the Arab-Israeli conflict and the political forces in that region. We believe that the *Washington Report* is worth every bit of energy and money that we invest."[18]

The *Washington Report on Middle East Affairs* is widely respected for its balanced coverage of the politics of Muslim countries and the Middle East generally. Paid subscribers total over twenty thousand, making its circulation the largest among magazines that focus on the Middle East.

Dartmouth College has taken a dietary step toward interfaith conciliation. It will soon offer halal and kosher meals to Muslim and Jewish students. Sponsors hope it will help promote harmony among "those with a history of conflict."

In late 2000, the Catholic Theological Union, the nation's largest Catholic graduate school of theology and ministry, launched the Catholic-Muslim Studies Program to commemorate the approaching millennium. Muslim speakers at the inaugural ceremony included Talat Othman, a Chicago developer who chairs the local Council of Islamic Organizations, and Dr. M. Cherif Bassiouni, who observed that "the United States is probably the best place in the world where a revival of Islam can link with Christianity and Judaism to establish the common bonds of these three monotheistic faiths."

James Denny, Catholic philanthropist in Chicago, became the chief sponsor of the program after a visit, with his wife, Catherine, to schools in Palestine. He lamented:

"I never before fully appreciated the common heritage that Islam and Judaism and Christianity share. Once you are exposed to all that history you start asking yourself, isn't that enough of a basis to form some avenue of understanding and cooperation? The public dialogue is dominated by the extremes.

"The people in the middle of both faith communities, who don't know anything about each other, are led and influenced by people on the fringe."[19]

Notes:

1. *Journal-Courier*, 2-18-1990, p. 6.
2. *USA Today*, 4-28-2000, p 12E.
3. *Washington Report on Middle East Affairs*, 10-92.
4. See Appendix A: "A Friendly Note From Your Muslim Neighbor."
5. Zogby International poll, 7-15-1977.
6. Zogby International poll, 3-29-1993.
7. "This We Believe," Findley Associates, Zogby Survey, 5-18 to 7-19, 1998; John Zogby, interview, 9-3-1998.
8. William Baker, *More in Common Than You Think*, p. 61.
9. Ibid., p. 56.
10. Ibid., backcover.
11. Ibid., backcover.
12. Ibid., backcover comments.
13. Ibid., p. 16.
14. Ibid.
15. Ibid., p. 17.

16. Ibid., p. 43.
17. *Hope,* Nov.-Dec. 1997, pp. 51–52.
18. Interviews, 8-23-1999.
19. *Logos* Fall 2000, (Catholic Theological Union).

Chapter 9: Students Lead the Way

Nineteen sixty-three was an important year for Muslims. In America's heartland, Muslim students took the first steps in confronting America's stereotypes of their religion. On the East Coast, a Dartmouth College student helped motivate Malcolm X to reject anti-white racism and black separatism, then provided support when the controversial Black leader became engulfed in the national hysteria that followed the assassination of President John F. Kennedy.

It was a year that heralded advances for the nation's fast growing Muslim population, progress that would come in small but significant steps over the next two decades, then break into great strides during the last years of the twentieth century.

Progress was long overdue.

For years, U.S. Muslims endured religious discrimination, some of it violent. Even the non-physical abuse has been painful: taunts, ridicule, anonymous phone calls, job discrimination, racial profiling, delays at airports for questioning, and even the indignity of strip searches by customs officials.

Until recently, Muslims have not responded to abuse in an organized way. In fact, they had little organization for any purpose. Even today, only a small fraction of the adults—perhaps less than 5 percent—are affiliated with an Islamic organization of any type.

For two decades, the principal Muslim organizations limited their activities and services almost entirely to their members. They did little to provide information to non-Muslims or bring Muslim grievances and aspirations to public attention. Poorly organized and reluctant to "make waves," most Muslims suffered in silence.

These self-imposed restraints are coming down. From firsthand observation, I know that all major national Muslim organizations now sponsor substantial outreach programs, and several of them exist only for that purpose. During my journey through Islam, I have addressed assemblages sponsored by most of the organizations that are listed in these chapters and have become acquainted with almost all of the individuals who are mentioned.

In this gradual but steady transition, students have led the way.

Thirty years ago, only the Muslim Student Association [MSA] provided outreach activity. It was founded early in 1963 on the Champaign campus of the University of Illinois, an organization of college students who saw the need for solidarity in their own ranks and better understanding of Islam among students and townspeople of other faiths. Chapters soon appeared at other major colleges and universities, often serving entire communities with lectures, exhibits and seminars, all of them open to the public.

Later in the same year that the MSA came into being at Champaign, Ahmed Osman, a student from Sudan, helped found an MSA chapter at Dartmouth College and a few months later unwittingly set in motion a process that ultimately brought about a vast improvement in the unity of Muslims in America, and prepared the way for major advances in interfaith understanding.

Osman happened to be at the right place at the right time with the right message. He took part in a brief, unscheduled public discussion with Malcolm X, a controversial Black who then served as the assistant to Elijah Muhammad, the founder and leader of the Nation of Islam. The remarkable sequence of events began one Sunday afternoon in Harlem, where Osman and a fellow student were sightseeing during a break from studies at Dartmouth.

At the time, I had just begun my second term in Congress, but, although I strongly supported civil rights legislation on Capitol Hill, Malcolm X was not in my range of interests. I wanted to help African-Americans gain the right to vote, buy any house they could afford, and eat in any restaurant and stay in a hotel or motel of their choice. Still influenced by the false stereotypes learned in childhood, I knew almost nothing about Islam or the Nation of Islam organization. In my thoughts, Malcolm X was nothing but a troublemaker who hated white people. My image of him came mainly from viewing the television program produced by Mike Wallace and broadcast on CBS entitled, "The Hate That Hate Produced." It focused on the harsh, un-Islamic views that Malcolm X was expressing at that time.

Osman's sudden personal association with Malcolm X proved to be the beginning of a friendship with historic consequences. Their meeting and subsequent correspondence were a principal factor in the fiery leader's decision to renounce the racist policies of the Nation of Islam and leave the organization.

I heard the details of this important chapter in Malcolm X's life in conversations with Osman thirty-eight years later. I also learned that, despite the large amount of biographical material already published about Malcolm X, these facts had not previously been made public. Osman readily talked privately about his experiences but was reluctant to provide them for publication. In a lengthy discussion one afternoon in Chicago on Labor Day 2000, he explained: "Muslims are taught modesty. We shouldn't blow our own horns, so to speak, and I don't want anyone to think I am bragging about what happened. I am not a hero. I just happened to have some unusual experiences with one of the great figures in the advancement of human rights in America." He relented when I argued that his experiences should be published for the benefit of people who want a correct understanding of the factors that led this man to make historic contributions to the growth and unity of U.S. Muslims.

Osman's encounter with Malcolm X was pure happenstance. He and his friend were strolling down a Harlem avenue when they noticed an announcement on a building named Muhammad's Temple Number Seven. A poster invited the public to hear

Malcolm X speak there that afternoon, and Osman and his com-
panion decided to attend. Osman recalls the afternoon's events,

"We were welcomed at the door by neatly-dressed guards who
politely checked our pockets for weapons, then ushered us into a
large meeting room where nearly five hundred people were already
gathered. Malcolm X spoke for nearly three hours to an enthralled
audience.

"When he finished his speech, I had the good fortune to be
recognized to ask a question. After introducing myself as a student
from Sudan, I complimented him on his eloquence and on the
positive things he said about Africa. Then I said some of his
comments troubled me. I said, 'Islam, as I understand it, makes no
distinction on race, nationality, or color. But in your speech you
condemned white people.'

"At that point, the crowd got restless, and I heard calls
demanding that I sit down. Malcolm X quieted them by saying, 'Let
him speak his mind. Let's hear what he has to say.' Then I said, 'It
seems to me your criticism of white people violates the teachings
of Islam.' Malcolm X, to loud applause, responded firmly in these
words, 'As a young student from Sudan, you don't understand the
problems that Blacks face in America.'

"After the lecture, to my surprise, Malcolm X invited me and
my friend to have supper with him at a restaurant next door.
We couldn't stay, but, before we parted, he and I exchanged
addresses. A few days later, I mailed him several books on Islam.
He responded in a letter, thanking me for the books and stating that
he wanted to buy extra copies for people at the temple. In the
months ahead, he wrote several other letters to me, all of them
thoughtful. I, of course, responded to each of them."

Osman recalls that in the midst of the correspondence, President
John F. Kennedy was assassinated. During the mourning that
followed, Malcolm X made a remark that made him the center of a
national controversy that raged until his own assassination fifteen
months later.

A brief exchange with a newspaper reporter provoked the controversy. Malcolm X had just addressed a rally in New York City, during which he made several references to the career of the slain president, but, in keeping to the instructions of his leader, Elijah Muhammad, he did not comment on the assassination. After the rally, the reporter asked him to comment on Kennedy's death. Malcolm X responded brusquely, "The chickens have come to roost." He did not explain why he used that phrase, and the reporter assumed that Malcolm X wanted it known that Kennedy deserved to die, and he reported the comment in that light. His "chickens" remark was printed and broadcast nationwide and interpreted as a slap at the universally mourned president.

Later, Malcolm X insisted to friends that he meant something quite different. He intended to convey the idea that the climate of hate and violence caused by racist extremism in American society had created an atmosphere that provoked terrible violence.

Osman declares, "Malcolm X did not mean to applaud Kennedy's death. Far from it. He meant only that you harvest what you sow, that Kennedy was the victim of the racist extremism that pervaded the nation." He believes the off-the-cuff statement triggered a chain of events that actually led to the assassination of Malcolm X himself. The public rage, Osman reasons, helped some of Malcolm X's critics drive a wedge between him and Elijah Muhammad: "They lost no time in exploiting the rage to their own ends, hammering on the wedge they had already put in place between the mentor and his disciple."

Because of the public uproar, Elijah Muhammad ordered Malcolm X into silent isolation for ninety days. He was instructed not to speak in public, talk to any member of the Nation of Islam, participate in Nation of Islam activities, or even visit Nation of Islam facilities.

Osman recalls that Malcolm X submitted dutifully to the instructions, but during that time of isolation and silence, he took another big step on his journey to orthodox Islam. Barred from Nation of Islam Temples, he began attending Friday prayers at the Islamic Foundation of New York, where Osman sometimes prayed.

The Center was directed by Dr. Mahmoud Al Shawarbi, an Egyptian professor on leave from the University of Cairo.

Osman noticed a change of tone in the letters he was receiving from the banished leader:

"He began to question some of the Nation of Islam principles, and I soon realized that he was, by then, fully committed in his private thoughts to orthodox Islam. This realization prompted me to join Al Shawarbi in meeting with Malcolm X to urge him to undertake the Hajj, the pilgrimage to Mecca. When, at the meeting, Malcolm X said he had no funds for the trip, I suggested that he borrow what he needed from his sister, Ella, who lived in Boston. She resided on Massachusetts Avenue near Symphony Hall, had a prosperous real estate business, and owned several houses. She had been 'in and out' of the Nation of Islam in earlier years, but had finally reverted to orthodox Islam.

"Malcolm X made the request for funds, and Ella readily agreed. Before leaving, he cut all ties with the Nation of Islam, and in the presence of Al Shawarbi renounced all teachings of the organization that were contrary to mainline Islam. This qualified him for a visa that enabled him to enter Mecca for the Hajj."

Malcolm X traveled alone to Cairo where he joined a party of pilgrims on a flight to Jeddah, the next stop in the journey to Mecca. During the flight he described the diversity of the group on his notepad: "Packed in the plane were white, black, red, and yellow people, blue eyes and blond hair, and my kinky red hair. All together, brothers! All honoring the same God, all in turn giving equal honor to each other." Osman observes: "What he was seeing and feeling contradicted his previous teachings and experiences."

At the Jeddah airport, he was required to stay at the Pilgrims Compound until his conversion to Islam was authenticated. After waiting two days, he made a call to Dr. Omar Azzam, as suggested by a friend in New York just before his departure. Before making the call, he was unaware that Azzam was the brother-in-law of Prince Mohammed Al Faisal, the son of the late King Faisal. Malcolm X almost immediately became a state guest and placed in a residence suite at the Kandra Palace Hotel before going to Mecca.

The stand on Mount Arafat, Osman relates, is the climax of the Hajj: "It is soul-searching. Every pilgrim stands there in full humility, stripped of his worldly titles and possessions, equalized in humanity with his fellow pilgrims. Simply put, the Hajj is a rebirth of an individual. When asked by his companions what impressed him most about the Hajj, Malcolm X responded, 'The brotherhood! The people of all races, colors, from all over the world coming together as one. It has proved to me the power of the One God.'"

From Mecca, he wrote to his family and friends, among them W. Deen Mohammed, the son of Elijah Muhammad:

"Never have I witnessed such sincere hospitality and the overwhelming spirit of true brotherhood as is practiced by the people of all colors and races.... For the past week, I have been utterly speechless and spellbound by the graciousness I see displayed all around me by the people of all colors.... There were tens of thousands of pilgrims from all over the world.... But we were all participating in the same ritual, displaying a spirit of unity and brotherhood that my experiences in America had led me to believe never could exist between the white and the non-white.

"America needs to understand Islam, because this is the one religion that erases from its society the race problem.... I have never before seen sincere and true brotherhood practiced by all colors together, irrespective of their color. You may be shocked by these words coming from me, but on this pilgrimage, what I have seen and experienced has forced me to rearrange much of my thought patterns previously held and to toss aside some of my previous convictions.

"In the words and in the actions and in the deeds of the 'white' Muslims I felt the same sincerity I felt among the black African Muslims of Nigeria, Sudan, and Ghana.... I could see from this, that perhaps if white Americans could accept the Oneness of God, then perhaps, too, they could accept in reality the Oneness of Man—and cease to measure, and hinder, and harm others in terms of their 'differences' in color."[1]

Osman laments the fact that the major media never recognized Malcolm X's change of religious and racial outlook, his complete break with the Nation of Islam, and his unqualified acceptance of mainline Islamic doctrine.

After his death, *The Saturday Evening Post* published this comment: "If Malcolm X were not a Negro, his autobiography would be little more than a journal of abnormal psychology, the story of a burglar, dope pusher, addict, and jailbird, with a family history of insanity, who acquires messianic delusions and sets forth to preach an upside-down religion of 'brotherly' hatred."[2]

"On every occasion," Osman noted, "Malcolm X stated that in the past he had made sweeping indictments of all white people. He said he would never be guilty of that again, as he knew that some white people are truly sincere, some truly are capable of being brotherly toward a black man. But the media took no note of these comments and did not change its stance towards him, dead or alive."

In contrast, Malcolm X had a good rapport with white college students. He was heavily in demand as a speaker on campuses and invariably received standing ovations. He wrote, "I do believe... the whites of the younger generation, in the colleges and universities, will see the handwriting on the wall and many of them will turn to the spiritual path of truth—the only way left to America to ward off the disaster that racism inevitably must lead to." [3]

Osman recalls Malcolm X's experience at Dartmouth: "It was the most memorable visit of any guest speaker at the time. Without involving the school administration, the students invited him and asked me to facilitate his acceptance. A delegation of students welcomed his arrival at the airport and enjoyed the warm person-to-person discussions with him over dinner and following his speech at the fully packed Spaulding auditorium. The following day, the students joined him for breakfast."

On February 21, 1965, almost fifteen months to the day after Kennedy's assassination, Malcolm X was shot to death while he was preparing to address a rally at Audubon Ballroom in Harlem. The African-American press was united in mourning his passing, but the "white" media reported his life in harsh, negative terms. Overseas, the slain leader's life had sympathetic coverage, especially in Africa and Asia. This prompted a curious reaction from Carl Rowan, the African-American who directed the U.S. Information Agency at the time. He showed examples of laudatory foreign coverage to U.S. reporters and said, "All this about an ex-convict, ex-dope peddler who became a racial fanatic."

The moment Osman learned of the assassination, he took a Greyhound bus from Dartmouth College to New York to offer his condolences and assistance to the bereaved, as well as destitute, Malcolm X family. Living with neighbors because their home had been firebombed a week earlier, the family asked him to help arrange an orthodox Muslim funeral and bury Malcolm X, as he wished, under his chosen Muslim name, El-Hajj Malik El-Shabazz.

When the assassination occurred, Sheikh Ahmed Hassoun, a Sudanese Muslim scholar, was sitting in the front row with Malcolm X's family. He is the one who prepared the body for burial according to Islamic rites by removing the clothes, washing the body with water and perfumes, then wrapping it in white linen shrouds. Hassoun had come to New York from Mecca, commissioned by the World Muslim League to help Malcolm X establish Muslim Mosque, Inc., in Harlem.

Burial occurred after a week of public mourning. Osman recalls, "During the week, more than thirty thousand people viewed the body, protected by hundreds of extra-duty policemen. The police lined rooftops, searched people on the streets for weapons, and blocked street corners. It was perhaps the tensest week in the community's history. Despite threats and insults, the Muslim Student Association of the United States and Canada, observing a religious mandate, decided to take a stand and attend the funeral."

Other Muslim leaders did not. It fell to playwright-actor Ossie Davis, his wife, actress Ruby Dee, and Osman to conduct the services. Ruby Dee read messages of condolences from world leaders. In his eulogy, Osman said he spoke as an African who knew Malcolm X intimately. He noted his genuine conversion to mainline Islam and closed his remarks with these words:"He attained the highest aspiration of any Muslim, to be martyred fighting for justice and human equality."

In the final eulogy, Davis's deep voice echoed:

"Here, at this final hour, in this quiet place, Harlem has come to bid farewell to one of its brightest hopes....

"Many will ask what Harlem finds to honor this stormy, controversial and bold young captain -and we will smile... if you knew him, you would know why we must honor him: Malcolm was our manhood, our living, Black manhood. This was his meaning to his people. And in honoring him, we honor the best in ourselves... And we will know him then for what he was and is - a Prince -our own Black shining Prince -who did not hesitate to die, because he loved us so." [4]

Osman offers Malcolm X's own words for remembrance: "If I can die having brought any light, having exposed any meaningful truth that will help to destroy the racist cancer that is malignant in the body of America, then, all credit is due to Allah. Only the mistakes have been mine."

After the funeral, Osman helped raise funds for Malcolm X's impoverished widow and children. Some of the money was used to finance the pilgrimage of his wife, Beyhia Shabazz, to Mecca.

Osman considers his life greatly enriched during student days by his close association with Malcolm X, but he benefited as well from other unique, off-campus experiences. As a foreign student, he received a close glimpse of American life, thanks to a remarkable stipulation in the terms of his three-year scholarship at Dartmouth. The sponsors, members of the graduating class of 1956, offered Osman to spend all school holidays in the homes of the alumni who provided the funds. These family experiences led him to a deep appreciation of America as a haven for immigrants.

Notes:
1. Malcolm X, letter from Mecca,Muslim Mosque Inc., 1964.

2. Alex Haley, *The Autobiography of Malcolm X.*
    (New York: Random House, 1965) pp. 418-419
3. Ibid., p. 341
4   Ibid., p. 454

Chapter 10: Breaking the Silence

A few years after Ahmed Osman's encounter with Malcolm X, two national Muslim organizations were functioning. The first, the Islamic Circle of North America [ICNA], began its work in 1971, followed in 1982 by the Islamic Society of North America [ISNA]. Both organizations initially offered a wide range of services to Muslims before adding outreach activity.

ICNA, based in New York, replaced a group founded in 1968 to serve Urdu-speaking Muslims. ISNA, with headquarters in Plainfield, Indiana, was organized by a group of leaders of the Muslim Student Association.

The two organizations have similar goals. Both struggled for financial survival in the early years but by 2000 were on solid footing. Both sponsor widely-attended national conventions, provide disaster relief in many foreign countries and charitable and educational services to Muslims in the United States and Canada. They issue books and leaflets on a variety of Islamic topics.

ICNA functions nationwide through local chapters, as well as national institutions. It publishes *The Message,* a monthly magazine edited by Zaheer Uddin, who also serves as secretary-general of the ten-thousand member organization and as executive director of the Center for American Muslim Research and Information [CAMRI]. The center sponsors conferences, lectures, and publications, as well as educational and research programs. Beginning in 1983, ICNA began a unique service, called MSI Financial Services Corporation, that provides Muslims with an alternative to conventional interest charges when they need to borrow money.

ICNA pioneered in multi-media communication for all ages, using compact discs, VCR documentaries, and the Internet. It will soon publish a reference book on U.S. Muslims, to be titled *The Muslim Community 2000.*

The Islamic Society of North America publishes a monthly magazine called *Islamic Horizons,* manages a training center, and collaborates with Indiana University in offering college-level courses. In 2000, Dr. Muzammil Siddiqi, an India-born U.S. citizen and scholar, began his fourth year as president. Sayyid M. Syeed is secretary-general. As a student, Siddiqi was chairman of the Muslim Student Association of the United States and Canada [MSA]. He later served as director of the Islamic Center in Washington, D.C.

The organization's direct membership is about eleven thousand, and by February 2000, it had, by Syeed's estimate, provided personal services to more than one million U.S. Muslims. ISNA acts as an umbrella organization for regional and specialized Muslim groups, including the Muslim Student Association. Syeed reports, "In just three years, the number of organizations that the society serves has risen from three hundred and twenty-five to four hundred."[1] In October 2000, ISNA sponsored a workshop on domestic violence, attended by fifty Muslims leaders from various parts of the country.[2]

Support for the society was evident in 1997 when more than twenty thousand Muslims attended its national convention, held that year in Chicago. I participated in the agenda and noted attendance so great that police were required to keep traffic moving in the corridors of the Conrad Hilton, the center of most of the convention programs. Anticipating a further increase in attendance, the event was held in 2000 at the Hyatt Convention Center near Chicago's O'Hare Airport, where attendance exceeded thirty thousand.[3]

Siddiqi applauds the American environment: "American Muslims live in perhaps the most democratic country in the world, one that provides unlimited opportunities for growth."[4]

Muslims are making steady progress in educational services. Schools for Muslims thrive at all levels in major cities nation-wide.

Among more than one hundred and fifty elementary schools, the New Horizon School in southern California may be the best known. It maintains two campuses, one in Pasadena and the other in Orange County, and is headed by Necva Ozgur, an educator of Turkish ancestry. Her goal is providing each student "with an excellent academic education and firm founding in moral and ethical conduct based on Islamic teachings." She adds, "Teaching our students life skills—like problem solving, conflict resolution, and empathy—and instilling in them values and habits of personal responsibility, honesty and justice are the school's gift." Student body and faculty represent a broad mix of races and nationalities.

Several Muslim schools offer high school instruction, in addition to elementary education.

East-West University, a Muslim-inspired institution of higher learning in Chicago, is training students for the professions and public service, with emphasis on economically-disadvantaged young people. Located in the heart of the Loop on Michigan Avenue in Chicago, it is the first major U.S. institution of higher learning headed by a Muslim scholar. Muslims are prominent members of its board of trustees and student body. Founded in 1980 and headed since its inception by Dr. Wasiullah Khan, it offers a broad curriculum at the baccalaureate level and plans graduate programs in the next few years.

In the 1999-2000 academic year, a faculty of thirty members—fifteen of them full time—served a student body of seven hundred. In September 2000, when the university celebrated its twentieth year, enrollment reached eight hundred. Khan anticipates that the student body will grow to two thousand within three years. At the anniversary observance, U.S. Rep. David Bonior, deputy leader of Democrats in the U.S. House of Representatives, received an honorary doctorate degree for leadership in interfaith causes.

The American Islamic College, founded in Chicago in 1982, offers Islamic courses, as well as instruction in the Arabic language. Its founder and president is Dr. Asad Hussein.

The Muslim scholarly community is served by several organizations. The International Institute of Islamic Thought, founded in 1981 and based in Herndon, Virginia, publishes a quarterly journal, *The American Journal of Islamic Social Sciences*. The United Association for Studies and Research, established in 1999 in Annandale, Virginia, issues *The Middle East Affairs Journal*, a quarterly first published in 1998. *The American Muslim*, a monthly magazine sponsored by Imam W. Deen Mohammed's Muslim American Society, began publication in January 2000.

The Center for the Study of Islam and Democracy, directed by Radwan A. Masmoudi and based in Burtonsville, Maryland, and the Circle of Tradition and Progress, directed by Professor Antony T. Sullivan at Ann Arbor, Michigan, focus on interfaith and institutional relations.

With the debut of two national public policy organizations — the American Muslim Council [AMC] and the Muslim Public Affairs Council [MPAC] — in 1989, political activity became a major, organized Muslim activity. AMC is based in Washington, D.C., and MPAC in Los Angeles. Both have professional staffs that advance varied agendas at an ever-increasing pace.

As explained by executive director Aly Abuzaakouk, AMC's objectives are to advance Muslim policy goals at the federal level and enlist Muslims in the American political process: "The more we participate, the more people will listen to us. We want our community to play politics, starting from the Parent-Teacher Associations and continuing to Pennsylvania Avenue in the nation's capital. We tell them, 'If you are voteless, you are weightless in this society.'"[5]

AMC pioneered in several activities that brought Muslim concerns to national attention. In 1991, it helped establish an organization of military personnel called Muslim Military Members and has since co-sponsored activities of the organization. Later that year, President George Bush encouraged religious tolerance by sending the organization a supportive message at the conclusion of its first Hajj pilgrimage to Mecca, and Imam Siraj

Wahhaj, a leader in AMC, became the first Muslim to offer prayer during a session of the U.S. House of Representatives.

As the agent for the Islamic Society of North America, AMC encouraged the establishment of Muslim chaplains in the U.S. Armed Services, and on December 3, 1993, Captain Abdul Rasheed Muhammad became the first Muslim chaplain in U.S. history. There are now eight among the various military services. Each wears the Islamic Star and Crescent as an identifying insignia.

AMC helped to establish the National Islamic Prison Foundation in 1993 to help serve the needs of "Muslims who have converted while in prison, who are still serving sentences, or who are reentering society after incarceration."

The organization maintains a busy pace in various legislative and foreign policy initiatives, recently supporting legislation to outlaw secret evidence in legal proceedings of the U.S. Immigration and Naturalization Service. In 1992, it issued a widely-cited booklet entitled, "The Muslim Population in the United States." The organization has issued a series of public papers, including one dealing with responses to anti-Islamic hate crimes and several editions of a Muslim legal directory and guide to legal rights. The council later initiated a Muslim-Catholic project to combat terrorism.

In 1992, the council broke new ground in partisan endeavor by polling Muslims on political issues and sponsoring hospitality suites at the national presidential nominating conventions. In 1996, it initiated a program of voter outreach, identifying topics of concern to Muslims, surveying Muslim political preferences, and producing a guide on voting procedures.

About five thousand Muslims provide financial support for the council and also participate in choosing the organization's leadership. Abdurahman Alamoudi helped to found the organization, served for nine years as executive director, and now directs its affiliate, the American Muslim Council Foundation.[6]

The Muslim Public Affairs Council, although not affiliated with the American Muslim Council, undertakes complementary activity. It seeks "to foster a positive, constructive relationship between American Muslims and their elected representatives and to make Islamic ethical values available to the American political process."

In 1996, it presented a paper to the U.S. Senate on the concept of an Islamic democracy and three years later one for the State Department on U.S. counterterrorism policy. In April 2000, it sponsored entertainment media awards, recognizing Warner Brothers Studios for exposing, in its production of the "Three Kings," the plight of the Iraqi people as the result of economic sanctions enforced by U.S. military forces.

Salam Al-Marayati, its national director and one of its founders, is prominent in Los Angeles civic activities. I first met him at the Islamic Center of Southern California in Los Angeles during my 1986 book tour. He addresses school and religious groups, writes editorial page commentaries for major U.S. newspapers, is a frequent guest on television programs, and has organized several forums in Washington, D.C., for legislators and other policy makers.

Al-Marayati has learned that critics of Israel can become targets themselves. In 1998, he became the center of nationwide attention when U.S. Representative Richard Gephardt, Democratic leader of the U.S. House of Representatives, noticed his scholarly work as a leader of MPAC and nominated him to the Federal Terrorism Prevention Commission. It was a logical nomination, as Al-Marayati is a frequent commentator on antiterrorism. He contends that a program of eradication cannot succeed if it is limited to the apprehension and punishment of the individuals guilty of terrorist acts. It must also, he believes, try to redress the just grievances that give rise to senseless violence.

Despite these credentials, pro-Israel lobbying groups protested so strongly that Gephardt withdrew the nomination. Their main complaint was Al-Marayati's frequent criticism of Israel for its mistreatment of Palestinians. The withdrawal proved to be a pyrrhic victory for those protesting, because the publicity over Gephardt's capitulation embarrassed the congressional leader, a star in the Democratic Party constellation, and, at the same time, brought to public attention Al-Marayati's case for the redress of Palestinian grievances.

A year later, Al-Marayati's critics, among them the Zionist Organization of America, tried unsuccessfully to discredit him as he provided leadership in a popular Muslim-Jewish dialogue in Los Angeles. One of the protesting groups urged Jewish leaders to "shun" him, as well as all other Muslim leaders who had helped to establish the dialogue series. They charged him and the editors of *The Minaret,* the monthly magazine of the Islamic Center of Southern California, with being "Holocaust deniers," people who question the fact that Jews were systematically exterminated by Nazi Germany during World War II. Those protesting criticized the editorial content of the magazine and tagged Al-Marayati as a "denier" because he shared office space with the magazine staff.

The charges were unfounded and preposterous, according to Ramsey Hakim, chairman of MPAC's board of directors. Meeting with media, he said, "Sharing office space is not the issue.... The issue here is to silence voices that are not so pleasing to special interest groups accustomed to tactics of intimidation.... The Muslim Public Affairs Council, *The Minaret,* the Islamic Center of Southern California, as well as all mainstream Muslim organizations, have always considered the Holocaust as the most heinous crime committed in modern history. As Muslims suffer the trauma of genocide in the Balkans, Chechnya, and China, and in so many other places, they are cognizant of the need to speak out against hate and intolerance that leads to persecution and eradication of any ethnic or religious group."[7]

Al-Marayati did not move his office, and, despite the controversy, the interfaith dialogue went forward successfully with Al-Marayati remaining in its leadership. It was hailed nationally as a model for constructive discussion.

In June 2000, the lobbying organizations again turned on Al-Marayati, sparking a controversy in one of the most hotly contested congressional races in the nation, the bid for reelection by U.S. Rep. James Rogan, a California Republican who attained national prominence in 1999 as one of the House managers of the Senate impeachment trial of President Clinton. The Democratic National Congressional Campaign Committee targeted Rogan for defeat in the November 2000 voting, and provided heavy support to his Democratic opponent, State Senator Adam Schiff.

Al-Marayati and other Muslims became points of controversy when Jason Cabel Roe, Rogan's campaign manager, was quoted in the *Los Angeles Times* as making demeaning remarks about them. *Times* reporter Michael Finnegan quoted Roe as saying that Schiff's appearance at a community program cohosted by Al-Marayati "raised some questions about the associations [that Schiff] plans to keep," if elected. In a reference to Al-Marayati's prominence as an advocate for Muslims, Roe was also quoted as saying, "It seems to me odd that Senator Schiff would feel comfortable, especially as a Jew, to be participating in this event."

The newspaper account prompted protests by Muslim leaders, among them Hussam Ayloush, executive director of the Council on American Islamic Relations for Southern California, who denounced Roe's comments as "an attempt to treat American Muslims as an outcast community."

Because of the controversy, Roe offered to resign as campaign manager. Rogan rejected the offer but personally visited Al-Marayati to deliver a letter of apology for Roe's remarks. When the two met, Rogan told the Muslim leader that messages from "special interest groups" had prompted Roe's statements to the *Times* reporter. Al-Marayati later told news media, "What concerns us is that special interest groups from outside the district have turned Congressman Rogan from one who has been traditionally open and respectful towards our community to one who has shut the door on dialogue and civilized discourse."

Maher Hathout, M.D., a senior adviser to the Muslim Public Affairs Council, told reporters, "Until Roe makes a formal apology, the meeting with Mr. Rogan can only be viewed as a step in the right direction." Two days later, Al-Marayati received a letter of apology in which Roe stated his "deep respect for the Muslim community." A week later, Finnegan stood by his report, stating in a phone interview that his controversial article was accurate.[8] On November 7, Rogan lost his bid for reelection, receiving 43 percent of the votes.

In July 2000, Gebhardt made amends to the Muslim community by joining Al-Marayati in a Capitol Hill forum on "American Muslim Experiences." The forum was sponsored by the Interfaith Alliance, an organization headed by Rev. Welton Gaddy, a Baptist minister in Monroe, Louisiana. Gephardt told the forum, "Muslims, one of the most ethnically diverse groups in America, are underrepresented in public life and suffering from misunderstanding and discrimination."

Among those participating were Dr. Hathout and Rabbi David Saperstein of the Center of Reform Judaism, both members of the Interfaith Alliance board of directors. Others on the panel were U.S. Rep. Amo Houghton, R-NY, and three Muslims who serve as staff members on Capitol Hill: Jameel Aalim-Johnson, office of U.S. Rep. Gregory Meeks, D-NY; Soheila Al-Jadda, office of U.S. Rep. Dennis Kucinich, D-OH; and Asim Ghafoor, office of U.S. Rep. Ciro Rodriguez, D-TX.[9]

Al-Marayati has enjoyed other pleasant moments. In 1998, responding to the request of Mrs. Clinton, he and his wife, Laila Al-Marayati, M.D., organized a White House celebration marking the end of Ramadan, the Muslim month of fasting. A year later, they jointly received the prestigious World Citizen Award at a dinner sponsored by the United Nations Association of Los Angeles.

Like her husband, Laila Al-Marayati is prominent as a Muslim leader and spokesperson. She is a founder and former chair of the Muslim Women's League. In 1995, she served on the U.S. delegation chaired by First Lady Hillary Rodham Clinton that participated in the UN World Conference on Women held in China. In early 1999, President Clinton appointed her to the Commission on International Religious Freedom.

Talat Othman of the Islamic Center of Chicago and Hathout made history in the summer of 2000 when they became the first Muslims to offer prayers at the national presidential nominating conventions of the two major political parties. Othman offered the benediction at the end of the first day of the Republican Party convention in Philadelphia and Hathout gave the opening prayer in Los Angeles at the session of the Democratic Party convention that was addressed by President Bill Clinton and First Lady Hillary Rodham Clinton.

A fifth major Muslim group entered the national scene in 1992 when Agha Saeed, a California professor who had just received a doctorate degree in rhetoric, founded the American Muslim Alliance [AMA], an organization devoted exclusively to encouraging Muslim participation in political parties and the electoral process.

The AMA had a running start in Texas where an organization called the Texas American Muslim Caucus had already been encouraging Muslim partisan activities for two years. Its chairman, Syed Ahsani, reports that caucus members helped to elect twenty-five Muslims to public office in 1996 alone. The organization's purpose, as explained by Dr. Nizam A. Peerwani, is "to foster a positive perception of Islam and Muslims and to promote Muslim interests through participation in the political process."[10] It is now the Texas branch of the AMA.

One of its members, Dr. Amanullah Khan, belonged to the inner circle that helped Texas Governor George W. Bush win the presidency in 2000. Member Barakat Ali also has top Republican ties, and other members have personal relationships with Democratic Party leaders.

In 1999, the caucus urged Muslims to bestir themselves. It declared that U.S. Muslims are "the world's wealthiest Islamic community" and urged them to "stop blaming 'the West' and pointing fingers at others for our own shortcomings." Twenty-seven Texas Muslims agreed to be candidates for election as delegates to party conventions.

Members provide financial support to selected candidates of both major political parties, locally and beyond. In 1996, they raised $60,000 for the re-election of a Republican, U.S. Senator

Phil Gramm of Texas. They also contributed substantially to the reelection to the U.S. Senate of Tom Harkin of Iowa and Tim Johnson of South Dakota, both Democrats.

Through the AMA, Saeed expanded Muslim political action nationally. While carrying a full-time university teaching load, he travels extensively to further the national political organization he has set in motion. By 2000, the Alliance had a sixty-member national secretariat and network of more than four hundred leaders, consisting almost entirely of volunteers. By then, ninety-three chapters were functioning in thirty-one states, fourteen in Canada alone. Total AMA membership was about seven thousand.

Saeed's rise to prominence has been rapid. When we first met in 1985, he was a graduate student already committed to the political empowerment of immigrants. Six years later, he telephoned to outline his plan to bring Muslims into the nation's partisan mainstream. In a Los Angeles hotel room in February 2000, he explained AMA strategy: "Our main goal is to organize Muslims in the mainstream of public affairs, civic discourse, and political party activity in all fifty states. We believe that political power is not a function of numbers alone but is a combined product of initiative, innovation, and determination. We need to transform our pent-up frustration, anger, and pain into creative and meaningful steps for self-empowerment."[11]

His research discloses more than 521,000 elective offices in the United States. "Muslims presently have been elected only to a handful of these offices. They need to be awakened to their full potential in the American political system." He predicted that Muslims are numerous enough in California, Texas, New Jersey, Michigan, Florida, Illinois, and New York to be a crucial influence in presidential elections and in closely contested races within those states.[12]

A number of smaller groups help to advance policy goals and train Muslims for leadership in the public arena.

In two years, the American Muslim Union, headed by Mohamed Younes, a Patterson, N.J. industrialist, attained a membership of 2,000 and assisted the Metropolitan Muslim Federation, led by Magdy Mahmoud, in sponsoring major Manhattan rallies held during 2000 and 2001 for Palestinian rights.

Ziad Asali, M.D., a Muslim who owns the Christian County Medical Clinic in Taylorville, Illinois, heads the Association of Arab-American University Graduates and serves on the board of a number of other nonprofit organizations that focus on human rights in the Middle East. He serves as an adviser to the American Arab Anti-Discrimination Committee, where his wife, Naila, is the chairman of the board of directors.

Marghoob and Renae Quraishi sponsor the Muslim Student Network in Washington, D.C. Each summer this program brings together ten to twenty of the top Muslim students in universities for assignments as interns in various government offices. In off-hours, the students are instructed by attorneys and scholars in international, U.S., and Islamic law. Each student receives housing and a modest stipend.

Asifa Quraishi, the daughter of the sponsors, writes, "These students will likely be very influential on the American Muslim political scene in the future, given their early training and exposure."[13] While engaged in graduate law studies at Harvard University, she sponsored another unique Muslim service. She directed an e-mail discussion group of Muslim attorneys and law students. In 1999, the panel consisted of about one hundred subscribers. She finds law a profession of growing interest in the Muslim community: "It is clear that as more Muslims become involved in the legal system overall, the more interest and awareness there is in creating a coherent, political voice, one that is interested in domestic as well as foreign issues."

Nashville, Tennessee, is a major center of Muslim initiatives for interfaith understanding. Throughout the Gulf War, local churches, with Muslim support, sponsored citywide public lectures. Zainab Elberry, once saluted by the *Nashville Tennessean* as a "one-person embassy," and her economist husband, Nour Naciri, are widely recognized for their initiatives to broaden understanding of Islam. Elberry began her work in 1985 when she chaired the United Nations "Peace Links" celebration. She frequently writes articles and letters to editors, one of which was published in *USA Today*. During the Gulf War, she organized a "Middle Eastern Women's Dialogue," in which six Arab-Americans met regularly with the same number of Jewish Americans.

Mohammed and Sayda Yussef sponsor a Nashville radio program called "Islam in Focus," inviting listeners to call in questions. Ali El Mousawi, an immigrant from Iraq, represents the Nashville government in the resettlement of refugees from Muslim countries. Abubakar Bah is a member of the Tennessee Human Rights Commission. Dr. Arshi Nasseh has been an interfaith leader for a quarter of a century. In 1980, she was recognized as Nashville's "Woman of the Year" and is known informally throughout the city as "Mother Arshi" for her charitable work.

Sadiq Mohyuddin, M.D., provides leadership for the large and growing Muslim population in the St. Louis area. He helps direct the assimilation of more than ten thousand immigrant Muslims, a part of America's humanitarian resettlement program following the civil war in Somalia that came to a head in 1991. He founded charitable clinics in both St. Louis and Lahore, Pakistan. Mohyuddin is active in civic programs and, for several years, served as chairman of the St. Louis Council on World Affairs. He has lectured widely on world mosques and served as media chairman for the 1998 ISNA convention, held in St. Louis. As a part of the agenda, he organized an interfaith session, explaining that "Muslims like to see human rights recognized and endorsed on one standard throughout the world."[14]

In the Chicago area, Talal Sonboli, M.D., and Talat Othman, a developer, are prominent in the Federation of Muslim American Organizations, a group that promotes cooperation among the various Muslim communities in Chicago and its suburbs. One of its goals is improved cooperation between African-American Muslims and others in the Muslim community. Othman recognizes that there are differences but believes these "will be worked out over time."[15]

Four people are among the Muslims promoting interfaith understanding in neighborhoods near Chicago. Miriam Zayed, a teacher in the public school system, was appointed to the Humanities Council by Illinois Governor George Ryan. A Democratic Party precinct captain, she protested against anti-Arab bias in schools during her unsuccessful campaign for election to a non-partisan local school board. Author Ray Hanania cites her campaign as "uplifting Arab-Americans and Muslims in local politics."

Sammer Ghouleh is an author and artist. Her latest book, *Treasured Misfortunes,* centers on spina bifida, a disease afflicting Shahida, her young daughter. Her poetry about challenges facing Muslims and Arabs appeared in two earlier books. She is a leader in Palestine associations and conducts instruction in Arabic for young people. She has published several coloring books for children and a collection of greeting cards, all of which center on Islamic and Arab themes. "I am Muslim, but I feel it is important to participate in the larger society and be unified under the goodness of God's message."

Two other Muslims divide their time between politics and civic causes. Khalil Shalabi, born in Palestine, is a businessman, active in Arab-American organizations, and a leader in the Democratic Party. Saffiya Shillo works in voter registration as a deputy registrar and serves on a panel that helps first-time youthful offenders. "Rather than send them to court where they might face harsh sentences, we strive to direct them into community service."[16]

Michael Wolfe of San Francisco, a free-lance producer of documentary films, is working with Alex Kronemer of Washington, D.C., to advance interfaith understanding. He produced a widely-praised documentary on the pilgrimages to the shrines at Mecca and Madina. It was broadcast nationwide by the Public Broadcasting System.

A visible, energetic, and successful organization that helps Muslims down the political road came into being in 1994. Three Muslims, Nihad Awad, 37, Omar Ahmad, 38, and Ibrahim Hooper, 43, established the Council on American Islamic Relations, better known by its CAIR acronym.

Awad and Ahmad were born in a Palestinian refugee camp in Jordan. They did not meet until years later as students in Minneapolis, where they became acquainted with Muslim convert Ibrahim Hooper, a native of Canada who had a master's degree in communications and was working for a local broadcasting station.

Ahmad, now an officer in a high-tech firm in Santa Clara, California, provided the startup funding for CAIR and is chairman of its national board of directors. Awad and Hooper are employed full time in CAIR leadership. As national director, Awad concentrates on organization, while Hooper takes charge of communications. Their Washington-based organization focuses on defending the civil rights of Muslims, defending Islam against stereotypes, and training Muslims in news media relations.

The new organization won immediate praise and cooperation from the American Muslim Council, whose founding executive secretary, Abdurahman Alamoudi, recalls: "We were delighted with the CAIR program and promptly voted to close down our own activities on civil rights and legal defense. The division of responsibility enabled our organization to devote more attention and resources to its other vital programs. It is a happy marriage."

Since its inaugural year, CAIR has won an impressive string of victories. By 1999, it had helped aggrieved Muslims protest victoriously in more than two hundred varied episodes of bias. According to Awad, CAIR won redress—apologies or policy reforms—in all cases but four. Late in the first year of CAIR's existence, I visited their small office suite in a modest building on Washington's K Street. They had just employed a receptionist, a decision that increased CAIR's staff by 50 percent. Their desks were piled high with challenges, and their quarters were as cramped as their budget. CAIR's outlay in its first year of operation was under $100,000. At its annual dinner in October 2000, fundraising yielded $300,000 that one evening alone.

When I interviewed Awad five years later, CAIR's budget had risen to nearly $2 million, and its full-time staff, although it had grown from three to sixteen, remained overloaded. Requests for help and information flooded e-mail and FAX equipment. One of the two men who handled the tide of incoming requests estimated their backlog of messages at nearly one thousand. By then, CAIR had established full-time regional offices in Santa Clara, Los Angeles, Columbus, and Dallas, and chapters in thirty-five cities.

A few days after the interview, I attended the opening of a new regional office in Queens, New York. Each CAIR office is financially self-supporting and has its own board of directors. Awad reports with pride that women as well as men are members of the national board of directors as well as the regional boards.

In May 2000, CAIR moved its national headquarters into a large building that it purchased at 453 New Jersey Avenue, SE, almost in the shadow of the U.S. Capitol. The extra space will enable the organization to expand its training and outreach activities.

The move was a major milestone for the young organization and its leaders. Awad reflected on the organization's achievements: "CAIR has already trained several thousand Muslims in media relations. It introduced publicity campaigns for the holy days of the Hajj and Ramadan. In 1995, the first Ramadan campaign produced three hundred fourteen news articles and the number climbed steadily to more than fourteen hundred in 1998."

From its earliest days, CAIR has utilized electronic communication to summon Muslims to action. My FAX machine hums almost every day with reminders of CAIR vitality. The organization issues news reports and appeals to about 40,000 FAX machines and Internet addresses. CAIR's campaign of assistance was a major factor in enabling Bosnia to become independent from Serbia in 1992.

The messages reach, among others, leaders at more than fifteen hundred mosques and Islamic centers. Awad notes their importance: "They address hundreds of thousands of Muslims who attend Friday congregational prayers and other weekly Muslim events. We know that CAIR bulletins often form the theme of Friday sermons. We can't be sure how many Muslims attend Friday prayers, but the number could reach more than a million. We find that most CAIR activists are second-generation Americans. This means they are comfortable in the English language and familiar with Western culture. We hope soon to have a computer database of a half million activists." He also sees the need for Muslim influence in professions related to public policy. "Whenever I speak to Muslim groups, I urge students to become majors in journalism, law or political science. Journalism is especially important, and we urge Muslim adults to establish scholarships in that field. Muslims must become active in the nation's offices where news reports and headlines are written."[17]

CAIR provides guides to educators and employers and guidance to Muslims who encounter discrimination or wish to gain the cooperation of the media. The organization issues a quarterly newsletter that goes to all members nationally, and regional offices issue newsletters that focus on items of local interest. The national office issues an annual report on the status of Muslim civil rights. The 2000 report outlines three hundred fifty verified incidents of discrimination, denial of religious accommodation, harassment, and illegal discrimination—a 25 percent increase over 1999. CAIR coordinator S. Eric Shakir comments: "The dissemination of accurate information about Islam, coupled with increased social and political activism on the part of American Muslims, is the best solution to this problem."[18]

Requests for help frequently come from Muslims confronting employer regulations against beards and female headscarves in workplaces. Many Muslims consider beards and headscarves as religiously mandated, and CAIR has won an unbroken string of victories when these practices threaten jobs. But CAIR's best known victories have been against giants in filmmaking, magazine publishing, and manufacturing. In 1998, CAIR-inspired protest forced Nike, a leading manufacturer of sports equipment, to remake a line of shoes that had the Allah, the Arabic word for God, displayed prominently in script on the heel. Nike apologized, recalled the entire production run, removed the offending word, and, as a gesture of goodwill, financed the construction of playgrounds at several Muslim schools and made donations to a number of Islamic charities.

CAIR gained respect in the film industry by helping to persuade DreamWorks SKG to make changes in the movie script for "Prince of Egypt," before its premiere in December 1998. In its Spring 1999 newsletter, CAIR reported that "during its four-year production schedule, the studio worked closely with Muslim, Jewish, and Christian groups to ensure historical accuracy and to eliminate sources of stereotyping." Dr. Maher Hathout, a leader of the Muslim Public Affairs Council, served as a principal consultant to the studio.

When Twentieth Century Fox refused to remove stereotype language and episodes from a movie called "The Siege," CAIR shifted its attention from Hollywood to a nationwide protest campaign that included newspaper advertisements and other publicity about the film's unfair images. Several major newspapers and television stations covered the controversy. *The New York Times* published a CAIR editorial commentary adjacent to one written by the film producer.

At dozens of cities nationwide, CAIR organized a unique program for patrons emerging from theater showings of the film. Awad explains. "When patrons left after viewing the movie, they were pleasantly surprised to find Muslims with smiling faces inviting them to a nearby mosque for a tour, refreshments, and information about Islam. In all, seven thousand movie patrons in various communities responded." Participation was especially strong at mosques in Northern California and the Washington, D.C., area. More than four hundred non-Muslims attended the open house at a mosque in Ann Arbor, Michigan. One hundred fifty attended the one in Nashville, an event covered by *The Nashville Tennessean* and all three major television stations.

Awad believes the campaign created goodwill for Muslims among movie fans and had a role in causing the film to show a $20 million loss. "Maybe the film industry learned a $20 million lesson."

IN THE POLITICAL ARENA

Zainab Elberry
Insurance Sales

Inayat Lalani, M.D.
Family Clinic

Naz Haque, DDS
Children's Clinic

CAIR's Capital Headquarters - The national staff of the Council on American-Islamic Relations (CAIR) standing outside the organization's new building near the U.S. Capitol, Washington, D.C.

MUSLIM BLOC VOTING

MUSLIM CANDIDATES FOR CONGRESS

Omar Ahmad
CAIR Board Chairman

Ibrahim Hooper
CAIR Communications

Eric Vickers
Civil Rights Attorney

Maher Hathout, M.D.
Public Affairs Council

Aly Abuzaakouk
AMC Executive Director

Elias Zenkich
Industrialist

ELECTED TO N.Y. SCHOOL BOARDS

CONGRESSIONAL AIDE

Nathaniel Ham
Railroad Manager

Morshed Alam
Chemist

Suhail Khan
Press Spokesman

Rev. Robert H. Schuller, (left) with **Sheikh Salah Kuftaro**
Hour of Power Pastor   *Syrian Muslim Scholar*

W. Deen Mohammed
Muslim American Society

Professor Ali A. Mazrui
Albert Schweitzer chair
Binghamton University

Islam A. Siddiqui, Ph.D.
USDA Undersecretary

Professor John L. Esposito
Georgetown University

Richard H. Curtiss
Author, Editor

Larry Shaw
State Senator

William Baker, Ph.D.
Author

Leaders of American Muslim Organizations meet Governor Bush at the Governor's Mansion in Austin, Texas during Presidential Campaign 2000

Muzammil H. Siddiqi, Ph.D.
ISNA President

Zaheer Uddin
ICNA Leader

Laila Al-Marayati, M.D.
Muslim Women's League

Nour Naciri, Ph.D.
Economist

Andrew Patterson
Author, Teacher

Talat Khan, M.D.
Family Clinic

Rally for Jerusalem - Glimpses of the crowd of more than ten thousand Muslims from across the nation who rallied on October 28, 2000 at Lafayette Park, across the White House, to protest Israel's abuse of Palestinians and its control of Islamic shrines in Jerusalem.

M. Osman Siddique, the first Muslim to be a U.S. ambassador, and Mrs. Siddique.

Secrecy Issue - U.S. Rep. Thomas Campbell protests against use of secret evidence.

Eid Postage Stamp - Muslim leaders unveil the Eid stamp at the Islamic Educational Center in Maryland.

The Pope greets Muslim leader - Archbishop Rembert Weakland from Milwaukee introduces Dr. M.A. Cheema, President of AMC, to Pope John Paul II.

First Muslim Navy Chaplain - Mangi Noel (right) of Norfolk, Virginia is commissioned in a 1994 ceremony as the first Muslim chaplain in the U.S. Navy.

Imam Leadership Conference - Participants gather on U.S. Capitol steps.

Voter Registration Campaign - Muslim women display T-shirts promoting "Your Values… Your Voice… Your Vote."

CAIR has had other successes. Challenging insensitive, biased comments about Islam, the organization has elicited apologies from prominent people and institutions, among them NBC show host Jay Leno, radio commentator Paul Harvey, U.S. Representative Jim Saxton, R-NJ, Chicago law firm Mayer, Brown and Platt, and National Public Radio. CAIR helped to organize American Muslim Voter Registration Day on Friday, September 15, 2000.

The organization's biggest triumph came when publisher Morton Zuckerman, owner of *U.S. News and World Report,* apologized in print for falsely charging in an editorial that centuries ago the Prophet Muhammad once violated a treaty with Jews. Awad was furious. He said, "It was a bold lie, and an attack on the Prophet, who never violated any treaty. When I told Zuckerman that he would face a protest from Muslims if he failed to apologize promptly and clearly in print, he brushed off the warning, saying, 'Be my guest.'

"CAIR issued an Action Alert on the Internet and by FAX. Three days later, Zuckerman was on the phone, urging CAIR to halt the protest. Zuckerman's secretary told CAIR, 'Our offices are paralyzed. We can't get anything done.' Zuckerman pleaded, 'Please bring this to an end.' I told him, 'We can't stop the protest, but you can.' He responded, 'I'm apologizing to you right now over the phone.' I said, 'That's not good enough. You must print a clear apology on the same page where the lie about the Prophet appeared.' Zuckerman said that he would, but in the magazine's next issue, he published only a vague comment. It was not an apology."

CAIR immediately called a news conference outside the magazine's Washington offices, where other national Muslim leaders joined CAIR in announcing that they would urge Muslims to intensify pressure on Zuckerman's magazine. The response was heavier than before, and Zuckerman quickly complied with Muslim demands. He published a personal apology in the space that customarily carries his editorials.

Awad calls it an important victory: "Muslims stood their ground. They did not break. They forced a powerful publisher, for the first time, to issue a clear, unequivocal apology to Muslims.

We've been able to remove a psychological barrier. Muslims no longer feel helpless in the face of abusive discrimination. They have a new confidence in themselves, a feeling that they can protect their own dignity as human beings. They now know that, by working together in a common cause, Muslims can make a difference."[19]

The Muslims who are engaged in organizational and public policy activities have made impressive strides in interfaith understanding, but they constitute only a small fraction of Islam's community in America. The membership lists and the attendance at the annual conventions of the two largest organizations, ISNA and ICNA, provide an informal measure of the number of Muslims who participate in organized activity. Even the most generous projections suggest that the total is less than two hundred thousand.

The rest—more than six million other Muslims—remain silently on the sidelines, unsupportive even with their checkbooks.

Notes:

1. Interview, 3-1-2000.
2. *Chicago Tribune,* 10-13-2000, p. 8, sect. 2.
3. Siddiqi, Interview, 10-29-2000.
4. *Pakistan Link* , 9-1-2000, p. 1.
5. *Washington Times* 7, 17-2- 2000, "Weekly," p. 23.
6. *AMC: Our First Five Years,* (11-96).
7. MPAC e-mail release, 4-19-2000.
8. CAIR, 6-22-00; MPAC statements, 6-24-2000 and 6-27-2000; and phone interview with Finnegan, 6-28-2000.
9. MPACUSA notes, 7-17-2000.
10. American Muslim Caucus Yearbook, 1996-1997.
11. Interview with Saeed, 2-22-2000.
12. Interview with Saeed, 10-3-1998.
13. Letter, 4-5-1999.
14. *Alton Telegraph,* 8-4-1998, Alton, IL., p.2.
15. Interview, Talat Othman, 12-27-2000.
16. Ray Hanania interview, 6-18-1999.

17. Interview with Nihad Awad, 2-3-2000.
18. CAIR e-mail release, 4-18-2000.
19. Interview, 5-22-1999.

Chapter 11: The Path to Partisan Success

S tep by step, U.S. Muslims, after being quietly on the sidelines for years, are gaining prominence in government and demonstrating skill in politics. They are getting elected to public office, helping other candidates win, providing leadership in political party and government policy activities, and establishing a presence in the judicial branch of government.

As electoral victories have emerged, some may be called large and some small, but to Muslims, there are no small victories. Whether the office won is a non-salaried job as a party precinct committeeman or prestigious membership in a state legislature, all victories are large.

Four years ago, Democrat Larry Shaw, an African-American who attained business success as the manager of cafeterias in fifteen military installations, starred as the only Muslim ever elected to a state legislature. He was first elected to the North Carolina House of Representatives in 1994 and two years later won a seat in the State Senate. Religion has never been a topic of controversy in his political career and is seldom mentioned by his fellow legislators. Shaw says, "They see me as a businessman, rather than in terms of my religion." He became interested in Islam as a teenager while studying the life of Malcolm X, the Nation of Islam leader who later embraced mainline Islam. In November 2000, Shaw was unopposed in his bid for reelection.[1]

The same day, two other Muslim Democrats were elected to state legislatures. Aisha W. Abdullah-Odiase was elected to a second term in the Rhode Island House of Representatives, and Saghir Tahir, chairman of the New Hampshire chapter of the

American Muslim Alliance, won a seat in the New Hampshire House of Representatives.

Tahir, a native of Pakistan, says he finds no religious bias in his district: "My family and I are the only Muslims in my constituency of twelve thousand eligible voters, and we have never sensed any prejudice. If other Muslims find prejudice, maybe they should ask themselves what they are doing for their country." A graduate engineer who specializes in roofing and insulation problems for major corporations, Tahir says: "I am trying to give back something in exchange for the wonderful life my family finds in America."

In 1998, Wisconsin Circuit Judge Hamdy Ezalarab became the first Muslim elected to the bench in the United States. He is the founder of the Fitchburg, Wisconsin, chapter of the American Muslim Alliance. Reelected in 2000, Ezalarab now shares the judicial distinction with two other Muslim judges, David Shahid of Indiana and Abdul Majeed of Florida, both elected on November 7, 2000. Attorney Arik Alikhan of Los Angeles is another trailblazer, the first Muslim to become an Assistant United States Attorney, an important position in the federal judiciary.

J ourneying along the electoral path, some Muslims are viewing close-up the rough-and-tumble face of partisan activity, experiencing the ugly religious and ethnic bias that sometimes poisons the process, and rejoicing when good citizens wash away the poison.

On one occasion in November 1997, Muslims played a crucial but unplanned election-day role just before the polls closed in a municipal election in the small city of Hamtramck, Michigan. They proved that a tiny handful of votes can make a large victory. The community's population is nearly 20,000—40 percent Polish Roman Catholic and 20 percent Muslim. Most of the others are Christians of various denominations.

The late-voting Muslims caused Mayor Robert Kozaren to lose his bid for an eleventh two-year term to Gary L. Zych by a margin of nine votes. A Roman Catholic, Zych campaigned vigorously for Muslim support. Late on election day, a group of his supporters noted a low turnout in predominantly Muslim precincts. This prompted them to race to the local mosque where they pleaded successfully for votes as Muslims completed evening prayers. Their appeal persuaded one hundred and seventy Muslims to cast votes in the hour before polling places closed.

When votes were counted, the unofficial tally showed Zych ahead by three votes. The official tally tripled his margin to nine. "A landslide," Zych observed with a chuckle. If Muslims had not responded in the final hour of voting, Zych would have lost by one hundred and sixty-one votes.

In one of his first decisions as mayor, he named Shahad Ahmed as multicultural director and Nevrus Nazarko as income tax director—the first Muslims ever appointed to administrative positions in the history of Hamtramck's municipal government.

A year later, a group of Kozaren's diehard supporters organized a group called Concerned Citizens for a Better Hamtramck and secured enough signatures to force a special city-wide election in June 1999 on the question of removing Zych from office. Voters rejected the proposal, but the citizen group did not abandon their assault. When the mayor announced that he would seek another term in the regular election six months later, the protest group secured approval from City Clerk Ethel Fiddler for several of their members to serve as official challengers during the voting on election day. This meant they could remain inside polling places during the voting and challenge citizens whose eligibility they wished to question.

Imad Hamad, Detroit regional director of the American Arab Anti-Discrimination Committee, learned of this move a week before the voting and sent an appeal to Michigan Attorney General Jennifer Granholm. In it, he expressed concern that challenges might be made "solely on the basis of national origin" and urged her to "ensure that duly registered voters are not discriminated against or harassed in the voting process."[2] At the same time, Mayor Zych notified the state election bureau that Fiddler, a close friend of Robert Zalewski, chairman of the citizen group, might not keep the challengers from "abusing the law."[3] Michigan law authorizes challenges only against people whose eligibility to vote is disputed for reasonable cause.

On election day, despite these precautionary moves, the voting rights of a number of "foreign looking" people were wrongfully challenged. Some were asked to produce passports before voting, even though they displayed cards certifying their eligibility. A number of others agreed, sometimes under strong protest, to take an official oath of citizenship while in the polling place. Several other citizens, offended at the unusual demand, persisted in refusal and ultimately were permitted to vote without taking the oath. Still others, after observing the intimidating hassle in the polling places or learning about it from friends, did not attempt to vote.

Zych told a reporter, "It's clear from the evidence we have that they [the challengers for the citizen group] specifically targeted the Muslim community."[4]

A review of forty-nine people whose right to vote was challenged showed that forty-five had "Arab or Bangladeshi" names. Several citizen group challengers acknowledged to a newspaper reporter during the voting that they made challenges only against voters with "foreign" names or those who did not speak English well. One said candidly that he had no reasons for the challenges he made.

Susan Dunn, a prominent member of Concerned Citizens for a Better Hamtramck, told a reporter during the voting that she challenged certain voters in order to "assure the purity" of the voting. Shamsul Ali, a native of Bangladesh who has lived in the United States for twenty-six years, the last eight in Hamtramck, was upset when Dunn questioned his citizenship. Relating his experience to a reporter, he said, "They don't ask any other people. Why did they ask me?"[5]

During the voting, Fiddler received complaints of illegal challenges. While visiting polling places where the complaints originated, she cautioned citizen group challengers to avoid violations, according to witnesses, but did not withdraw the authority of any of them or threaten to do so.

D espite the intimidating, day-long hassle, the voters reelected Zych to a second two-year term, this time by a margin of sixty-nine votes—"a 700 percent increase over the first time around," Zych noted with a smile.

The controversy did not end when the votes were counted. At a hearing conducted by the Hamtramck Human Relations Commission, Osia Ali entered this statement: "When my father went to cast his vote in the Third Precinct, he was unlawfully asked to take an oath. He thought it was wrong as he never had to do that before. So he walked out. He was led back into the building by a lawyer and told not to let his voting rights be taken away because of such distractions. So he cast his vote but was very upset. When I heard about this, I refused to go to the polling place, because I didn't want to go through such problems." Lisa McQuire, a challenger in behalf of Zych, testified that Richard Marecki, acting for the Concerned Citizens group, challenged the citizenship of Siraj Ahmed, even though Ahmed had already voluntarily produced his passport when he requested a ballot. Asked to explain this challenge, Marecki said only that Ahmed "looks like a non-citizen."

Another Zych supporter, Charles F. Cirgenski, said that he watched as Concerned Citizens challengers Dunn and Juanita Ford questioned the citizenship of fourteen people. He said that Dunn, when interviewed on camera by a Detroit television reporter, denied that she was challenging voters based on their ethnicity. When the reporter told her that the list of the people she challenged contained only names that seemed to be Arabic or Bengali, Dunn told the reporter the interview was over and walked away. Cirgenski added, "What I witnessed left me disheartened. I was enraged by the entire way in which Susan Dunn and Juanita Ford acted. It was with malice and arrogance, and without justification."

David Puls, another member of the Zych team, testified that some of the women who were challenged wore traditional Islamic attire. He added that, when the citizen group representatives were asked why they made challenges, these were typical replies: "No special reason." "Look at the way he/she is dressed." "Listen to the way he/she speaks English." or "He/she can hardly write to fill out the form."

Virginia Winiarski testified, "This election was very embarrassing. Voters who looked like foreigners were rudely pounced upon. I have worked on elections for about twenty-seven years, and have never before seen anything so childish." Nagi Saleh, born in Yemen, had his vote challenged despite the fact that he has been a U.S. citizen for many years and has voted consistently in Hamtramck. He lamented, "I have never been questioned before."

Frederick Zajdel echoed the testimony of several other witnesses when he said, "At no time did I see challenges being made against Caucasians or African-Americans."

After a review of the testimony, Nancy Rue, an attorney in the U.S. Justice Department, concluded that City Clerk Fiddler's staff failed to halt the abuse of people with "dark skin and distinctly Arab names," even after it was plain that the challenges against them were lodged because of "of physical appearance alone." As a consequence, although making no criminal charges, the Justice Department filed civil charges against Fiddler, as well as the City of Hamtramck, and demanded reforms in election procedures. One of the reforms requires that some Arab-Americans be among the workers employed in future elections. At the time, no Arab-Americans were within the pool of about two hundred workers maintained by Fiddler's office.

The Hamtramck Citizen, in an editorial two weeks after the voting, charged that challengers for Concerned Citizens for a Better Hamtramck attempted to intimidate a group of voters known to support Zych and "thumbed their nose at the law and shamefully targeted Arab and Bangladeshi voters." The editorial denounced the tactics as "ugly and un-American" and added: "Trying to prevent and intimidate voters from exercising a fundamental constitutional right is a cowardly act. Hamtramck has long held out the welcoming arm to immigrants, making it easy for them to make their first start in this country. Concerned Citizens desecrated that legacy."[6]

Nouhad El-Hajj, publisher of Detroit's *Arab American Journal*, believes that the Muslim role in Zych's nine-vote victory in 1997 has special significance: "It was proof to Muslims that they can make a difference on election day, and a reminder to all of us that every vote is important." It also demonstrated the importance of aggressive campaign work, even in the late hours before polling places close.

The electoral defeat of the proposal to remove Mayor Zych from office and his subsequent triumph over bigoted election-day tactics should inspire others who enter the political arena to stand firm for their legal rights. Those who bow to intimidating tactics simply whet the appetite of the bullies.

T he list of politically active Muslims is growing.

In New York, the nation's second largest state, two Muslims are bright stars in the political firmament, one a Democrat, the other a Republican.

In 1996, Democrat Morshed Alam, a forty-one-year-old chemist born in Bangladesh, became the first immigrant from South Asia to win election to a public office in New York City, winning a seat on the non-partisan New York City District 29 School Board. Two years later he established himself as a politician with a future when, despite the opposition of his party and union leadership, he received 41 percent of the vote and nearly upset the re-election bid of veteran Republican State Senator Frank Padavan in Queens.

In the campaign, he faced heavy odds. The Queens *Times Ledger*[7] reported: "Alam received no support from the Democratic Party machine, which refused to recognize him as the party candidate. While candidates anointed by the Democratic Party organization enjoyed the largesse of union money and contributions from residents within their districts, Alam was forced to solicit money from outside the district and target fellow Bangladeshis from across the country to finance his campaign."

U.S. Senator Patrick Moynihan defied the party line by endorsing Alam's candidacy, a gesture that *Newsday* of Queens called "rare." In a letter to Alam, Moynihan wrote: "I rarely issue individual endorsements of candidates for local office. I have chosen to make an exception in this case because of your compelling record. These achievements as well as your thoughtful voice on behalf of new Americans from South Asia, all augur well for your every success." Alam also received support from Chinese-Americans, among them Jimmy Mend, a prominent Chinese-American who lamented to a reporter: "We have so many Asian-Americans in Queens and not a single [elected] representative from our community."

A lam speaks with energy, confidence, and sincerity as he explains how he campaigned: "My wife and I worked long hours every day for more than a year, right up to election day. As she went down one side of a street, I went down the other. We knocked on thousands of doors, many thousands."[8] His hard work paid dividends. "I was able to attract support from most parts of the political spectrum by emphasizing my concerns as a parent and taxpayer. While my belief in traditional morality and family values helped me win support from conservatives, my activism in labor and immigrant issues helped me reach out to more liberal forces."

Campaign funds were difficult to raise, but election results far exceeded his expectations. Before starting his campaign, he believed he would need a campaign chest of $200,000 to achieve his goal, 15 percent of the total vote he expected to be cast. When votes were counted, he received nearly three times that percentage despite campaign expenditures of only $35,000. He said Padavan spent about $500,000. A few days after his narrow loss in the State Senate race, he began a new campaign, this one directed at election to the City of New York city council in 2001.[9] This time he expects support from the Democratic Party and labor unions, because he believes the leaders of these groups now see him as a winner.

While campaigning, Alam mentioned his religious affiliation only on the few occasions when questions were raised. He explains,

"I emphasize inclusion, rather than exclusion. We [immigrants] are a part of American society. It is high time that we act as a part, instead of separating ourselves from the mainstream. Where our numbers are small, we should form coalitions. In our campaigning, we reached beyond skin color and ethnicity. My supporters reflected various professional, civic, religious, and political organizations—a mini-Rainbow Coalition, dazzling in its diversity." In May 1999, Alam won re-election to the school board, a constituency that is mainly African-American. He received the second highest vote among nineteen candidates. The new board elected him vice-chairman.

He is receiving wide media attention. On December 22, 1999, he was featured on the front page of *The New York Times*. In the day's major article, reporter James Dao reviewed Alam's ambition and quick rise in politics: "As a teenager, Morshed Alam dodged enemy soldiers to deliver food to Bangladeshi independence fighters. And as a student at Dhaka University in the 1970s, he endured police beatings to organize pro-democracy demonstrations against the nation's newly formed military regime." Dao wrote that, with a headstart that impressive, Alam's plunge into America politics came as no surprise. Alam emigrated to Jamaica, New York, in 1985 and eleven years later was on the school board.

The New York Times published on page B-11 of the same issue a large picture of Alam addressing a recent meeting of the New American Democratic Club, an organization that he founded. The newspaper described the club as "kaleidoscopic as the city itself." Attending were immigrants from Korea, Taiwan, India, Pakistan, Colombia, and Bangladesh, as well as African-Americans from Brooklyn. Alam provided the newspaper's "Quotation of the Day": "Politics is the same everywhere in the world. Nobody wants to give up power. But times are changing."

In 1997, New York Republican Governor George E. Pataki presented him with an award for community service. In March 2000, Alam won unique presidential recognition. He was the only person of South Asian origin who joined President Clinton on Air Force One for the chief executive's tour of India, Pakistan, and Bangladesh.

Alam believes foreign-born residents constitute about 60 percent of New York City's population and urges them to register and to vote. He distributes a five-page guide on grassroots politics that concludes with these words: "The way to meaningful participation [in politics] does not require us to surrender our identities or lose our values. We can do well for ourselves and good for American society by swimming in the mainstream instead of staying apart and watching others move ahead."

Neither racial nor religious bias proved to be a problem to a Muslim candidate in another part of Queens. In 1996, a predominately white, Christian constituency elected Nathaniel Ham, a 47-year-old African-American Republican, to membership on a Queen's school board located near the one to which Alam was elected the same year.

In winning the seat, Ham's total vote topped by fifty-eight votes the board chairman's bid for reelection tally. He recalls, "A few activists for my opponent tried to make religion an issue. They were aware that I chose a Muslim name—Najeeb Hameed—when I converted to Islam ten years ago, and they occasionally suggested that people ask me for my real name." None did, and Ham believes that the tactic backfired.

Ham is the superintendent of the South Shore Branch of the Long Island Railroad and a resident of New York's Half Hollow Hills neighborhood. Reared in South Carolina as a Baptist, he became a Muslim as the result of "long walks and long talks" with a Muslim neighbor. He said he was attracted by Islam's universality and its tolerance of other religions. "Islam taught me to respect other people and to avoid personal criticism." Ham's wife is a Roman Catholic and their children, he believes, are inclined toward Islam. A newcomer to Republican Party ranks, he enjoyed the non-partisan school board campaign. Would he like to be elected to Congress? "That possibility seems very remote, but I would love to serve there. It would be a wonderful opportunity."

A lthough Jim Bates of San Diego, now living in Idaho converted to Islam after serving two terms in the U.S. House of Representatives, no Muslim has been elected to Congress. Several Muslims have sought election, all unsuccessfully, but most of them proceeded with enthusiasm, confident that, win or lose, candidacy is a valuable experience.

In 1998, Democrat Eileen Ansari made an unsuccessful bid in a Los Angeles congressional district, and two years earlier, Sayed Jaleel Ahmed, an Illiinois Muslim, lost his bid for the Republican nomination for U.S. Senator to Peter G. Fitzgerald, who won the office in the November voting. In 1992, Bombay-born Nizar Hai, vice-president of United Muslims of America, made a strong but losing bid for the Republican nomination for Congress in California's thirty-first District.

In the 2000 primary elections, Bill Quraishi achieved the distinction of being one of the first Muslims in California to be nominated by a major political party as its candidate for election to the U.S. House of Representatives. He won the Republican nomination in California's fourteenth district but lost in November.

In other voting that day, Maziar Mafi, a young attorney and a Democratic leader in Orange County who immigrated from Iran at the age of fourteen, lost in his bid for the Democratic nomination for Congress in the forty-seventh district, and Khalid Jafri failed to receive the Republican nomination in the forty-third district. In Missouri, Attorney Eric Vickers, an African-American and a rising voice in St. Louis politics, campaigned unsuccessfully for the Democratic nomination in Missouri's first district.

I n a Chicago district, Elias Zenkich, an immigrant Muslim who became a successful manufacturer, twice sought election to the U.S. House of Representatives. In 1992 and again in 1994, Zenkich, a Republican and a native of Bosnia, lost his bid to unseat Democrat Dan Rostenkowski, powerful chairman of the House Ways and Means Committee. He says, "I'm glad I ran. I came a lot closer both times than I expected. In this country, everyone can participate in political life, and it's important to seize opportunities to work within the system. I am helping in the presidential campaign this year, and I am trying to help in the ethnic communities in Chicago." In April 2000, he became treasurer of the newly-formed Chicago regional chapter of the American Muslim Alliance.

When Zenkich, now sixty-five, arrived in Chicago from Bosnia at the age of twenty, he was alone, broke, spoke only German, and had no acquaintances. A German-speaking clerk in a delicatessen provided the lead to his first job—working in a machine shop. While working there, Zenkich learned English and earned a college degree in engineering by attending night school. At the age of thirty, he founded Xenex Corporation, a firm that manufactures equipment and disposable supplies for hospitals. Like Morshed Alam, Zenkich won his first foray into politics by winning election to a district school board.

He finds, to his regret, that most Muslims stay out of politics. "There are about 350,000 Muslims in the Chicago area, and about 25,000 of them are Bosnians. They all should be taking part, but they aren't. This is their country—and a great country. Unfortunately, most immigrants bring too much baggage from the old country." With a chuckle, he adds, "They shouldn't bring any more old ideas and other stuff than they can put in one carry-on case. That's enough. They need to get new luggage here. Said another way, they should become active in American politics. Most of them are used to living under a dictator and seem to have trouble adjusting to the political opportunities in America. They know things are different here, but they hold back. If they jump in and get to work in politics, they can make a difference."

Zenkich is optimistic about the future for U.S. Muslims but troubled by what he sees as disinterest of young people in politics. "They need politics just as much as politics needs young people. Politics is an honorable profession, but, unfortunately, it has been abused in recent years. You might say it has been prostituted, and this has turned off a lot of young people, but they should do their part to straighten things up. If they get into politics, they will find it a great experience. I expect a Muslim renaissance here, one that will be good for everyone."[10]

A man who immigrated from Iran as a young adult waited until the age of sixty-seven to enter politics. Ali Alemi of Timonium, Maryland, earned a Ph.D. degree and had a long career in higher education before turning to the partisan arena. In 1994, he campaigned for the Republican nomination for a seat in Maryland's State Assembly, knowing it would be mainly a learning experience. Alemi lost the nomination but won friends. "I knocked on 940 doors and received 735 votes. I had about $6,000 to spend in the campaign and finished with $600 left over for my next one. My opponent received 13,000 votes and ended up $60,000 in the red."

Alemi's daughter, Lily, now a medical student, served as campaign manager. His most effective campaign literature was a simple leaflet, copied without change from a design by Emily Murphy, age seven. On each side of a photograph of Alemi she had hand-printed, "He's cool."

He found campaigning enjoyable, even at night in bad weather. "People were totally surprised to find me going door to door in a heavy rain. Some said they wished I were a Democrat so they could vote for me. I assured them that I needed Democratic votes. Many were very hospitable, wanting me to come inside and sit down for tea and talk. Several said I was the only candidate to call at their homes in twenty years or more. Some asked me to telephone them later. I said I would, and I did."

Alemi received little coverage in the news media, and his Iranian background created a few problems. When the primary election was over, he learned that several people had criticized him in calls broadcast on radio talk shows. "They mentioned that I am Iranian and reminded the radio audience that Iranians had locked up U.S. diplomats for more than a year when Jimmy Carter was president. They also claimed that Iran had done terrible things to Jews. Of course, I had nothing to do with any of this, but the calls no doubt hurt my vote a lot."

In March 1999, Alemi was elected without opposition to a four-year term on the state board that oversees state pensions. Asked about future candidacy, he said, "I hope to run for the State Assembly again in 2002. It's my way to pay back something for the advantages I've had in America." Then he adds a qualifying sentence, demonstrating that he has learned an important lesson in politics: "I will run provided my wife approves." If Alemi gets the required domestic approval and runs again, he will find ardent supporters, I believe, among the people he stopped to visit, especially those he telephoned after promising to do so.

T he list of Muslims who are learning campaign techniques and seeking election to state and local offices is growing.

A North Carolina Muslim had an eighteen-year career in public office. Nasif Rashad Majeed, a former pilot in the U.S. Air Force with combat experience in Vietnam, won election to four consecutive two-year terms on the Charlotte City Council. He served ten years earlier in municipal positions, including five years on the housing board. He is now engaged in international trade.

In California, Syed Mahmood won the Republican nomination in the eighteenth assembly district but lost in the general election. Others campaigned, unsuccessfully, for party nominations. Republican Riffat Mahmood lost in the thirteenth assembly District in California. In Atlanta, Karim Shahid, a professional land surveyor and vice-president of Citizens for Justice, lost the Democratic nomination for state assembly.

L ateefah Muhammad, a Muslim attorney who served for four years as the first Muslim on the Tuskegee, Alabama, city council, failed in her bid for election as mayor in November 2000. In Prospect Park, N.J., Muslim businessman Hassan Fahmy, who earned the Medal of Merit from President Ronald Reagan for civic achievement, won a council seat in the Burough of Prospect Park. Both are Democrats.

In 1999, proving that candidacy can be a learning experience, California Republican Sheraly Khawaja, lost his bid for treasurer of the City of Montebello by two hundred votes. "I blame myself for losing. I failed to go after absentee votes that I believe would have made the difference. But I learned a lot during the campaign and did well in public debates with the other two people seeking the office." A leader in his Rotary club and other civic activities, he plans to seek election to the Montebello city council in 2001.

Muslims are getting elected in substantial numbers as delegates to political conventions, both state and national. Thirty Muslims served as delegates to the August 2000 Democratic National Presidential Nominating Convention.

S ome Muslims campaign for entire slates of candidates, while others focus their energies behind individuals, and some put issues above party affiliation.

Talat Khan, M.D., of Los Angeles is a registered Republican and a member of the Republican Senatorial Inner Circle on Capitol Hill, where membership signifies generous donations, but she is bipartisan in her campaigning. She is faithful to the Republican Party up to a point, but she crosses the line to support vigorously, openly, and generously Democratic candidates who support causes to which she is personally committed.

Talat is a busy woman. She is forty-nine, a native of India, married, the mother of three school-age children, and a captain in the U.S. Air Force Reserve. She conducts a busy practice in gynecology and pediatrics in Alta Loma, besides maintaining a close involvement in professional, civic, charitable, and Muslim organizations. She is the founder of the Muslim Free Clinic, open without charge to all citizens. She campaigns against abuse of women, noting that female students encounter unique challenges if they are Muslim. "They are singled out because they wear the head scarf and cannot participate in some physical education activities, like swimming, because they would have to expose their bodies and thus violate the Islamic requirement of modesty."[11]

In recent years, Talat has provided leadership in the electoral campaigns of nineteen individual candidates—a few more of them Democrats than Republicans. She worked as a fundraiser and campaigner for Republican Rob Guzman in his two unsuccessful quests for election to the U.S. House of Representatives, but she also campaigned publicly for Democrat Bill Clinton in both of his campaigns for the presidency. She supported California Democrat

Barbara Boxer in her race for the U.S. Senate, Democrats George Brown of California and David Bonior of Michigan in their bids for re-election to the U.S. House of Representatives, and Democrat Rima Nashashibi in her campaign for election to the California State Assembly.

The complexity of Talat's political loyalty may mystify political novices, but it is not unusual: "I am a lifelong Republican—a registered one—but, in exceptional cases, I have contributed financially to the campaigns of Democrats and voted for them."

L oyalty motivates one Muslim political leader in California to focus on a specific Republican candidate, while it leads another to provide support to the entire Democratic Party slate of candidates. Both have emerged as role models for Muslims entering politics.

In November 1999, Suhail A. Khan, thirty-five, began serving as press secretary and campaign spokesman when U.S. Rep. Thomas Campbell of Campbell, California, announced his candidacy for the Republican nomination for U.S. Senator. Khan continued in that role after Republicans chose Campbell to oppose the reelection bid of Senator Dianne Feinstein, a Democrat. Before taking the assignment, Khan served as Campbell's legislative assistant in Washington. In 1997, I heard him address a large Muslim audience in Chicago, where, speaking with confidence and sincerity, he received rapt attention as he described his staff responsibilities. The campaign attracted national attention to both Campbell and his Muslim spokesman.

K han is not the first Muslim to have a major staff position on Capitol Hill. That distinction belongs to Khalil Munir, who served for several years as press secretary for Rep. Edolphus Towns, a Brooklyn Democrat. More than a dozen Muslims now work on Capitol Hill for Members of Congress.

Campbell became a favorite among Muslims, when he sponsored the Secret Evidence Repeal Act, legislation to outlaw secrecy in deportation hearings. He declared that the secrecy is a violation of constitutional rights of due process. When he first introduced the bill, twenty-five immigrants were being held for possible deportation based on secret testimony. Twenty of them were Muslims or Arabs, or both. By year's end, the bill was reported from the Judiciary Committee. By then, it had over one hundred co-sponsors. The only organizational opposition came from the Anti-Defamation League and the American Jewish Committee. With Ray LaHood, R-IL, my congressman, David Bonior, D-MI, and Mark Sanford, R-SC, as co-sponsors, Campbell won a legislative skirmish for immigrants in June 2000 when his amendment to prohibit funding of secret evidence cases won House of Representatives approval in a bipartisan vote of 239 to 173.[12] It was one of the few times in history that a majority in the House rejected the recommendation of major Jewish organizations. The American Jewish Committee expressed "deep regret."

It was viewed by Muslims as a victory for their religious community. In a June 2000 poll of seven hundred and fifty-five Muslims, 87 percent said they believe the Islamic community is the main target of the Immigration and Naturalization Service's controversial authority to use secret evidence in its proceedings against persons accused of unlawful immigration. The poll was conducted by Zogby International for the American Muslim Council, one of the earliest and strongest critics of the secret evidence law. Under it, such evidence is withheld from the accused but can become the basis for deportation. Campbell also opposed the continuation of economic sanctions against Iraq, contending that they cause great hardship for innocent people.[13]

Salam Al-Marayati praises Campbell. "He is always willing to listen to Muslim concerns. He's accessible, and that's important."

On election day, Feinstein received 56 percent of the vote, Campbell 36 percent. In a review of the congressional races, *The Jerusalem Post* cited only the Feinstein-Campbell race as being of concern to pro-Israel lobbyists and political action committees. It reported that pro-Israel forces united behind Feinstein because "...Campbell... has been outspoken on issues of the Arab-American community and is considered anti-Israel."

R ima Nashashibi, another Californian, is a political role model
for Muslim women. A Palestinian born in Jerusalem and
educated at the American University in Beirut, she lives in Orange
County and has long been prominent in California's Democratic
Party. With a smile, she says, "I have two full-time jobs, one
working for an insurance company to earn my living and the other
volunteering in Democratic politics."

Her commitment and enthusiasm have propelled her up the
party ladder, but she is also a leader in nonpartisan heritage
projects. She established an endowment that rewards individuals
who register Arab-Americans to vote and organizes projects that
preserve Palestinian arts and fashions.

At forty-five, she has a remarkable, groundbreaking record in
partisan politics. She was the first Muslim elected to serve as chair
of the Democratic Party of the sixty-seventh assembly district and
as vice-chair of the Democratic Party of Orange County. She was
also the first to be selected for several statewide party assignments.
In 1998, she sought the Democratic nomination for the State
Assembly and ran a close second, receiving 41 percent of the votes
cast. She is glad that she ran—"It was the best experience of my
life"—and looks forward to the next opportunity. Nashashibi says
that religion did not emerge as an issue in the campaign, at least
publicly. "To my knowledge, it was never mentioned, but most
activists in the district know I am Muslim because we had worked
together very closely in Democratic politics for many years. I am
proud to be a Muslim and have never tried to conceal it."

H ow can Muslims get started in politics? Nashashibi responds:
"Exactly the same way other citizens get started. Go to the
headquarters of the political party you like and offer to help. Or, if
a campaign is under way, go to the headquarters of a candidate you
especially like. Or, go to an elected official and offer to work as an
intern or volunteer. Local party leaders can point you in the right
direction."

Will Muslims feel comfortable as volunteers? "Of course. They
will enjoy the variety of people and situations. Some party activists

are dignified and refined. Others can be brusque and coarse at times. You will find prima donnas and boisterous people who shouldn't be taken seriously, but most are down-to-earth, nice people. They are a fair cross-section of the American people. Volunteers have the opportunity to meet candidates for public office and get acquainted with them as human beings, and not just as poster pictures or TV ads."

Should Muslims mention their religion when they volunteer? "There is no need to do so. Does a Christian, a Jew, or a Buddhist state his or her religion when volunteering? They do not. I didn't say anything about religion when I first volunteered. Muslims should volunteer as American citizens, not as Muslims. When you get to the party office, just explain that you don't have experience in politics and are eager to learn so you can help good candidates get elected."

If religion comes up, what should Muslims say? "Above all, don't be defensive. Be matter-of-fact about your religion. Usually, it will be enough to say that Islam is like Christianity and Judaism in many ways. For most people, that is enough detail, but if the discussion continues, you will have the opportunity to clear away some of the stereotypes. You can also mention that you have a lot of acquaintances in the Muslim community, and you may be able to get some of them to vote on election day and perhaps be campaign volunteers."

Are Muslim women welcomed to party politics? "Of course. The more the better. I'm a woman and a Muslim. In some Muslim countries, women tend to stay in the background, but not in America. All of the top elected state officials in Arizona happen to be women. Women are gaining prominence in all professions, not just in politics. I heard the other day that women are now more numerous in law schools than men. America is no longer just a man's world."

Will Muslim women who wear the traditional headscarf and long, loose-fitting dresses be welcome and feel comfortable? "They will be just as welcome as the Muslim women, like myself, who wear Western attire. At first, they may get a glance or two, but once they get acquainted, their attire won't make a bit of difference."

Nashashibi adds, "The people that make up the Democratic Party are as diverse in their motivations and interests as they are in their personalities and manners, and I suppose that the same is true in the Republican Party. For some of them—many of them—it is a matter of principle. For what I would call the political junkies, it's the excitement, the highs and lows, that come with election years. Year after year, they invest their time, energy, and money in the party. It's like betting on a horse or rooting for a baseball team. Once they are committed, many of them stay no matter what happens on election days or in between. If their 'horse' loses, some campaign workers may lose interest and drop out, but most will not. They remain loyal through thick and thin. People with that outlook are the bedrock of the party.

"For a lot of them, it's somewhat like a religious affiliation. Most Muslims have followed the religious path of their parents. The same is often true in politics. A lot of Democrats followed the political preference of their parents, and Republicans the same. Some may hope the affiliation and active work for a political party will lead to a good job in government. And sometimes that happens. Then, too, in the Democratic Party, any volunteer has a chance to be chosen for an appointive office. Some people become active for the party's social life. There are events to attend, some of them for just party members.

"I believe that most active Democrats want good government and like what most Democratic candidates and elected public officials stand for. Still, I don't underrate the excitement that comes with political activity. The most thrilling and satisfying part of party work is watching the returns come in on election night for the party as a whole and for the candidates you are supporting. It's like watching the Super Bowl or the World Series. A lot of elections are settled by just a few votes. When the party's candidates win, great! When they lose, those who were in there plugging still can go home with a certain satisfaction. They have no regrets about working hard in a good but losing cause. And besides, there's always tomorrow. Another election is always just ahead."

The substantial number of U.S. Muslims who accepted responsibilities in the 2000 political arena is heartening, partly because it was nearly empty of names four years before. Muslims are sometimes called a sleeping giant, because almost all Muslims keep idle substantial assets, financial and otherwise, that could be transformed into political influence. The law of inertia, a powerful force that is well known in physical science, is just as powerful within would-be politicians.

One afternoon, while conversing in the cloakroom just off the floor of the U.S. House of Representatives, Tim Lee Carter, a physician who left a medical practice in Kentucky to serve as a Member of Congress, offered a bit of wisdom gleaned from forty years in politics: "The hardest part of getting elected to Congress is deciding to run." I had never thought of it that way, but he was right. That first step is the biggest of all.

Most Americans—not just Muslims—stay away from politics, and candidacy, because of that challenging first step. In fact, they seldom vote. Nearly one-half of eligible voters fail to enter the polling places even in presidential elections. In some local elections, the turnout is five percent or less. A handful of votes often decide elections.

Non-voters should be ashamed of themselves. In failing to perform that basic duty of citizenship, they dishonor a great heritage and squander a precious right. All power and policy originate in the voter, and through politics the citizen can help shape government action at all levels. Over the years, I have heard many people say, "I stay away from politics. It doesn't pay to get involved." Some are more specific: "Getting into politics may hurt my career, keep me from getting a better job." "It's sure to hurt business." "I'd rather help worthy causes that are less controversial."

N ihad Awad, the national director of the Council on American Islamic Relations, summarizes the excuses for inaction that he hears most often from Muslims: "It's pointless to try." "It is wasted effort." "One person can't get anywhere." "The system is corrupt and immoral. We shouldn't sully ourselves by taking part." "We're afraid that if we get into politics, the FBI will start bothering us. For that reason, I won't even sign a petition."

Understandably, immigrants from countries where political activity is prohibited or discouraged may feel reluctant to take a public role in the electoral process in America. They need to be reminded, however, that political endeavor is a citizen's highest calling. Those who strive for good government serve their own loved ones, as well as all other citizens.

In classes for new citizens, immigrants learn that the right to vote is the most important of all rights, because, in America, the individual citizen has the opportunity to help exercise sovereign power. In every constituency, each voter—no matter how poor, no matter what his or her station in life may be—is equal to every other citizen when votes are counted.

Like other citizens, Muslims often underrate their own potential. Most people mistakenly assume that a large bank account and politically powerful friends are essential to success in politics. The historical record proves otherwise.

For example, Paul Simon of Illinois, a Democrat I have known and admired for fifty years, entered the political arena with no partisan connections and only a few dollars in his pocket. A Lutheran, his life is one of the great success stories in American politics. Noted for personal integrity and achievements in public policy, he won acclaim in the Illinois legislature, in Congress, and as a presidential candidate before taking an academic position at Southern Illinois University.[14]

P oliticians of Simon's quality seem to be in short supply, partly because of politics' shady reputation. Like all other human endeavors, political activity is far from pristine. It can be seamy, corrupt, mercenary, opportunistic, and wasteful, and some emerge from political activity with their reputations tainted. Even U.S. presidents sometimes go astray and fall hard from their pedestal.

The late Ambassador Adlai E. Stevenson II, who served in Springfield as governor of Illinois for two terms, once observed, "Honesty is next to Godliness. In Springfield, it's next to impossible." Stevenson, twice chosen as the Democratic candidate to oppose Republican Dwight D. Eisenhower for the presidency, may not have been joking when he made that statement.

At that time, despite Simon's endeavors, corruption lingered in the corridors of the Illinois State House in Springfield. A state senator confided one day that he had just come from a private meeting where he saw $40,000 in cash used to buy votes on pending legislation. Political misbehavior occurred on both sides of the political aisle. When Democrat Paul Powell, a popular secretary of state, died, investigators found shoeboxes full of currency in a closet in his hotel apartment. Cronies said that the money accumulated because Powell followed a personally profitable practice during his long political career. He routinely kept half of each political contribution for his own personal use. When he died, one of his contemporaries quipped, "He had a heart attack when he opened a shoebox and found shoes in it."

Nowadays, whether in Washington or in Springfield, campaign money is distributed in bigger bunches but more subtly. Very few Members of Congress, I believe, put money intended for campaign expenses in their personal bank accounts, but most of them welcome big donations as the expense of campaigning keeps soaring. One day I asked Tennyson Guyer, a House colleague from Ohio who was noted for his fine sense of humor, how he planned to vote on a pending bill. He looked up from his seat in the House chamber and, with an impish grin, said, "I haven't yet been financially advised."

Influence peddling is big business in Washington, providing full time employment to more than ten thousand people. Laden with money for political campaigns, these lobbyists exert far greater influence on legislators than citizens in their constituencies.

244 Silent No More

But these somber realities about the political arena should not discourage outsiders from entering it. To the contrary, they constitute a powerful incentive for good people to participate. Lobbyists are able to advance special interests only because individual citizens neglect their own responsibilities. People who engage honorably and stick to principles need have no fear that political involvement will taint their reputation or cause personal embarrassment.

Nihad Awad has detected a steady, fundamental improvement in the attitude of Muslims toward political activity: "We are witnessing a major shift. A lot of Muslims are having a change of heart. People who in the past donated only to mosques now also give generously to candidates for office. They are motivated by the tangible results and successes of grassroots efforts of the Muslims who are pioneering in politics.

"People who have had anxieties in the past are reconsidering. Some of the doubters of yesterday are now active in politics and enjoying the experience. They recognize how open the U.S. political system really is, and have come to realize that if they don't speak up and try to be an influence themselves, they can't expect others to speak on their behalf."

Ninety-six percent of the seven hundred fifty-five Muslims polled in June 2000 believe that Muslims should get involved in local and national politics.[15]

Rima Nashashibi advises citizens to avoid appearing defensive about their religion when entering political activity. By being matter-of-fact about Islam and its common links with Christianity and Judaism, Muslims will put new acquaintances at ease and enhance mutual trust and friendship.

But there are times when forthright assault on religious stereotypes is prudent, and 1960 was such a time. It marked a politician's historic victory over religious stereotyping.

It is commemorated in our home in a painting by our artist neighbor, Ollie Noll. It displays the front page of the November 6, 1960, issue of *The Pike County Republican,* a weekly newspaper that I owned at the time. The headline announced that ballots cast the previous day had elected John F. Kennedy to the presidency and me to the U.S. House of Representatives.

I t also signified a major advance against bigotry. In the 1960 campaign, Kennedy used political action—and acumen—to erase an ugly and persistent religious image that plagued the entire nation.

Early in his campaign, his Roman Catholic affiliation became a major, vexing issue. Dark predictions surfaced repeatedly that Kennedy, as president, would be manipulated by the Vatican, implying that Pope John would influence Kennedy to favor Roman Catholic public policy positions. The rumors were an echo of those of thirty-two years before, when the same stereotyping became a major factor in the failure of Roman Catholic Al Smith's 1928 bid for the White House.

Earlier in his political career, Kennedy used good-natured humor to lighten religious prejudice. A former colleague, John Kyl of Iowa, gave me the details of one such occasion. Before he left the Senate for the White House, Kennedy told Kyl that Senator James Eastland of Mississippi had once accepted his invitation to speak in Boston at a Democratic Party dinner. Aware that Mississippi's Catholic population was small in contrast to the large one in Massachusetts, Kennedy called Eastland aside before entering the dining hall and told him that Irish and Polish Catholics would be prominent in the audience. He cautioned him against saying anything that might offend them.

Eastland responded in his southern drawl, "Don't worry, son. I know how to handle this crowd." He began his speech by declaring his love for Irish and Polish Catholics, then added, "It's just those damned Roman Catholics that I can't stand." The diners, mostly Roman Catholics, laughed uproariously at Eastland's gaffe.

In his presidential campaign, Kennedy laid aside the light touch. He dealt seriously and directly with the religious issue and succeeded in turning the anti-Catholic stereotype to his advantage. On the campaign trail, he kept reminding audiences—correctly— that the U.S. Constitution "establishes no religious test for the presidency" and asserted just as often that religion should not become an issue in the campaign. Because of this repeated emphasis,

Kennedy made religion a major, persistent campaign issue, but his deft handling of it won him interfaith applause—and votes.

Once Kennedy became president, the anti-Catholic stereotype quickly disappeared, and I believe it is gone forever. This advance in religious tolerance is one of Kennedy's most important legacies. His use of political action in eradicating the stereotyping of Roman Catholics may inspire those who wish to correct misconceptions of Islam.

Another Democratic President, Bill Clinton, lifted Muslims to new levels of prestige in the political realm. During his second term, he appointed M. Osman Siddique, a Washington, D.C., businessman, as ambassador to Fiji, the first Muslim appointed to a U.S. ambassadorial post, and named Dr. Islam A. Siddiqui as deputy secretary of the Department of Agriculture, the first Muslim to occupy a position second only to a cabinet secretary. Siddiqui moved up the ladder in USDA after a long career as a scientist in California's department of agriculture.

Notes:

1. Interview, 12-17-2000.
2. Letter by Hamad of ADC, 10-29-1999.
3. *The Hamtramck Citizen,* 3-30-2000.
4. *The Detroit News,* 11-4-1999.
5. The Detroit News, 11-4-1999.
6. *The Hamtramck Citizen,* 11-18-1999.
7. *Queens Times Ledger,* 11-12-1998.
8. Interview, 5-23-1999.
9. AMA message, 8-21-2000.
10. Interview, 2-18-2000.
11. Interview, 10-24-1999.
12. CAIR Alert, 256.
13. AMC news release, 8-28-2000.
14. See Appendix B, "The Committee-of-One."
15. CAIR poll, 7-7-2000.

Chapter 12: The Muslim Bloc Vote

M uslims made political history during the 2000 presidential election, and, thanks to longstanding friendships as well as happenstance, I was an eyewitness as major steps toward the community's political maturity were taken.

Six leaders I met years ago emerged as the architects of success.

When we first met in 1985, Agha Saeed was already mentally sketching the Muslim political organization, the American Muslim Alliance [AMA], that he later founded.

During the same year, I had a glimpse of Salam Al-Marayati, who later became the director of the Muslim Public Affairs Council [MPAC].

Nine years later in Washington, D.C., just a few months after they established the Council on American Islamic Relations [CAIR], Nihad Awad and Ibrahim Hooper entered my life. I first met Omar Ahmad, chairman of the CAIR national board of directors, in July 1997, when I took part in a conference Saeed organized in St. Louis. My acquaintance with Yahya M. Basha, president of the American Muslim Council (AMC), did not begin until 2000, but I had long been acquainted with AMC's pioneering work in political activism since 1990, endeavors advanced by its first executive director, Abdurahman Alamoudi, and followed up beginning in 1998 by his successor, Aly R. Abuzaakouk.

The men make a formidable team. Awad, Al-Marayati, Abuzaakouk, Hooper, and Alamoudi are employed full time in the cause. The others devote many hours to it but earn their living in their professions, Saeed in education, Basha and MPAC's Maher Hathout in medicine, and Ahmad in technology.

When I think of Saeed, Alamoudi, Awad, and Hooper, the word driven comes to mind. They seem always in motion, never easing up. From my first discussion with Saeed in his small student apartment in Berkeley, I have never found him detached even for a moment from his goal of Muslim political action. I find the same intensity in Awad. During one of his rare, relaxed, reflective moments, he told me, "I've decided to dedicate my life to this cause." Ahmad, Abuzaakouk and Hooper probably have said the same thing to themselves, if not to others. Hooper is a serious, skilled writer who is totally fixed on the task of communication. Al-Marayati works in a more relaxed manner, reaching beyond the Muslim population in interfaith endeavors. The AMC, headed by Basha, has long worked in the partisan arena, making the presence of Muslims felt in the Administration and the Congress.

During the 2000 campaign, their talents meshed well. With the enthusiastic support of the rank and file of their own organizations, they formed a union and became a political powerhouse. They are largely responsible for writing one of the most momentous chapters in recent political history.

B y the time the presidential election campaign began, U.S. Muslims were ready for political leadership. Troubled by challenges to their civil rights at home—especially the use of secret evidence in deportation hearings and profiling at airports—and threats to Muslim interests in the Middle East, they entered the partisan arena in earnest.

Deep concern over the future of the Holy Land—especially Jerusalem—counted heavily. After first tending for the candidacy of Vice-President Al Gore, they shifted strongly to Governor George W. Bush. They abandoned Gore mainly, I believe, because of his deep attachment to Israel, particularly his acceptance of an undivided Jerusalem as its exclusive capital, and his guarded but clear support for the relocation of the U.S. embassy from Tel Aviv to Jerusalem.

While sympathetic to a number of the domestic policies advocated by Gore, Muslims had other, higher priorities. They pinned their hopes, faint though they may be, on Bush for U.S. policies in the Middle East that are fair to Arabs as well as Israelis.

They resented the failure of the Clinton-Gore administration—and its predecessors, both Democrat and Republican—to oppose aggressively Israel's claim to the entirety of Jerusalem. To Muslims, the relocation of the U.S. embassy would signify Washington's official acceptance of Israel's claim to the Holy City, a claim that violates the United Nations' prohibition against the acquisition of territory by force and serves as a precedent for other rogue states to acquire land by force from weaker neighbors.[1]

Gore underscored his attachment to Israel when asked what he would do as president if the Palestinians declared statehood outside the peace process. Gore responded, "I would consult with the government of Israel to see what the most helpful response from Israel's view might be."[2]

In conversations over recent years, Muslims have often expressed their strong resentment over the acquiescence of U.S. administrations in several developments they regard as pernicious. Chief among them:

- Israel's annexation of East Jerusalem which includes Al-Haram Al-Sharif [Arabic for the Noble Sanctuary], Islam's third holiest shrine;
- its harsh treatment of Palestinians living in the Occupied Territories;
- its biased policies that have prompted a steady increase in the number of Jews residing in East Jerusalem and in Jewish settlements in the West Bank and Gaza District; and
- the continuation of U.S. air assaults and economic sanctions against Iraq.

The air assaults began in 1991 when several Arab states joined the United States, Great Britain, and France in military attacks that forced Iraq to end its military occupation of Kuwait.

After Iraqi forces were driven out from Kuwait, the United States and Great Britain continued the air attacks, justifying them as a means of restricting Iraqi air operations and enforcing the sanctions. They were not authorized by the U.S. Congress or the United Nations and, in my opinion, clearly violate the terms of the War Powers Resolution, which I co-authored. Aside from the question of legality, they are counterproductive. They inflict casualties on innocent Iraqi civilians and cause destruction of their property, but they do not harm Saddam Hussein, Iraq's dictator. Indeed, they help him maintain, even strengthen, his political power and win him undeserved sympathy.

Sam Husseini, communications director of the Institute for Public Accuracy, explains why Palestinians are upset: "While the Israeli government has been talking peace for the past six years: Palestinians have seen fifty thousand more Jewish settlers illegally put into the West Bank and Gaza; Israel has demolished nearly one thousand Palestinians homes; there has been a threefold increase in Palestinian unemployment; the Israelis have arrested thirteen thousand Palestinians; and they have restricted Palestinians' freedom of movement, keeping them on little Swiss cheese patches of land on the West Bank."[3]

The veneration Muslims feel toward Jerusalem arises mainly from the city's close association with Islam and the night journey of the Prophet Muhammad to Jerusalem which is mentioned as blessed in the Quran: "Glory to (Allah) who did take His Servant (Muhammad) for a journey by night from the Sacred Mosque (the Ka'abah at Mecca) to the Farthest Mosque (al Aqsa Mosque in Jerusalem), whose precincts We did bless—in order that We may show him some of Our signs: for He is the One who hears and sees (all things)" (Quran 17:1). Muslims consider Jerusalem the spiritual home of all prophets and messengers of God. It was the first *qibla* (direction of daily prayers) for Muslims.

In a February 2000 national survey of 1000 American Muslims, commissioned by AMC, "the status of Jerusalem" was ranked as the second most important issue in a list of the ten issues of most concern.[4] In another national survey of 755 U.S. Muslims, in July 2000, the respondents cited the status of Jerusalem more often than any other political concern.[5]

Muslims see Israel's control of the eastern part of Jerusalem—long known as Arab East Jerusalem—as a constant threat to two mosques on Al-Haram Al-Sharif. One of them is the Al-Aqsa mosque, where the Prophet Muhammad prayed after his night journey from Mecca. The other is the Dome of the Rock mosque, from which the Prophet is believed to have ascended to heaven. These mosques are exceeded in Islamic importance only by those in Mecca and Madina in Saudi Arabia. Worldwide, Muslims face Mecca when they offer daily prayers, but in the early days of Islam, all faced Jerusalem.

In October 2000, *Haaretz,* a leading Israeli daily newspaper, editorialized on the worsening plight of Palestinians in Jerusalem and the Occupied Territories. It noted that seven years after the Oslo Accords were signed, Israel has yielded security control of only 12 percent of the West Bank and has, in effect, frozen Palestinian economic development. One of Israel's most extreme measures was making further cuts in the allotment of fresh water available to Palestinians in the Occupied Territories, an apportionment that was already only a fraction of the amount provided to Jews.

The newspaper questioned the sincerity of government policies toward Palestinians during those years: "Was Israel really giving up its attitude of superiority and domination, built up in order to keep the Palestinian people under its control? More than seven years have gone by, and Israel has security and administrative control of 61.2 percent of the West Bank and about 20 percent of the Gaza Strip, and security control over another 26.8 percent of the West Bank."[6]

A month before the presidential voting, U.S. Muslims were disturbed by the highly-publicized visit to Al-Haram Al-Sharif by would-be Israeli prime minister Ariel Sharon, the man who was censured by the Israeli government for his role in the 1982 massacre of nearly two thousand Palestinians in Beirut refugee camps of Sabra and Shatila. Sharon's visit to the Islamic shrine was widely viewed as a deliberate provocation. During the protracted violence that followed Sharon's visit there, it became apparent to U.S. Muslims that the fate of their shrines in Jerusalem is inextricably bound to the future of the Palestinians who live there.

The violence provoked harsh anti-Arab and anti-Muslim comment in the United States. Newspapers seemed almost unanimous in blaming Palestinians. *The Virginian-Pilot* newspaper, in its October 13 issue, quoted former Secretary of Education William Bennett, usually known for thoughtful opinions, as saying: "There is no moral equality between Israel and the Palestinians. One is a nation of violence and terrorism, and the other is one of democracy and peace."

The same day, the Associated Press quoted Franklin Graham, vice chairman of the Billy Graham Evangelistic Association and son of noted evangelist Billy Graham, as saying: "The Arabs will not be happy until every Jew is dead.... They all hate the Jews. God gave that land to the Jews. The Arabs will never accept that. Why can't they live in peace?"

Los Angeles Times syndicated columnist Cal Thomas stooped still lower, calling Islam "murderous." He cited it as "the threat of the present and the immediate future." *New York Post* columnist Rod Dreher wrote: "As the only outpost of the West in that savage and irrational desert, we owe the Israelis our loyalty.... The Israelis, whatever their failings, are fighting for us and for our civilization." The same day, MSNBC's Don Imus called Yasser Arafat a "dishrag head."[7]

In a rare exception to this abuse, Charley Reece, one of the few U.S. columnists who writes candidly about U.S. complicity in Israel's abuse of Palestinians, castigated official Washington: "American politicians would serve America better if they simply would be honest. All they have to do is say, 'Look, there are few Arab votes in my elections, so, for my own selfish reasons, I support Israel right or wrong.' That's a lot better than blaming the victims and making the United States look absurd and hypocritical in the eyes of the world. People all around the world know the score in American politics, but it enrages them when American politicians try to cover up their vote-selling by blaming innocent people."[8]

D uring a pre-election mass rally for Jerusalem in Lafayette Park, across from the White House, more than ten thousand Muslims heard a series of speakers discuss the plight of Palestinians and the threat to other Muslim interests in the Holy Land. It was sponsored by the National Task Force for the Crisis in Jerusalem and supported by seventeen National Muslim and Arab-American groups in the country.

In one of the spirited program's highlights, a group of orthodox rabbis from Brooklyn received enthusiastic applause when they stepped to the speakers' platform to show support for Palestinian human rights. Observing the Sabbath, their vows kept them from speaking to the crowd that day, a Saturday, but they stood silently on the platform while Saif Abdur Rehman, read their prepared statement of solidarity and sympathy: "We condemn the actions [of Israel] in these past weeks. The justice of the current situation lies entirely with the Palestinian people. They have been dispossessed. Political control over the land belongs to them."

The series of speakers divided their attention between concern for Palestinians and alarm over the future of Jerusalem. W. Mahdi Bray, president of the Coordinating Council of Muslim Organizations, a group that serves community groups in the Washington area, shared the management of the agenda with representatives of the sponsoring organizations. Abuzaakouk of AMC, declared: "Jerusalem is in the heart of every Muslim. Our administration must show fairness and not favoritism brokering a just peace."[9]

In my contribution to the program, I strayed from the non-partisan theme by focusing on the upcoming presidential election. Pointing to the White House just a block away from the immense gathering, I asked whether Muslims wanted a man heavily committed to Israel to serve as chief executive and commander-in-chief during the next four years, a period when decisions fundamental to Jerusalem's future may be made and the Middle East may even find itself embroiled in war.

I told the group that I hung my head in shame three days earlier on learning that my former colleagues in the U.S. House of Representatives approved, 365 to 30, a resolution that condemned the victims, not the perpetrators, of the violence that had engulfed Israel and the Occupied Territories during the previous month. The resolution denounced the beleaguered Palestinians, armed mainly with stones, and sympathized with Israel, whose high-tech military forces by then had killed one hundred and fifty-four Palestinians and injured over seven thousand others. The Israeli death toll was eight. The resolution repeated the bias expressed in a letter, dated October 12, in which ninety-four U.S. Senators urged President Clinton to "condemn the Palestinian campaign of violence" and "express American solidarity with Israel." The letter praised Israel for its "restrained response" and urged Clinton to put pressure on PLO leader Yasser Arafat to stop the civil strife. During the debate in the House of Representatives, four brave representatives spoke in opposition to the resolution—Democrats John Dingell of Michigan, Jim Moran of Virginia, and Nick Rahall of West Virginia, and Republican Dana Rohrabacher of California. Dingell told his colleagues, "The Israelis must realize that the Palestinians have a legitimate right to an independent state and to return to their homes, just as the Palestinians must realize Israel has a right to exist and desires safety and security.... I wonder why this legislation, in pinning blame solely on the Palestinians, fails to explain why Palestinians are angry."

D uring the rally for Jerusalem, one of the speakers unintention- ally stirred controversy over Islam's terrorist stereotypes. Abdurahman Alamoudi, a longtime leader of AMC, received shouts of support from the audience when he queried them on how they felt about Hezbollah and Hamas. Reporters covering the rally misread the exchange as an expression of Muslim support for terrorism.

When Alamoudi learned of their interpretation, he protested: "It was an expression of support for the exertions that the two organizations have undertaken against Israel's violation of the human rights of Palestinians and other Arabs. Israel has inflicted terror on Arabs, not the other way around. Moreover, terrorism and subjugation are violations of Islam."

The controversy prompted the Muslim Public Affairs Council [MPAC] to issue a statement reiterating its "stand against terrorism, based on Islamic grounds of zero tolerance on violence against civilians." Its executive committee stated its support for "legal and political means" to end the double-standard U.S. officials use in responding to acts of terrorism: "This double-standard overlooks Israeli acts of terrorism, even when Israeli forces engage in gross human rights violations." MPAC deplored "attempts by pro-Israel lobbies to marginalize the role of Muslims in U.S. politics." It added, "This effort has led to desperate campaigns of stereotyping and scape-goating against Muslim groups that represent the mainstream of citizens."

The national reaction was so intense, however, that Alamoudi issued a statement apologizing for "emotional statements" that were "interpreted as supporting terrorism." Sensing that the coverage of the episode might worsen the stereotypes of Islam, he offered to resign from his position as a senior official of AMC, an organization he had helped to guide throughout its existence. His offer to resign was refused by AMC leadership.[10] The national uproar over Hezbollah and Hamas was prompted by news reports that were broadcast or published after the conclusion of the program. The rally was one of the largest and most enthusiastic ever staged by Muslims.

D uring the presidential campaign, Muslims responded mainly to issues, not to a political party or personality.

Among those seeking the presidency, Ralph Nader was the unchallenged hero of Muslims. They admired his long, constructive service as a consumer advocate, his knowledge of public issues, eloquence, and proven integrity. So have I. During my years in Congress, I frequently saluted his commitment to worthy goals and respected the army of "Nader Raiders" that worked in his varied causes. I could always bring a smile to Nader's face when I asked when he intended to run for president as a Republican.

Muslims of Arab ancestry felt a close kinship with Nader, the first candidate of that heritage to run for the nation's highest office. Moreover, Muslims were pleased during the closing weeks of the campaign when he publicly deplored the lethal violence Israelis have been inflicting on Palestinians and demanded that sanctions against Iraq be lifted. They noted with approval that the Green Party, whose banner Nader carried, recommended that U.S. aid to Israel be suspended.

The Muslim decision to vote for Bush was what pollsters would call episode-specific. Many Americans, not just Muslims, favored Nader for the presidency over the two leading candidates, but they recognized that he was not a serious contender. Through his position as the Green Party candidate, he was attempting to build the party into an institution large enough to influence public policy in the future. His fans, by the thousands, recognized that Nader had no chance to win the presidency in 2000, and ultimately cast their votes elsewhere.

I n early 2000, polls showed the Democratic Party more popular among Muslims than the Republican Party. One conducted by AMC in late 1999 showed two-thirds of 844 respondents not affiliated to any political party. Others were closely divided between Republican and Democratic candidates. Another poll conducted by Zogby International showed 46 percent of Michigan Muslims leaning toward the Democratic Party, 26 percent maintaining an independent stance, and only 18 percent favoring the Republican Party.[11] In a June 2000 national survey of Muslims, 31 percent of those responding said the Democratic Party best represented their interests. Only 17 percent favored the Republican Party. Forty-three percent said they were either undecided or believed that neither major party was addressing their basic Muslim interests. Sixty-four percent supported Republican positions on moral issues, such as abortion and same-sex marriages. The Democratic Party got 56 percent favorable rating on social issues and 41 percent on economic. Muslims in thirty-seven states were surveyed. Fifty-six percent of those polled have a graduate degree, and 25 percent reported a household income of more than $100,000.

Dr. Mohamed Nimer, CAIR research director, said: "This survey shows that Muslims are independent voters, and that they will support those candidates who address their concerns."[12] A lonely dissent was heard in Dearborn, Michigan. Danny Agemy, 25, after hearing his instructor, Imam Hassan Qazwini, urge students at the University of Michigan to vote, protested, declaring, "God forbids any Muslim from participating in the elections of a non-Islamic state." Qazwini responded, "We should pursue our rights in the society we choose to live in. If I keep myself excluded, I am not influencing anybody." After class, Agemy distributed brochures that called voting "treason against Islam."[13] Agha Saeed believes the Muslims who share Agemy's views on voting constitute a tiny and dwindling minority. A survey of mosque leaders showed that 89 percent publicly urged Muslims to vote.[14]

M uslims were summoned to bloc voting for the presidency, as well as to the issue of Jerusalem, in a widely reprinted editorial by Richard T. Curtiss, executive editor of *The Washington Report on Middle East Affairs,* bimonthly magazine. In its June 2000 issue, he wrote, "Muslims from all ethnic backgrounds and from all social classes can agree on Jerusalem." He linked the fate of the Palestinians in the Holy Land to the plight of U.S. Muslims: "Until the Palestinian problem is solved, it is going to be increasingly difficult to be a Muslim in the United States. The Israeli lobby, with its incredible influence in the media, is going to continue to depict all Arabs and all Muslims as 'terrorists'—to be restricted, thwarted, ridiculed, and even deported for the 'security' of the non-Muslim community."

In a darkening sky, Curtiss found a ray of hope: "Solving the Palestine problem… can bring immediate benefits to everyone seeking to raise his or her children as Muslims in America. Israel is the issue around which the otherwise diverse American Jewish community has united and developed power. The theft of [the Palestinian] nation and of Islamic and Christian holy places, can work just as well for Muslims and Arab-Americans."

Curtiss urged Muslims to unite behind one candidate when they vote: "If Muslim voters demonstrate the discipline this year in such a close election, to turn out their communities to vote, then vote as a bloc, and publicize their vote, the United States will never again be the same. Its Middle East policy will become evenhanded for the first time since the creation of Israel. U.S. policy in South Asia may be liberated from the current influence of the Israel-India alliance."

He expressed his personal preference for Bush but said the act of bloc voting is more important than the identity of the candidate Muslims choose to support.

He noted that in the 1996 campaign, Muslims failed to establish bloc support for a presidential candidate but succeeded in two races for the U..S. Senate. Muslim support proved crucial in the election of two Democrats, Robert Torricelli of New Jersey and Tim Johnson of North Dakota, to the U.S. Senate. Early in the campaign to fill an open seat in New Jersey, Muslims endorsed Richard Zimmer, the Republican candidate. When Zimmer, concerned about Jewish reaction, announced that he did not seek the endorsement, this statement prompted members of the American Muslim Alliance, in what Curtiss called a "masterpiece of organization," to switch their support to Torricelli. This transfer of votes gave Torricelli a narrow victory, and, on several subsequent occasions, he publicly credited Muslims with providing the winning margin.

During the same year, out-of-state Muslims were upset when Republican Senator Larry Pressler of North Dakota supported legislation to end U.S. aid to Pakistan, a Muslim country. Although the distressed Muslims could not vote for the Democrat, Tim Johnson, they provided him with campaign funds that proved essential in his slim victory over Pressler.

C urtiss observed that Muslims are uniquely situated to exert political influence nationally: "By chance, or divine providence, according to your viewpoint, most Muslims, and a very high percentage of Christian Arab Americans, are concentrated in major metropolitan centers of a very few states. They are the tri-state area around New York City, as well as in Ohio, Michigan, Illinois and California. In a very close election, if most of the Muslim votes are cast as a bloc, the Muslim vote probably will determine which candidate wins in those states."

Muslims should not be deterred, he wrote, by the fact that they constitute only 3 percent of the American population. He noted that the pro-Israel lobby, representing at most only 2 percent of the population, is generally rated as the second most-powerful lobby in the United States, more powerful than the lobbies for guns, tobacco, teachers, or any of the others. Only the American Association of Retired Persons, claiming to represent 25 percent of the population, is rated more powerful than the lobby for Israel.[15]

After writing that article, Curtiss suffered a light stroke that put him temporarily on the sidelines. At the AMA national convention in Los Angeles on September 30, I heard his daughter, Delinda Hanley, read, to strong applause, his summons to bloc voting. It was the first time I had focused on his message, and, during the remaining weeks before election day, I quoted his words whenever I addressed gatherings, including CAIR's national convention on October 7 in Washington, D.C.

B y far, the most important factor that prompted Muslims to vote as a bloc for Bush was the unity and perseverance of the leaders of the four principal Muslim public policy organizations: the American Muslim Alliance [AMA], the Council on American Islamic Relations [CAIR], the American Muslim Council [AMC], and the Muslim Public Affairs Council [MPAC].

AMC's pioneer leader Abdurahman Alamoudi had summoned Muslims to unity in January 1998, when he wrote: "The time has come to establish a coordinating council of American Islamic organizations." In the article, he elaborated on ideas he had presented at the 1997 AMA convention.[16]

In May 1998, two years before the presidential campaign, representatives of the four groups formed the American Muslim Political Coordination Council [AMPCC]. Dr. Agha Saeed, the founder and chairman of AMA, served as the first coordinator.

Later in 1998, AMC's Abuzaakouk followed up by urging national Muslim organizations to invite candidates for public office to their meetings, and directing the national distribution of voter registration kits, a campaign that received coverage in *The Washington Post*, on *National Public Radio*, and other media.

In February 1999, after agreeing to work on a joint agenda, the group reached beyond the Muslim community by meeting with the Council of Presidents of Arab American Organizations. Those attending, in addition to representatives of the four Muslim groups represented in AMPCC, were leaders of the American Arab Anti-Discrimination Committee [ADC], Arab American Institute [AAI], the National Association of Arab Americans [NAAA], and the Association of Arab University Graduates [AAUG]. The meeting resulted in full agreement over four key issues: Jerusalem, the Secret Evidence Repeal Act, profiling, and establishing September 1999 as "The Voter Registration and Education Month." It also led to long range cooperation in registration, civic education, and leadership training.[17]

M uslims began organized campaign activities early in 1999. For several weeks before primary elections, working through its ninety-three chapters in thirty-one states, the AMA network instructed Muslims gathered in schools and mosques in the electoral process, the role of political parties, and the contents of the ballot. It issued primary voting recommendations in all major states. In California, a post-election analysis showed that 82 percent of the candidates and ballot propositions recommended by AMA were successful. In April, AMA leaders urged Muslims to volunteer their help during the presidential nominating conventions.

In July 1999, AMC President Basha organized a meeting in Detroit where representatives of seven national Muslim organizations met with Governor John Engler of Michigan, an early leader in the presidential campaign of George W. Bush. They presented Muslim concerns to Engler in a discussion that was the first contact between U.S. Muslim organizations and a principal organizer of the Bush candidacy.[18]

In the late spring and summer of 2000, all four Muslim policy organizations sponsored workshops in major cities for candidates, campaign volunteers, and prospective voters.

At its annual convention, held June 22-25 in Washington, D.C., AMC instructed delegates in campaign issues, procedures, and voter registration. It distributed instructions for campaign volunteers, and later developed a base of Muslim voters, published positions taken by individual candidates, and placed these documents on the AMC website.

Voter-registration activities came to a climax on September 15, designated as Hesham Reda Voter Registration Day, in recognition of the pioneering work of the director of MPAC who had died a few months earlier. Earlier, Reda chaired the first AMC chapter in the nation. Registration tables were set up in mosques, Islamic centers and schools throughout the country. [19]

The most dramatic step toward nationwide Muslim unity occurred during the annual Labor Day convention of the Islamic Society of North America [ISNA], held near Chicago's O'Hare airport. At the end of his remarks to an audience of more than ten thousand Muslims, Agha Saeed announced that AMPCC had decided to put aside all other campaign issues and recommend bloc voting by Muslims in the presidential election. He said the council, after interviewing the principal candidates, would announce its recommendation for the presidency two weeks before the voting.

Concluding his remarks, Saeed invited to the speaker's platform Omar Ahmad and Nihad Awad of CAIR and Basha and Aly R. Abuzaakouk of AMC. Noting that MPAC had earlier pledged its support, Saeed brought the audience to its feet by declaring, "We are not fighting. We are united. And two weeks before the election, we will make up our collective mind, and issue an advisory for the presidential candidate."

To a roar of approval from the audience, the Muslim leaders joined hands and raised them high as they shouted, "We will make a difference!" The pledge was repeated in wave after wave of audience response.[20]

AMPCC officials announced their decision to support Republican George W. Bush for president during a news conference on October 23 in Washington, D.C. It occurred eighteen days after the group had a fruitful interview in Detroit with the

Texas governor. At the news conference, Saeed explained: "Governor Bush took the initiative to meet with local and national representatives of the Muslim community. He also promised to address Muslim concerns on domestic and foreign policy issues." Basha credited Bush for speaking out against "secret evidence and airport profiling."[21] Aware that Gore had cancelled an appointment with AMPCC leaders, Ibrahim Hooper, communications director for CAIR, said: "The main factor was the governor's accessibility to Muslim leaders." He added, "He is our best bet to do away with secret evidence [in deportation hearings]."

Others speaking during the news conference were Omar Ahmad and Nihad Awad of CAIR; Abuzaakouk of AMC; Salam Al-Marayati of MPAC; and Eric Vickers of AMA. Representatives of the Islamic Society of North America [ISNA] and the Islamic Circle of North America [ICNA] attended as observers.[22]

The spokesmen were not more specific about Bush positions, because Bush himself had not been more specific. The endorsement, in great measure, was a rejection of Gore, who they felt had been unresponsive to Muslim interests. The endorsement was reported widely by national media and circulated to Muslims through e-mails, notices in mosques and Islamic centers, and sermons by Imams during congregational prayers on Friday before the election. In supporting the decision, two of the principals, Saeed of AMA and Al-Marayati of MPAC, departed from their well-known allegiance to the Democratic Party.

Three days after the endorsement, Bush elaborated his views on profiling in a videotape message provided to Basha. In it, Bush said, "Airline travelers have experienced harassment and delay simply because of their ethnic heritage. Such indiscriminate use of passenger profiling is wrong and must be stopped. The security of our country and our people is of course the foremost consideration. Yet, that does not justify a disregard for fairness, dignity, and civil rights."[23]

N o sooner had Muslim leaders announced the campaign for Bush than Democrat Hillary Rodham Clinton, the wife of

President Clinton, offended Muslims by returning $1000 to Abdurahman Alamoudi of AMC and $50,000 that members of the American Muslim Alliance [AMA] had contributed to her campaign three months earlier. Clinton announced the refund on October 26, three days after AMPCC endorsed Bush.

Clearly fearful of a backlash from New York's large Jewish and pro-Israel population, Clinton declared, "I strongly disagree with the positions taken by this group [AMA]. Every penny of [the $50,000] is going back." She accused the Muslim donors of making "offensive and outrageous" statements and said Agha Saeed, president of the alliance, supported the Palestinian use of "armed resistance" against the Israelis. She received immediate applause from Jewish organizations for the refund decision, but Saeed protested: "I am pro-Palestinian, but at the same time I am willing to have a reasonable settlement with the Israelis. I have also said that I support the peace process and that the conflict [in the Middle East] was political, not theological. But none of those things are being mentioned."

Salam Al-Marayati said he "got a sinking feeling" when he read about Clinton's decision. "It was happening again," he said. "Agha Saeed was successful in unifying the Muslim vote and for the first time in creating a voting bloc. It is no surprise that he is now the target. It happens to any of us who is successful in gaining access for Muslims."

Dean E. Murphy wrote in *The New York Times*: "As Mrs. Clinton's campaign aides began returning about one hundred checks from members of the American Muslim Alliance, Muslims across the country were reminded of how difficult it remains for them to make inroads into American politics and how disputed remarks about other parts of the world can derail the acceptance of Muslim Americans here. They also contend that extremist views by Muslims carry far greater negative consequences for Muslim Americans than extremist remarks in support of Israel do for Jewish Americans."[24]

In a surprising twist to the campaign, New York Muslims ultimately embraced Clinton's candidacy. They found the campaign tactics of her Republican opponent, U.S. Rep. Rick Lazio, even more offensive than Clinton's decision to refund the contributions.[25]

At one point, Lazio supporters used a telephone blitz to accuse Clinton and U.S. Muslim organizations of being linked to groups behind the bombing of the USS *Cole* in Yemen, an explosion that killed seventeen U.S. sailors. A *Washington Post* reporter called the calls "political pornography." After waiting a week, Lazio denied responsibility for the accusation but called the funds that Clinton returned "blood money." He charged that she hosted Muslims at White House events, as if such hospitality was somehow sinful.[26] Despite Clinton's refund decision, New York Muslims helped her to an easy, 12-percent victory on election day. The contest was the nation's most closely-watched non-presidential campaign of the year.

Noting the controversy, Dr. John L. Esposito, director of the Center for Muslim-Christian Understanding at Georgetown University, remarked, "Americans have been raised in a country that is predominantly Judeo-Christian. Their experience with Islam is negligible. What they have to operate on is stereotypes."

An AMC news release declared, "It is totally un-American to turn against Muslim and Arab groups and use them as scapegoats at election time." It added that it is unfair to deny First Amendment protection rights to individual American Muslims "for views they may express as citizens of a free society."

An organization called Jews for Racial and Economic Justice condemned the anti-Muslim bias in the New York race, as well as in a campaign in Georgia. In an Atlanta-area congressional district, Republican candidate Sunny Warren followed Lazio's example, accusing her opponent, U.S. Rep. Cynthia McKinney, a Democrat, of taking "blood money" when she accepted contributions from Muslims. After responding that "racist innuendo and hate-mongering have no place in an election campaign or any respectable discourse," McKinney coasted to reelection with a 20 percent margin over Warren.

CAIR concluded, "All the political candidates who engaged in Muslim-bashing in their campaigns were defeated."[27]

Although not recognized in major media, Florida Muslims deserved credit for clearing George W. Bush's path to the White House. His statewide margin in the official count was so thin that any of several forces and factors could be cited as important, if not crucial, but, in my estimate, the impact of Muslim bloc voting towered above all others.

The Texas governor started from a low point in his eleven-month climb to a Muslim landslide. A series of surveys chronicled his ascent.

In December 1999, the eve of the 2000 primary elections, a survey of 734 eligible Muslim voters, commissioned by Dr. Mohamed Nimer, CAIR's director of research, showed only 25 percent supporting Bush. Fifteen percent favored Democrat Bill Bradley and 15 percent were in Vice-President Al Gore's corner. The others were undecided.[28]

When Bradley dropped out as a candidate four months later, most of his Muslim support went to Gore. In June, a poll of 755 Muslims, commissioned by AMA, showed 33 percent for Gore, with Bush up only slightly at 28 percent. Almost one-fourth of those surveyed were undecided. Sixty-four percent reported voting in the 1998 general election and 90 percent said they planned to vote on November 7.[29] A Zogby International Poll, commissioned by AMC in April 2000, showed the political diversity of the Muslim community, with 46 percent inclined toward the Democratic Party and 16 percent toward the Republican Party. It also showed that 25 percent consider themselves liberal and 29 percent conservative. By mid-September, a survey showed a sharp increase for Bush. In a poll of 1,022 eligible voters, 40 percent favored Bush, 25 percent Nader, and 24 percent Gore.[30] By October, the tide had shifted.

In the final eight weeks of the campaign, Muslim support for Bush nearly doubled. A CAIR election-day exit poll of 1,774 Muslim voters, a sampling large enough to assure reasonable accuracy in projections, disclosed 72 percent for Bush, 19 percent for Nader and 8 percent for Gore. Thirty-eight percent said they voted for the first time, close to the 42 percent finding in an AMA-sponsored exit survey. Responses to the CAIR poll came from almost every state: 22 percent were from California, 10 percent from Virginia, 8 percent each from Illinois, Maryland, and New York, 7 percent from Texas and 6 percent from New Jersey. Sixty-nine percent of the respondents were male. Sixty-eight percent were thirty-nine years of age or younger.[31]

T he importance of Muslim bloc voting is underscored by its magnitude, as well as its focus. Accepting seven million as the Muslim population on election day, 70 as the percentage of those who are eligible to vote, and 65 the percentage of those actually voting, the national turnout of Muslims on election day came to 3.2 million. At 72 percent of the total, the Muslim vote for Bush totaled 2.3 million, while 256,000—8 percent—supported Gore. About 900,000 of the Muslims cast ballots for the first time, more than triple the total turnout for the vice-president. An exit poll of Muslims conducted by the American Muslim Alliance showed 80 percent voting for Bush. An AMC exit poll of 732 Muslim voters showed 68 percent for Bush, 10 percent for Gore, and 18 percent for Nader.

The percentage for Bush was even higher in Florida, the home of many AMA and AMC chapters and the state that proved to be pivotal in the long wrangle over who won the presidency. On election night, Dr. Sami Al-Arian of Tampa, an AMA leader, directed a   telephone survey of three hundred and fifty Florida Muslims who had voted. It showed that Bush received 91 percent of the votes, Nader 8 percent, and Gore 1 percent. Even after making allowances for the limited extent of the survey, it remains impressive evidence of a powerful Muslim tide for Bush.

Applying the assumptions used in the national analysis and accepting 200,000 as the statewide Muslim population, 140,000 Florida Muslims were eligible and 91,000 actually voted. If 80 percent—a conservative estimate—voted for Bush, this means he received 72,000 Muslim votes. If 8 percent—a generous level—voted for Gore, his total vote came to 7,238. Taking CAIR's report that 38 percent of Muslim voters cast ballots for the first time, 26,600 of the Muslim votes Bush received were from first-timers.

Al-Arian observed, "Political pundits have been slow in acknowledging the crucial, even decisive, role of the Muslim vote in Florida."[32]

During the presidential campaign, Muslims were largely ignored by Vice-President Al Gore, the Democratic candidate, and his allies, and, despite their near-unanimous turnout for Bush, they received relatively little attention during the Texas governor's quest for votes.

Bush made only one televised statement that bestirred Muslims, but it reverberated throughout the community. During a presidential debate with Gore three weeks before the voting, Bush sharply criticized government use of secret evidence in hearings on the deportation of immigrants. He denounced secret evidence as "not the American way" and declared, "We've got to do something about it." Muslims regarded the secret-evidence controversy as a major issue and took Bush's declaration as a promise of corrective action if he became president. Most Muslims believe they are the main target of secret evidence.[33]

Bush's comment may have been enough to motivate many of Florida's Muslims to enter polling places for the first time and cast their ballots for the Texas governor. American Muslim Council President Yahya M. Basha cited Bush's statement as "one of the highlights of this election and this campaign." He told the Associated Press that Bush had "obviously noticed" lobbying on the issue by the Muslim and Arab-American communities and added, "The Clinton administration talked about it but did absolutely nothing."[34]

The secret evidence controversy may explain why Bush's support among Muslims in Florida was above the national average. By election day, the controversy had long been a raging, much-publicized issue among Muslims nationally, but nowhere else with as much intensity as in Florida. The reason for this focus was the plight of Dr. Mazen Al-Najjar, a Muslim Palestinian on the faculty of the University of South Florida, who had been locked up in a Bradenton jail for three and one-half years. He was charged with holding a lapsed student visa and held without bond while he fought against deportation. In proceedings before a U.S. immigration court, evidence that he was not allowed to see was sufficient to convince the judge that he was guilty of supporting terrorist organizations in the Middle East. Al-Najjar denied the allegation, and his attorneys protested that the secrecy policy effectively denied him due process.

The Florida media prominently reported the court battles and the public protests, as well as the initiatives for Al-Najjar's relief that were undertaken in Congress. The Tampa Bay Coalition for Justice and Peace, a group organized and headed by Al-Arian, generated a steady flow of publicity in Florida, including more than one hundred feature articles and over fifty editorials and commentaries. All deplored the use of secret evidence. The *St. Petersburg Times* declared that "secret evidence is fundamentally unfair" and warned, "Al-Najjar's case speaks volumes about our nation's commitment to the principles of justice, and what it says isn't worthy of pride."[35] In October, the immigration judge who ordered Al-Najjar's incarceration reconsidered his decision.

Al-Najjar was released on an $8,000 bond on December 16, after being locked up for 1,306 days. Al-Arian's group praised the American Muslim Alliance, Professor David Cole, the American Civil Liberties Union, and U.S. Reps. Tom Campbell, R-CA, and David Bonior, D-MI, for supporting their endeavors. The group saluted Bonior as "truly the conscience of America."[36] Three days earlier, the American Muslim Council [AMC], also prominent in promoting Al-Najjar's release, celebrated the release of Dr. Anwar Haddam, a Muslim who had been held without charge for four years in a Stafford, Virginia, detention center, on the basis of secret evidence. AMC executive director Aly Abuzaakouk credited the release to "the sustained grassroots efforts of our community."[37]

Muslims were the main new political element in Florida, whose twenty-five electoral votes finally settled the outcome of one of the most protracted presidential contests in history. In the final certification, the Texas governor won Florida—and the presidency—by less than one thousand votes. In achieving that tiny margin, Bush benefited substantially from Muslim bloc voting.

Florida Muslims provided him with a net margin that exceeded 60,000 votes, sixty times his winning margin.

If Muslims had not voted as a bloc for Bush, the Florida outcome would not have been contested. Given the normal Muslim tendency toward Democratic candidates, Gore would have received, in my opinion, about as many Muslim votes as Bush. He would have emerged as the clear winner shortly after the polls closed.

There would have been no controversy over Florida election laws or procedures, hearings and judgments in state and federal courts, and vote-recounting spectacles. The word chad—dimpled, pregnant or otherwise—would have enjoyed public usage only as the name of a little known country.

The Muslim bloc voting success was not a sudden happenstance. It resulted from the hard work of many organizations and individuals who contributed over the years to the discourse on the importance of Muslim voting, as well as those who took part in the mobilization of voters during the 2000 campaign. Since its inception in 1990, AMC has made voter registration and Muslim participation in politics its sole objective. In the 1996 campaign, it published a guide for Muslim voters. The list of people and organizations mentioned in this chapter is not comprehensive. I am sure there are thousands of unheralded individual Muslims and dozens of organizations whose contributions are as significant as those who are mentioned.

Professor Sulayman S. Nyang, an expert on Muslim political behavior, calls the bloc voting "the result of a long process of consciousness-raising among the Muslims."

He adds: "To get such numbers of voters in Florida and elsewhere, all major national organizations had to galvanize to action many reluctant voters. These are members of our community who are apolitical for a variety of reasons. Some are continuing a tradition of political apathy and indifference from Middle Eastern societies where military, civilian or royal authoritarianism has made them allergic to politics. Others are still caught in the web of the 'myth of return.' Preoccupied with the idea of striking it rich and determined to return home laden with the Golden Fleece, these Muslims see America as a fertile ground for self-enrichment. In their view, political activity is simply a nuisance."

I n 2000, African-Americans did not dismiss the electoral process as a nuisance. They voted in nearly the same percentage as other Americans, but most of the Muslims—like other African-Americans—voted for the vice-president, following the long tradition of strong support for Democratic presidential candidates, a tradition that began with the election of Franklin D. Roosevelt in 1932. They did so despite the support Bush received from African-Americans during his years as governor of Texas, the near-certainty that he would name Colin Powell, an African-American, as secretary of state, and other African-Americans to high positions in his administration, and the prominence of AMA national board member Eric Vickers, an African-American civil rights attorney, in the Muslim campaign for Bush.

At the same time, organized African-American Muslims who opted for Gore avoided an open rupture with the pro-Bush forces. Two weeks before the presidential election, Ali Khan, leader of the Council for Good Government [CGG], joined a colleague, Ayesha Mustafa, in offering this advice to African-American Muslims: "While the Muslim American Society and the Council for Good Government encourage everyone to get out and vote on Tuesday, November 7, 2000, as your right and obligation, the weigh-in on who is the better candidate is up to you—as local and world events rapidly continue to unfold."[38] Khan's organization is closely affiliated with the Muslim American Society, a prestigious organization of African-Americans led by Imam W. Deen Mohammed.

It is noteworthy that the statement encouraged African-American Muslims to exercise their own judgment. Khan did not issue a call for bloc voting for Gore, although he did make an indirect endorsement of the vice-president. As Saeed later observed, "He left the door open for African-American Muslims to express their care and sensitivity for Palestine and other relevant international issues by voting for Bush." Khan's restraint in language must be accepted as a remarkable gesture of cordiality with AMPCC.

The African-American Muslim turnout on election day was substantial. The total population is 1.75 million, with 1.22 million of voting age. Analysis suggests that 50 percent, or 612,500, actually voted. Observers believe that about 15 percent— in all, 91,800—voted for Bush, nearly twice the 8 percent Bush received from African-Americans in general. It is likely that some African-American Muslims decided to stay away from the polls, rather than break ranks with either AMPCC or other Blacks.

Nyang believes African-American Muslims who voted for Bush were largely "those who have either assimilated successfully within the immigrant communities or are beneficiaries of the bourgeoisifying tendencies of the puritan ethics of the Nation of Islam and the patriotic Islamism of Imam W. Deen Mohammed."[39]

Recognizing the political importance of African-American Muslims, AMPCC leaders are now making arrangements for ongoing consultation and coordination with the Council for Good Government. They plan to work with African-American Muslims as other policy and partisan endeavors are undertaken in the future.[40]

On November 7, 2000, U.S. Muslim bloc voting brought about a major alteration of the American political landscape. As political leaders study the day's election returns, they will gain a new awareness of America's Muslim community and, accordingly, make substantial changes in their tactics in future campaigning for most offices, not just the presidency.

During the year, over seven hundred Muslims sought election as candidates, both Republicans and Democrats, for offices ranging from convention delegate and precinct committeeman to membership in state legislatures and Congress. One hundred and fifty-two candidates were victorious.[41]

In future campaigns, the Muslim tide may be even greater, given the above-average birthrate among Muslims, the enthusiasm that the year 2000 successes will impart, and the likelihood that African-Americans will be more prominent.

Inayat Lalani writes: "In the past, when we Muslims asked for the time of the day, Democrats, upon realizing our religious affiliation, would run without responding. Republicans would stop, give us the time of the day, and then run. As a result, although our natural immigrant, underprivileged instincts favor Democrats, we would hold our nose and often vote for Republicans. I suspect that, in the wake of the Muslim bloc voting success, things will change fast."[42]

In major political campaigns of the future, Muslims and their money are unlikely to be rejected—or Muslim candidacies neglected. In a dramatic turn from the recent past, most party leaders will compete aggressively for "the Muslim vote." Every serious contender for a major office will seek, not cancel, an interview with Muslim leaders. As Albert Gore lists errors in his presidential campaign, his failure to reschedule his cancelled date with AMPCC leaders may head the list.

During the presidential campaign, Muslims met all of the tests set forth by Richard T. Curtiss when he issued his call for bloc voting. They turned out the vote, voted in a bloc, and publicized their vote. These accomplishments may not immediately yield the new even-handed U.S. policy in the Middle East and South Asia that Curtiss forecast, but they surely are a big step in that direction.

After analyzing Muslim voting, Agha Saeed declares, "In this year's election, U.S. Muslims crossed the political Rubicon. They formed a new national coalition of voters." He is confident that Muslims will reach another important goal in the near future: "The election of a Muslim to Congress will have historic importance, not just for Islam, but for all America. It will immediately help to erase stereotypes within the entire congressional membership and beyond, and the person elected will become a role model for young Muslims who are considering a political career."[43]

Based on my experience in Congress, I agree with Saeed's appraisal and forecast. Nothing improves the congressional mindset better than direct personal acquaintance and fellowship. The arrival of a Muslim or two within the congressional circle will fundamentally and permanently dim the stereotypes that are now a fact of life on Capitol Hill.

Saeed and his colleagues have led Muslims to important attainments. The publicity yielded by bloc voting and related political activities will improve public awareness of the size and favorable character of the Muslim community.

Most Americans will be surprised as they learn of a new 2.3-million Muslim voting bloc, and impressed that all of the principal leaders of the four Muslim groups who organized the bloc voting are foreign-born citizens with degrees in higher education. All have proceeded with dignity, consideration, and professionalism, as well as spirited determination. Four of them—AMA's Saeed, MPAC's Hathout, AMC's Basha, and CAIR's Mohamed Nimer, hold doctorate degrees. And none seems inclined to rest on past laurels.

On November 26, two weeks before the presidential contest was settled, Agha Saeed invited Muslims to gather in Newark, California, to review the campaign just ended and make plans for those in 2002 and 2004. His invitation read: "Join us, if you want to help elect Muslims to Congress in the upcoming elections." Thirty-four Muslim community leaders attended, formed committees, and set an agenda for the next election cycle.

Notes:

1. Interview with Agha Saeed, 12-10-2000.
2. *Washington Report on Middle East Affairs,* June 2000, p. 22–24.
3. *USA Today,* 10-10-2000.
4. AMC release, 2-29-2000.
5. CAIR release, 7-6-2000.
6. *Haaretz ,* 10-18-2000.
7. MPAC bulletin, 11-7-2000; and CAIR bulletin, 10-18-2000.
8. *Orlando Sentinel,* 10-19-2000.
9. AMC release, 10-3-2000.
10. Interview with Abdurahman Alamoudi, 11-20-2000.
11. *Christian Science Monitor,* 11-2-2000.
12 CAIR release, 7-6-2000.
13. *Christian Science Monitor,* 11-2-2000.

14. Interview with Agha Saeed, 12-2-2000.
15. *Washington Report on Middle East Affairs,* June 2000, pp. 22–24.
16. Washington Report on Middle East Affairs, January-February, p.50.
17. AMC release, 8-16-1999.
18. AMC release, 7-28-1999.
19. Interview with Agha Saeed, 12-2-2000.
20. AMC release, 10-5-2000.
21. *St. Petersburg Times,* 10-24-2000;
    Los Angeles Times, 10-23-2000; AMA news release 10-23-2000.
22. AMC release, 10-26-2000.
23. *New York Times,* 10-27-2000.
24. *USA Today* ,10-26-2000.
25. *Washington Post,* 10-30-2000.
26. CAIR release, 12-7-2000.
27. CAIR Research, "American Muslims and the 2000 Elections," 12-18-2000.
28. CAIR news release, 7-6-2000.
29. AMC release, 20-8-2000,*Washington Times*, 20-9-2000.
30. CAIR news release, 11-2-2000.
31. CAIR news release, 11-14-2000.
32. CAIR news release, 11-17-2000.
33. Ibid., 11-17-2000.
34. *St. Petersburg Times,* 10-24-2000.
35. *St. Petersburg Times editorial,* 11-21-2000.
36. AMA news release, 12-12-2000.
37. AMC release, 12-13-2000.
38. *Muslim Journal,* 26, no. 5 (11-10-2000).
39. Interviews with Agha Saeed,
    Sulayman Nyang, and Eric Vickers, 12-26-2000.
40. Interview with Agha Saeed, 12-26-2000.
36. Interview with Agha Saeed, 12-1-2000.
42. E-mail, 12-22-2000.
43. AMA news release, 11-17-2000.

Chapter 13: The Challenge Ahead

As we confront America's false images of Islam, all must acknowledge that Muslims, like Christians and Jews, have a blemished history when it comes to religious tolerance. No one's laundry is spotless, but historians may discover that Muslim laundry has the least stains.

Over the centuries, leaders of all three monotheistic faiths have treated many non-believers with extreme brutality in gross violation of their own religious doctrines and principles. Stereotypes propagated by Christian leaders, for example, led to the slaughter of Muslims in Jerusalem during the Crusades and to the cruel execution of many Muslims and Jews during the Inquisition in Spain and France.

America's record is mixed. On one page is the idealism set forth in our nation's basic documents and expressed with regularity by U.S. leaders through the years. On another is our nation's splendid record as a place of refuge for people fleeing religious wars.

Other pages are smeared with religious intolerance.

Years ago, native Indians were scorned as heathens so dangerous that they had to be slaughtered. Slaughtered they were, and Christians did most of the slaughtering. America has the shameful distinction of being one of the few countries in the Western Hemisphere where settlers from abroad deliberately killed off the native population.

For nearly three centuries, U.S. citizens, mostly Christian, held African-Americans—many of them Muslims—as personal property, mistreated them in despicable ways, and routinely denied them the opportunity to practice their religion. A constitutional amendment ended slavery more than a century ago, but African-

Americans were terrorized by mobs and many of them murdered during the decades that followed. In all, nearly ten thousand were victims of lynching. For several generations, professed Christians, many marauding under the Ku Klux Klan banner, kept the descendants of slaves segregated from other citizens and ruthlessly denied justice in voting, housing, employment, education, and public accommodations.

Early in my congressional career, Democrat William L. Dawson, the first African-American to become a committee chairman in the U.S. House of Representatives, expressed the plight of his race to a white colleague: "If you think you have problems, just imagine what life would be like if you were black all over."[1] To this day, African-Americans are not fully accepted by much of the white community as equal before the law and before God. Despite the valiant endeavors of Rosa Parks, Malcolm X, Martin Luther King, Jr., and others, stereotypes still keep most of them segregated and denied opportunity and dignity.

Other ethnic and religious groups have also suffered from false images. In the first half of the nineteenth century, Mormons fled to Utah from mobs whose rage was fired by religious stereotypes. For years, Irish Catholics suffered employment discrimination. In the nineteenth century, the Know Nothing Party symbolized anti-Catholic sentiment.

"Gentlemen's" agreements kept Jews and African-Americans from housing and social opportunities until federal legislation outlawed such discrimination in the 1960s. The eradication of Hispanic stereotyping remains unfinished, long after Cesar Chavez campaigned for the rights of farm workers in the United States and migrant workers from Mexico.

During World War II, following wartime tradition, our enemies were stereotyped in demonic caricatures. Some of them were indeed demonic. In one of the worst chapters in human history, those anti-Christian leaders of Nazi Germany used racist and religious stereotypes to justify the wholesale, indiscriminate murder of Jews.

Throughout the violent, bloody Arab-Israeli conflict that began with the creation of Israel in 1948, the antagonists have stereotyped each other. On one side, Jews are denounced as "racists" for harsh discrimination against mostly-Muslim Palestinians. On the other, Palestinians are excoriated as terrorists unworthy of first-class citizenship. Some of the Jews oppressed under the Nazi regime are now the oppressors in the Arab-Israeli conflict. For fifty years, the leaders of the Israeli government—religious and secular Jews—using overwhelming military power augmented by massive aid from the U.S. government, have subjugated, dispossessed, brutalized, and stereotyped the Palestinian people, both Muslim and Christian. The support provided by the United States, pledged as it is to religious tolerance, has, in effect, supported these intolerant policies.

At times through the years, Muslim rulers have engaged in harsh religious stereotyping on a broad scale. Inayat I. Lalani writes: "There have been waves of intolerance against religious minorities—or subjugated majorities, for that matter—under Islamic rule in all countries and during all ages. Unfortunately, many Muslims will vehemently deny such behavior, or somehow try to justify it. Several Muslim rulers treated their non-Muslim adversaries and subjects with utmost cruelty. In the eleventh century, Al Mansoor in Moorish Spain and Aurangzeb in the seventeenth century in Mughal, India, come to mind. In 1398, Tamerlane pillaged Delhi and slaughtered one hundred thousand of its inhabitants, mostly Hindu, on the pretext that the Muslim rulers of the Delhi Sultanate were treating polytheistic and idolatrous Hindus too leniently. The treatment was not too lenient.

"The behavior of Suleiman the Magnificent as he retreated back toward Istanbul after the failed siege of Vienna in 1529 does not inspire admiration either. During that retreat he enslaved one hundred thousand boys. And one recoils in horror upon reading accounts of the recurring theme of fratricide that characterized the struggles for succession in Mughal India and Ottoman Turkey.

"At the same time, historians have noted, parenthetically but with impressive regularity, that on balance Muslim rulers have been more enlightened and have accorded non-Muslim subjects greater protection from discrimination and oppression than, say, Christian conquerors up until the beginning of the Enlightenment.

"At no time, did Muslim leaders engage in religious oppression that even approached the awful agony of death by burning at the stake and boiling in oil as inflicted against non-believers during the Christian Inquisition and the wholesale slaughter of Muslims in the Middle East by swords wielded by Christian Crusaders. There was no such thing as ecclesiastical Muslim authority examining one's faith in ridiculous details such as the Inquisitors presumed to do. Muslim leaders ordered no banishment, excommunication, or burning at the stake as retribution for straying from established dogma. The reason for such restraint must be found in the relatively liberal attitude of the Muslim scholars toward dissent.

"The Quran does not explicitly condemn slavery, but its terms were far less harsh under Islam, than, say, the plantation slavery of the ante-bellum South in the United States. The remission of slavery receives frequent and vocal approval and encouragement in the Quran.

"My humble conclusion is that intolerance and vindictiveness are hallmarks of declining or defeated societies. The triumphant become magnanimous and tolerant and even celebrate diversity when all threats to their hegemony have been neutralized. In this, we all—Muslims, Jews, Christians, and Hindus—without exception behave in a predictable manner."

I asked Lalani, a self-described Muslim modernist, to estimate the percentage of Muslims of his acquaintance who agree with his assessment of modern Islam. "Perhaps only 10 percent are willing to speak up as I have, but privately, I believe, many agree with me."[2]

The beginning of the Third Millennium may herald a promising new era for interfaith relations in the United States. Except for persistent anti-Muslim stereotypes and the intolerance sometimes exhibited by fundamentalist Christians, I find the American people celebrating religious diversity to a greater extent than ever before. This may mean, in an extension of Lalani's logic, that the U.S. government believes that it has neutralized all threats to its hegemony and can afford to be magnanimous.

My hope is that it reflects instead a determination on the part of the American people to give substance at long last to the ideal of religious tolerance that is so clearly expressed in our nation's founding documents. The achievement of this goal will, however, require sustained interfaith leadership that is highly-motivated, a human commodity that now seems to be in short supply.

Today, Muslims are the primary targets of intolerance, and, to an embarrassing degree, Muslim stereotypes are made-in-America. Two years ago, when I decided to test Islam's image within our own family, I received a sobering response. Learning that my mother-in-law, Kathryn Gemme, a devout Roman Catholic who follows national and world news closely at the age of one hundred and six, had read the draft introduction and the first three chapters of this book, I asked for her reaction. Her response: "I am probably like millions of other Americans. I always thought Muslims were strange, off-the-wall people. I got this impression from snippets of television news and newspaper headlines. Now I know better, but I am afraid most people don't."

Only in America is Islam closely and falsely linked in the public mind with terrorism. This stereotype exists beyond our borders, of course, but nowhere else has it flourished in recent years with comparable intensity and persistence.

The false images of Islam in America are partly a by-product of the Arab-Israeli conflict. The late I. F. "Izzy" Stone, a revered Jewish author and commentator, once told me, "When people are at war, it is normal for civil liberties to suffer." He explained that U.S. Jews, afraid about the future, feel that they "have to fight and keep fighting" against Israel's enemies as long as Israel itself remains on a war footing.[3] Many of America's fifty million fundamentalist Christians have similar sentiments, believing that the survival of a strong Israel is an essential part of God's plan. They view Muslims as a threat to that plan.

These Christians and many Jews feel they must remain hostile to Muslims, because Israel remains in a state of military alert against neighboring states that are largely Muslim. When a just peace brings Israel's military posturing to an end, the passion for Muslim stereotyping in the United States can be expected to subside.

Not all Jews are hostile toward Muslims. Several years ago, when the Islamic Center in Ft. Collins, Colorado, was ransacked and damaged, Rabbi Jack Gabriel was the first to show up with a hammer to help make repairs. When the mosque in Springfield, Illinois, was set afire, Rabbi Barry A. Marks arrived the next morning to offer help.

A major reason for the survival of anti-Islamic stereotypes is the reality that U.S. Muslims, despite their long, growing presence in America, remain largely unorganized. National leadership has only recently begun to take shape.

The need for sustained, constructive Muslim influence is especially apparent in the functioning of America's apparatus for the gathering and dissemination of news. American attitudes on terrorism and the other false images of Islam are heavily influenced by the few minutes of evening news provided by network television. These reports specialize in on-site coverage of a few shocking, violent events and rarely present more than two or three breathless sentences about any of them. This means that the words "Muslim" and "Islam" are usually brought to the attention of the American television audience only in relation to violence and other harsh, unpleasant events.

U.S. Muslims have little input on news coverage decisions in any medium, partly because only a few have ventured into journalism as a career. Most of the news published and broadcast in America is written by journalists who are uninformed or misinformed about Islam. In the absence of protests, news editors have no reason to be vigilant about erroneous reports on Islam and Muslims.

Among the editors and reporters in newsrooms—the work-places where reports and headlines are written for mass audiences—Muslims are virtually nonexistent. If Muslims were among those working in these centers, their very presence would have a beneficial impact. The collegial atmosphere that usually prevails in newsrooms, not to mention common courtesy, would cause other staff members to avoid stereotypes in what they write and edit about Islam.

Beyond the direct staffing of newsrooms and television studios, full time Muslim professionals are needed to provide quality Islamic perspectives and insights to the media. These specialists, if not employed by the media, should logically be part of the established Muslim organizational presence in the nation's major cities—Washington, D.C., and New York City, for example—that are acknowledged as the major news centers for disseminating news. Beyond being capable and experienced in news work, they must be able to attain and maintain a cordial relationship with news personalities so that they will be consulted as news events develop. They must be able to make convincing presentations on television and radio talk shows, interviews, and discussion programs. In addition, these specialists are needed to provide support to Muslims who provide similar services to news centers at the local level throughout America. The Muslim community is endowed with varied, journalistic talent, including a number of scholars and other professionals who already appear occasionally on local stations, but this reservoir must be nurtured and expanded.

At present, television audiences identify only one person, Louis Farrakhan of the Nation of Islam, nationally as a Muslim leader, even though the majority of mainline Muslims do not accept him as such. That fact alone should summon U.S. Muslims to identify, train, and support followers of Islam who can become nationally recognized and respected Muslim spokespersons. In time, Farrakhan may speak convincingly for the mainstream, but, despite his recent statement of conversion to accepted Islamic teachings, the memories of his past rhetoric will linger.

The scarcity of Muslim spokespersons nationally is not the only current shortcoming. Muslims are rarely found in senior positions in the federal government, whether elective or appointive. Only a few Muslims occupy positions at the state level. These voids in leadership handicap all citizens, not just Muslims. The followers of Islam are a growing, important part of America, and all citizens will benefit when Muslims assume roles affording them the opportunity to contribute wise counsel and balance in public policymaking.

The remedy lies in political action at various levels and in varied forms. This is no time to follow a wait-and-see policy. The stereotypes leave a damaging image so pervasive that Muslims should join non-Muslims in publicly undertaking aggressive, corrective steps that they may have considered unthinkable in the past. All citizens should respond to the call to political endeavor, but Muslims must accept their special responsibility and not leave the challenge to non-Muslims alone. If Muslims fail to act, they cannot reasonably expect others to fill the leadership gap. Inaction does nothing to lift the burden of stereotypes.

Muslims must undertake two vitally important steps that they alone can accomplish. In recommending these steps, I realize that I may venture into sensitive areas of personal behavior and tradition, but I take that risk because of the importance of removing stereotypes in the shortest time possible.

Here are steps I recommend:

First, Muslims should identify themselves publicly with Islam and seek ways to present the truth about their faith to non-Muslims.

Responding to stereotypes with reactive, corrective measures is essential, but proactive steps are equally important. "Accentuate the positive," the theme of a song that was popular years ago, is sound advice for Muslims. They should not wait for a crisis to occur before offering factual information about their religion.

As a first step, they should mark themselves as Muslims, so their own good behavior and worthy accomplishments will be identified with Islam. Exemplary conduct can be recognized by the public as Islamic only if the person is clearly identified as Muslim.

One day, I asked Rasha Yow, one of the few Muslims in our hometown, what she is doing to help erase false images of Islam. She responded, "I deal with them by personal example. I try to live by the high standards of conduct that my religion requires." Her policy, of course, is a commendable, essential commitment that I greatly admire, but her excellent personal behavior is not always identified with Islam. Like most other U.S. Muslims, Yow customarily wears nothing that identifies her faith—no distinctive pin, ring or clothing. A local acquaintance, learning that her mother is of Greek origin, wrongly assumed that Yow's religious affiliation is Eastern Orthodox. He was surprised when I corrected his assumption. Yow had not concealed her Muslim faith, but, like most other citizens, she felt no need to publicly identify herself with Islam. Muslims must put aside any such reluctance.

In some cases, clothing provides an adequate identification, for example, when women wear a headscarf or men wear a Muslim cap. But the majority of U.S. Muslim women wear a headscarf only when they are in a mosque or praying. Few men wear a Muslim cap.

Muslims can display their religious affiliation modestly but effectively by wearing a lapel pin, necklace, or ring that displays the word Allah, star-and-crescent, or some other visible linkage with Islam. A waitress taking Zainab Elberry's order for breakfast one morning in Nashville, remarked, "I notice your ring, so I won't bring you any bacon." Elberry smiled appreciatively. Her ring featured the star-and-crescent, signifying Islam, a faith that prohibits its adherents to eat pork. After his conversion, Malcolm X wore a ring bearing the star-and-crescent insignia. It was removed from his finger after his assassination.

From Amman, Jordan, April Szuchyt writes, "Back in America, many people comment on a charm I wear with the name of Allah inscribed on it. The responses ranged from, 'Oh, that is so cool!' to 'how exotic!'" She notes that some did not recognize the charm as an Islamic symbol, but she acknowledged that all of the reactions it evoked, no matter how uninformed, have the effect of opening conversations, even with strangers, that can help clear away stereotypes.

Many Christians wear a cross and Jews wear the Star of David to show their religious affiliation. While Muslim men do not customarily wear jewelry, a small lapel pin or ring will, in an unostentatious way, provide an important identification for men or women.

The lack of identification in Muslim attire sometimes reflects a deep personal problem. From my experience, I conclude that some Muslims—excluding Rasha Yow—find the anti-Muslim stereotypes in America so oppressive and embarrassing that they keep their religious affiliation a very private matter. Some of them even hide their faith, believing that they and their families are better off pretending to have no faith than being identified with a religion that many Americans view as radical and threatening. This policy is unfortunate and harmful, because it does nothing to eradicate false images.

Beyond wearing pins, rings, and necklaces, Muslims can take other important initiatives: distributing informational leaflets about Islam to neighbors and other acquaintances; offering to speak about their religion to service clubs, church and synagogue groups, and other gatherings; sponsoring informational advertising in local media. The advertising can be inserted in local newspapers and broadcast on radio stations at modest cost and can produce good results over a large area in a short period of time. The messages— those for personal distribution as well as advertising in media— must, of course, be prepared with great care so that non-Muslims will find them appealing.

Second, Muslims must defend their faith aggressively and publicly against misconceptions and misrepresentations, especially those expressed by professed Muslims.

When people identified as Muslims reportedly engage in bad conduct or express false or misleading interpretations of Islam, other Muslims must break their habitual silence and condemn these reports of un-Islamic behavior. To be effective, this must be done promptly, clearly, and publicly.

Newscasts and headlines in early January 2000 reported a protracted rampage by Muslims against Christians on several islands in Indonesia in what appeared to be gross Muslim violations of the interfaith tolerance required by Islam. To my surprise and disappointment, no Muslim denunciation of this reported injustice appeared in the news media. In the absence of publicized Muslim protests, non-Muslims are left to accept the reports, whether accurate or not, as evidence of Islamic intolerance and radicalism. The day the rampage was first reported, U.S. Muslims should have been speaking out, deploring the religious intolerance as reported, declaring it to be in violation of fundamental principles of Islam, and demanding that news media report their denunciations.

The anti-Christian violence in Indonesia may have been incited and organized by a rebellious military leader. It may have been politically motivated, not religiously. But its origin and the question of reporting accuracy are beside the point. Whenever misbehavior is wrongly attributed to Islam, U.S. Muslims should respond quickly and publicly.

For example, they should have denounced Osama bin Laden's call, in the name of Islam, for the indiscriminate killing of Americans and the Taliban for the un-Islamic treatment of women in Afghanistan. They should also have condemned the professed Muslims in the Philippines who, in April 2000, held innocent people as hostages, beheaded two of them, and threatened to keep killing hostages unless two Egyptians serving prison terms for complicity in the bombing of the World Trade Center in New York in 1993 were released. U.S. Muslims should have denounced the Philippine citizens for this savage abuse of innocent people and for defaming Islam by identifying their group as Muslim. So far as I have learned, no Muslims did so in an adequate and timely fashion. Four months after the atrocity, the Council on American-Islamic Relations [CAIR] urged an important step in the right direction when it called on the media "to exercise caution when reporting about the conflict [in the Philippines] so as not to indict the religion of the perpetrators."

CAIR explained, "Abu Sayyaf, a splinter group of the Moro National Liberation Army, is a separatist group trying to establish a predominantly Muslim entity [not an Islamic state] and secede from the Philippines. An Islamic state is ruled by religious law and is entirely different from a state run by a Muslim central government.... The actions of militant groups should not induce media professionals to paint all Muslims with a broad stroke through irresponsible headlines and inaccurate characterization.... Terrorism perpetrated by certain fringe groups of the Irish Republican Army has never been characterized as 'Catholic terrorism.' Orthodox Christian Serbs who committed pogroms against Bosnian and Kosovar Muslims have never been identified as 'Christian' murderers—and religious extremist settlers in the West Bank who randomly kill and maim Palestinians are almost never called 'Jewish terrorists.' In this context, the media is urged to apply the same standard when reporting about Muslims."[4]

Why the general silence of Muslims?

One explanation is offered by April Szuchyt: "I imagine that most Muslims, like myself, feel a dull pain in their hearts when faced with the reality that so many people in the Western world demonize them. There is a prevailing sense of confusion over this issue. Obviously, most Muslims are aware of the extremist groups who commit horrific crimes in the name of Islam, but, at the same time, most Muslims do not feel any association with these groups and therefore don't understand how or why people in the West continue to draw nonexistent parallels between them.

"I should add that in Islam, it is considered a big 'no-no' to criticize others. We have a saying that when a Muslim says something derogatory about another Muslim that is not true, the fault that is alleged will appear in the accuser's own behavior before he or she dies. Expressed another way, if I call someone a liar and it turns out that he or she is not, then I am the liar.

"We also believe that things aren't always as they appear on the outside, so it's very difficult to get a practicing Muslim to criticize another. In Islam, there is a lot of emphasis placed on giving people the benefit of the doubt. It is also part of Islamic teaching to conceal the weaknesses or sins of others. One shouldn't divulge such information to just anyone. It should be shared only with individuals immediately affected by the circumstances or with someone who has the knowledge and the ability to help correct the situation. But believe me when I say there is no shortage of Muslims criticizing others. I hear them doing it all day long!"

The Islamic requirement of restraint in personal criticism, cited by Szuchyt, should not keep Muslims from making a vigorous defense of the faith. I salute those who refuse to make personal accusations, but I am troubled when Muslim leaders fail to refute publicly and promptly representations of Islam that are erroneous. Muslims can condemn violations and misconceptions of Islam without condemning in a personal way the people who are responsible. Years ago, Rev. Billy Sunday, a popular Christian evangelist, set the right standard when he urged, "Condemn the sin, never the sinner."

Andrew Patterson offers another explanation for Muslim silence: "Many Muslims question the accuracy of Western news media in reporting news from Muslim nations." A prominent U.S. Muslim who requested anonymity supports Patterson's position: "Muslim criticism is scarce because U.S. Muslims distrust the reports from Muslim countries. Past experience shows that such reports are usually written by poorly informed reporters or persons with a political agenda. Or they come from people who are just biased and anti-Muslim. American Muslims do not want to be tools in the hands of media people who are selective in their reporting of Muslim issues. If Muslims are invited to appear only to condemn other Muslims, they prefer not to appear at all. If media coverage is balanced and gives a realistic view of Muslims societies, reporting the good as well as the bad, U.S. Muslim leaders would not be hesitant to air social issues. But since normal Muslim society is rarely depicted, and Muslim society is constantly presented only as being pathological, Muslim leaders do not want to add to this image."

These responses are illuminating but inadequate. They help to explain the general reluctance of U.S. Muslims to respond to stereotypes, but they do not excuse their silence. They do not absolve Muslims of the duty to condemn publicly injustices that are reported to have been committed in the name of Islam.

I sympathize with those who suffer in silence. I cannot, of course, put myself in the shoes of Muslim leaders who are reluctant to speak out, but I have some understanding of the frustrations they experience. Since my career in Congress began forty years ago, I have experienced frequent encounters with the media and occasionally have been upset at what I believed to be unfair treatment. On most of these occasions, I tried to conceal my resentment and maintain a cordial and cooperative relationship with offending editors and reporters. In doing so, I followed the advice of Paul Grote, a friend and wise country lawyer: "You can't beat the press or city hall, so never try." Today, he would add television and radio reporters to his "never try" list.

To my regret, I have not always followed Grote's counsel. As I look back on my congressional career, one of my main regrets was my failure, after votes were counted in the 1982 election, to make an immediate congratulatory telephone call to Richard Durbin, the man who defeated me. Instead, riding with Lucille and Diane, our daughter, several hours later, I stopped at Durbin's headquarters to congratulate him personally but found only the cleanup crew on hand. I left a brief written message of congratulations but made no attempt to telephone him at any time. For several days, upset over post-election news coverage that I considered unfair, I refused to respond to media inquiries.

This behavior made me look petty. Still worse, it deprived me of opportunities to thank the citizens who had supported me through the years and to demonstrate dignity and grace in defeat.

I understand the feelings of pain and outrage Muslims must feel when they receive biased and insensitive treatment in the media. But they harm their own cause if they fail to seize every opportunity for public comment about Islam. Each media interview affords an opportunity to cast their religion in a correct, positive light. By shunning such opportunities, they give free rein to reporters who are misinformed, including those who seem bent on characterizing Muslims as "pathological." If, as I believe, the news media tendency to misrepresent Islam and Muslims arises mainly from ignorance, Muslim silence is the worst possible reaction. If misconceptions, stereotypes, or plain lies go unchallenged, they inevitably will continue their corrosive course.

Although U.S. Muslims should not be held responsible for the misbehavior of other followers of Islam, all have a special duty to speak out when professed Muslims, no matter where they live, are reported to have cast their religion in a bad light. Perhaps they are prompted to remain silent by the general failure of U.S. Christians to condemn as un-Christian the misbehavior of other Christians, for example, the bloodbath Serbian Christians inflicted on innocent Muslims in Bosnia and Kosova during the period, 1995 to 1999. But it is a distinction with a big difference. The overwhelming majority of Americans—most of them Christians—know that the Balkan carnage violated Christian rules, but many, if not most, of the same Americans do not know that all violence against innocent people is prohibited in Islamic principles and doctrines.

Muslims are held responsible by poorly informed non-believers for the behavior of all professed Muslims, no matter how bad it may be. Everyone in a minority group—whether racial or religious—knows what it is like to be measured in that way. All have had the experience of being judged by unrepresentative stereotypes.

In the United States, African-Americans have suffered most of all. They suffered in the extreme during slavery, but stereotypes still afflict them today. Leonard Pitts, one of my favorite syndicated columnists, writes, as an African-American, "If we [blacks] were free, my behavior would bring another black man neither credit nor discredit, [but] as an African-American, one does not—cannot—move by oneself.... Each of us affects the rest of us and so, owes consideration to the rest of us..."[5]

Women are more numerous than men, but they too have suffered under chauvinistic stereotypes throughout history, some of the most painful occurring in Europe during the early part of the first millennium. Some were treated unfairly as if they were mentally deficient, vengeful, dirty, and dangerous.[6] Even today, eighty years after they won the right to vote, U.S. women struggle for equality in the work place.

When one Muslim neglects his duty as a citizen or behaves badly, all Muslims suffer. Every unchallenged image that misrepresents Islam—even the reports of occurrences in distant places like Indonesia, the Philippines, and Afghanistan—adds to the burden on U.S. Muslims.

Every Muslim should feel an obligation to defend his or her religion from misrepresentation, no matter where the reported abuse arises.

At first glance, the recommendations I have set forth may seem odd, awkward, or excessive to those accustomed to silence and inaction. In summoning U.S. Muslims to these initiatives, I realize that I am issuing a tall order. Most Muslims are unaccustomed to action in the public arena, even to correct misconceptions about Islam. Speaking out is a political act. Wearing a Star-and-Crescent or Allah pin is a political statement, not just a religious one.

It is not easy to break old habits, but breaking the silence about Islam is an urgent necessity.

*F*inally, all citizens—not just Muslims—should engage resolutely in partisan politics.

False images of Islam pose a formidable challenge and demand strong corrective measures. Abraham Lincoln responded to a great challenge in his time with an appeal that rings true today: "The occasion is piled high with difficulty, and we must rise with the occasion.... As our case is new, we must think anew and act anew. We must disenthrall ourselves."[7]

All citizens, not just Muslims, must recognize that Islamic stereotypes impose a heavy burden on American society. They are a nationwide blight. Across America, they stir ugly, base emotions that weaken public allegiance to cherished American principles of religious tolerance and the pursuit of dignity and decency for all people.

In Washington, they have already prompted our leaders to serious errors in foreign policy that harm vital national interests and have led to ill-considered, panic-driven domestic legislation. An example is the anti-terrorism law enacted in the wake of the Oklahoma City bombing that, in a clear violation of constitutional rights of due process, permits the government to arrest and expel immigrants on the basis of secret evidence. Several Muslims have already been incarcerated under this law.

The false stereotypes prompt government officials to focus exclusively on hunting down terrorists instead of giving serious attention, as well, to the grievances that sometimes lead desperate people to terrible violence.

Today's "occasion" is piled high with false images that handicap millions of American citizens, distort the vision of most of the others, and endanger our national well-being. Sulayman Nyang, although reporting a measure of progress, notes a daunting task ahead: "The political leadership now accepts Muslims as part of the American reality, but there's a lot of prejudice at the popular level."[8] Inayat Lalani writes: "The negative images and stereotypes of Islam and Muslims are really there and not just a figment of someone's imagination."[9]

To meet the challenge, we must think anew, act anew, and disenthrall ourselves of old habits and inhibitions. In the interest of justice and tranquility—in the home, in the neighborhood, throughout the nation and beyond—people of all faiths must reach out for correct comprehension of each other's religion and then work together for common goals. To that end, all Americans, not just Muslims, must accept a responsibility in politics.

The United States is one of the oldest democracies in the world, but it will always depend on the initiative and sustained commitment of its citizens. In his address at Gettysburg, Lincoln declared that America's constitutional democracy, conceived in liberty and dedicated to the equality of all people, remained an experiment "four score and seven years" after its birth. Today, it is still an experiment.

Those who work in the political arena to advance interfaith understanding and cooperation help keep the experiment robust and noble.

Notes:

1. U.S. Rep. John Kyl conversation, 6-10-1962.
2. Inayat Lalani letter, 1-20-2000.
3. Paul Findley, *They Dare to Speak Out,* p. 284.
4. CAIR release, 8-29-2000.
5. *Journal-Courier,* Jacksonville, IL 8-26-2000, p 8.
6. Alvin Schmidt, *Veiled and Silenced.*
7. President Abraham Lincoln's message to Congress, January 1862.
8. *Washington Times Weekly,* 7-(17-23)-2000, p. 23.
9. Letter, 5-2-1999.

Appendices

Appendix A:

"A Friendly Note From Your Muslim Neighbor…"

M uslims have much in common with Christians and Jews.

Muslims, like Christians and Jews, worship the One God, Creator of the Universe. Allah is the Arabic word for God.

Muslims, like Christians and Jews, consider themselves spiritual descendants of Abraham.

Muslims, like Christians and Jews, pledge themselves to prayer, peace with justice, harmony, cooperation, compassion, charity, family responsibility, tolerance toward people of other faith traditions, and respect for the environment.

All three faiths have spread worldwide. Because of geographic dispersal, within each faith exist several sects with slightly different interpretations of politics, family, dress, and social life.

We Muslims want you to know that –

Islam and democracy are compatible and complementary. Both rest on accountability, consultation, open discussion, delegation, and consensus. The opening words of the U.S. Declaration of Independence express deeply felt Islamic sentiments.

Muslims honor Biblical prophets, accord special esteem to Jesus and his mother, the Virgin Mary, and recognize as sacred the scriptures revealed to Moses and Jesus, namely the Torah and the New Testament.

Muslims are united in Islam, which means submission and peace. Submitting to the will of God and doing good define piety. The Quran is the final divine revelation, providing a complete guide for human behavior. Its text was revealed to the Prophet Muhammad between 610 and 632 A.D. Though revered by Muslims as the last of God's prophets, Muhammad is not worshiped.

Muslim women, like men, have the right to obtain an education, own property and engage in business, professions, and public life. Both women and men wear modest dress out of respect for public morality. If a society oppresses women or discriminates against them, it is in spite of Islam, not because of it.

The Muslim husband has the primary responsibility for family support, his wife for the household and children. Divorce is discouraged. Procedures vary by country, but either husband or wife may petition to dissolve a marriage. Polygamy, which was widely practiced in Biblical times, is subject to precise Quranic restrictions and is now seldom practiced, rarely where it violates public law, as in America.

Muslims assume personal responsibility for relatives and others in need. In Islam, a woman or elderly person is almost never obliged to life alone.

Muslims are committed to rules. Sadly, some people who say they are Muslims—like some professed Christians and Jews—grossly violate these rules and the rights of others. In doing so, they do not act as Muslims. It is erroneous to call them Islamic fundamentalists, a term unknown in Islam and used mostly in false stereotyping.

Jihad has two meanings: one, non-violent struggling within oneself for a life of virtue; the other, fighting for justice, a supreme goal in Islamic teachings. Islam eulogizes moderation and abhors extremism, terrorism, fanaticism, oppression and subjugation.

Muslims are proud to be Americans. They wish to be good citizens and neighbors by practicing their commitment to tolerance, charity, work, cooperation, and interfaith activities for community betterment.

[Note: The above text, prepared by Paul Findley, is not copyrighted. It may be copied and distributed, with or without attribution]

Appendix B:

The Committee-of-One

Muslims are finding that action by a committee-of-one is often the most effective way to challenge editors, commentators, and station managers to avoid the false images of Islam that surface regularly in the media. It can also be the best way to eliminate anti-Muslim bias when public policy decisions are made on Capitol Hill.

It has the advantage of splendid efficiency, because, acting alone, a person will usually find that opportunities for significant, satisfying victories are always within reach. Working mainly from home, the one-person committee can quickly set goals and decide strategy, but he or she must understand the keys to success.

Editors, reporters, and broadcast station managers do not relish accepting responsibility for false and misleading statements, and they dislike it even more when they have to correct errors publicly. This is true whether the errors were made innocently or maliciously.

Some media leaders—and Members of Congress—have deep-seated religious, racial, and political biases. I have found, however, that even those who are biased and enjoy putting Islam in a bad light want the public to view them as being fair-minded. They say they welcome the opportunity to correct mistakes, and when challenged by clear evidence of error, almost every editor, reporter, or station manager—as well as every Member of Congress—will agree to some form of public correction.

Even if the offending person stubbornly refuses to make any response to error, the challenge is worth the effort. The person responsible will almost certainly avoid false and misleading statements in the future, knowing that well-informed readers or listeners are apt to remain vigilant. In short, one person, acting alone, is almost certain to attain media and political victories and these successes will likely start a chain reaction in which others are inspired to create their own committees-of-one.

Most activists against stereotypes do not confine themselves to one-person endeavors. As they proceed down the path to success, they become acquainted with the work of established organizations and usually multiply their effectiveness by becoming a member of one or more of these groups, all of whom welcome new recruits.

Which path is the better—the committee-of-one or the larger groups? The question may suggest the answer offered by Yogi Berra, the baseball great of years past and legendary deadpan comic, when he said, "If you come to a fork in the road, take it." But people attacking bias need not limit themselves to taking the singular "it" path that Berra imprecisely recommended. They can take both forks in the road, because there is no need to choose. In my experience, I find that most people continue to act alone down the committee-of-one path but at the same time join traditional committees, knowing that they can accomplish some goals best by joining forces with others.

I have had long experience at both issuing and receiving complaints. First, as a reporter and sportswriter of a daily newspaper, then, in succession, as assistant editor of a monthly magazine, editor of a rural weekly newspaper, a Member of Congress, and, finally, as author of four books and scores of opinion columns. As newspaper editor, then legislator, I dealt almost entirely with controversial topics. I received outcries from people who wanted public policies changed, and I have also expressed demands of my own. Experience is a good teacher, and I have combined the lessons that I learned personally with those learned by other people, many of whom are winning daily battles in the news media against false images of Islam. The result is a road map with directions that will help your committee-of-one attain success. Below are other lessons, learned mostly from others on Capitol Hill, in case you are a reader who will take Islam-related problems directly to those who represent you in Congress.

How to Influence the Media

The following rules for dealing with the media are not my personal invention, although I endorse them. They are a distillation of common sense gained from discussions with old-timers in politics as well as those, including a number of Muslims, who have recently been tested in the fire of public policy competition.

First, in approaching local media, make sure you have accurate information about the person you will contact and the stereotype or error you will challenge. Keep a steno-pad or bound planner and pen by the chair where you generally read, watch, or listen. When a bad image about Islam comes to your attention, make a note then and there. Write down what was said or published. Be precise about when, where, by whom, and what was said or published. The more precise your record, the better chance for early success. If you are responding to a broadcast, note as closely as possible the exact words and the context in which they were used. If you are objecting to a statement about Islam in print, note the name of the periodical, date, page number, and author or person quoted.

Second, respond quickly by using your telephone. Don't put off your challenge until tomorrow. You will find helpful listings in the yellow pages of the telephone directory. Write key numbers on the cover of your steno-pad or planner so they will be at your fingertips each time a challenge arises. When you call, ask to speak to the person in charge—the editor of the periodical or the news editor of the television or radio station. When you make contact, give your name, and mention your mission. Request politely but firmly that the management broadcast or publish a correction or give you the opportunity to make the correction yourself. If your call is not relayed directly to the person in charge, ask that he or she call you as soon as possible.

If the anti-Muslim stereotype is expressed on a radio or television talk show, you may be able to secure an instant correction and apology from the host. The call-in numbers are usually repeated during such programs. If your call gets through while the host is on the air, the correction will likely reach most of the listeners who heard the stereotype expressed.

Third, in registering your protest, observe the "three Cs." Be calm, courteous, and considerate. Just state the facts. In making phone calls and writing complaints, never be harsh, demanding, or accusatory. Do your best to state your complaint so that the person on the receiving end will welcome it. If you use a verbal sledge-hammer, you may get your own adrenaline flowing and give yourself an emotional lift, but you are unlikely to elicit cooperation.

Always be calm and polite, no matter how provoked you may feel inwardly. Years ago, Clarence W. Kaylor, a Pittsfield, Illinois, businessman who retired from a successful career as an executive for Jewel Tea Company, offered me this advice, "An abusive letter is a waste of time and will do more harm than good. Try to write each letter so that it will create a good feeling." Years later, when I arrived in Washington, Marvin McLain, a lobbyist for the American Farm Bureau Federation, offered a similar suggestion, "If you feel you must write an angry letter, go ahead. But don't mail it." When I stopped one day at the office of the *Journal-Courier* in Jacksonville, Illinois, Cecil Tendick, a wise reporter-philosopher, recommended these rules for success, "Never threaten. Never beg. Never pretend you know it all."

Keep in mind that the people who receive your complaint are busy, under pressure, and often harried. No matter what they say, they don't really like to receive complaints and are apt to be defensive. Start off, if you can, with a compliment. Praise something constructive the station or newspaper has done recently and state your confidence that the periodical or broadcasting station employees always want to be correct and fair. That opener will help to ease any defensive impulse by the person whose cooperation you seek. But explain that you want corrective action. Firmly request promptness, explaining that you want to inform others. If action requires a public apology, explain why, clearly and firmly.

Fourth, provide updates on your activities to organizations that challenge stereotypes nationally. Prominent among these are the Council on American Islamic Relations, the American Muslim Council [AMC], and the American Arab Anti-Discrimination Committee [ADC].

Address information: CAIR, 453 New Jersey Avenue SE, Washington, D.C. 20003; telephone 202-488-8787;

FAX 202 659-2254; e-mail cair1@ix.netcom.com or URL:http//www.cair-net.org; ADC, 4201 Connecticut Ave., NW, Suite 300, Washington, D.C. 20008; telephone 202 244-2990; FAX 202 244-3196; e-mail adc@adc.org or http//www.adc.org; AMC, 1212 New York Ave. NW, Washington, D.C. 20005; telephone 202 789-2262; FAX 202 789-2550; e-mail amc@amconline.org

Fax your material or e-mail it but always also send a copy by regular mail. All organizations welcome phone calls but, in the interest of accuracy, they appreciate copies by postal service.

Fifth, follow up. Don't let your initial step be the last. If you maintain courteous pressure, you are almost certain to receive an apology and correction. Mail a statement giving details of the complaint to the person in charge, whether or not you have talked directly to that person. The letter will underscore your determination to get corrective action.

If you do not get a satisfactory response within a few days, pay a visit to the person's office, taking with you a memo of your complaint and, if possible, a few acquaintances who agree with your position. There is strength in numbers. Whenever a group of people stopped at my Capitol Hill office, I always felt obliged to spend a few minutes with them, no matter how busy I was, and even if they were not from the district I served.

A Guide to Success in Lobbying

To achieve maximum effect on Capitol Hill, you must understand political realities. Congress is a vital center of policy-making, one of the most important in the world. My knowledge comes partly from my own long experience as a representative and partly from the lessons that others have learned and shared with me. I spent twenty-two years on the receiving end of lobbying as a Member of Congress and two subsequent years writing a book about the activities of Israel's U.S. lobby. Since then, ten years as an officer of the Council for the National Interest have added to my education.

A glimpse into the busy life of a Member of Congress will help. I am the author of the words that follow, but the ideas that prompt the words come from manifold sources: former colleagues of both political parties; members of personal and committee staffs on Capitol Hill; veteran lobbyists who have a unique insight into life in the congressional fast lane and know firsthand techniques that generally produce good results and those that do not; the veterans of politics at the precinct and town levels; and the Muslims who have gained experience in Capitol Hill corridors. All are convinced that, with patience and commitment, acting alone or as a part of a delegation or larger organization, each citizen can become an important influence on Washington policy-makers.

Life as a Member of Congress is an exciting, sometimes exhilarating, existence. It is filled with a multitude of challenges and great opportunities for constructive work. It is also a life that is arduous and stressful almost every hour of every day. Members of Congress must constantly juggle competing demands on their time that come from a variety of sources. Among them are visits by people from the home district, some of whom will be armed with legislative requests, professional lobbyists who are helpful at campaign time and usually speak for influential constituents, and visitors who stop simply for a friendly chat and a souvenir photograph. These calls constitute only part of each day's challenges.

Members of Congress cannot wisely neglect legislative work. Most of them serve on two major committees and four subcommittees and almost always confront overlapping schedules. When schedules conflict, Members must make decisions—often difficult—about which meetings to attend. Committee work usually begins at 9:30 or 10:00 each morning, Mondays through Thursdays and sometimes on Fridays, followed promptly at noon by legislative agendas in the House of Representatives chamber in the Capitol Building. These sessions often last well into the evening.

In addition, Members always have a mountain of desk work, phone calls to return, mail to read and answer, and staff activities to direct. Staff members help, but the Member must provide direction and supervision.

The Hectic Congressional Pace

H ere is a typical week in the life of a Member of Congress:

Votes on pending legislation are at the top of the priority list for Members of Congress. They are rarely scheduled in the House chamber on Mondays or Fridays. This practice reflects the influence of the "Tuesday to Thursday Club," a name tagged on to Members whose home districts are reachable by air in about an hour. They are numerous enough to influence legislative scheduling. Their families reside in the home district, and these Members prefer to be in Washington only on Monday, Tuesday and Wednesday nights. If final action on controversial legislation is scheduled only on Tuesday, Wednesday, and Thursday, these Members can spend the other four nights at home, being with their families and mending political fences, without missing critical responsibilities in Washington.

When a Member arrives in his or her home district on a Thursday evening, a staff member is on hand with three-by-five cards that itemize a busy schedule for the coming three and a half days—Friday through Monday afternoon. The schedule commonly includes media interviews, town meetings, speeches to organizations, meetings with civic and political leaders, appointments with interest groups and individuals, in addition to office duties at the district congressional office.

All this comes to an end on Monday evening or early Tuesday morning, when the commuting Members return to the Ronald Reagan Washington National Airport. Awaiting their arrival are other sets of index cards covering obligations through the following Thursday evening. Included are appointments similar to those in the home district, plus committee and subcommittee schedules, and invitations for breakfasts, luncheons, receptions, and dinners.

Some members of the "Tuesday to Thursday Club" fly to their home districts every night. Rep. William A. Barrett told me one day that he flew home after House adjournment every evening so that he could meet constituents in his Philadelphia office before going to his residence. In contrast, Benjamin Rosenthal broke tradition of recent times by becoming the first New York City Member of Congress to move his family to the Washington, D.C., area.

Members of Congress who represent districts two hours or more flying time from Washington, usually spend an extra day in Washington and one less in the district. Otherwise, their schedules in Washington and in the home district are much the same as those in the "Tuesday to Thursday Club." Many Members who represent districts beyond the eastern seaboard persuade their families to live in the Washington suburban area.

Almost all Members of the House of Representatives must keep a watchful eye on the next election, as only a few of them have the luxury of representing districts that are considered politically safe. The life of Senators is much the same. Although they serve six-year terms, rather than the two-year span for Representatives, most Senators also maintain a hectic pace.

My Illinois district was never politically safe. For twenty-two years, I flew to the home district at least two weekends a month, sometimes three and occasionally four. In its last gerrymandered shape, my district stretched nearly two hundred miles east to west, and forty miles, north to south. This meant that I spent a lot of time driving across the country from one appointment to the next. There were moments when I envied urban Members of Congress whose districts might consist only of several blocks of tall apartment buildings.

Each day was busy and often hectic. In both Washington and the district, staff members, eager to accommodate constituent requests, tend to pack each available hour with appointments. I used to chide them by asking them to schedule restroom breaks along with other activities.

This glimpse will help the reader, figuratively, to walk in the shoes of those who represent you on Capitol Hill before you seek them out for a personal interview. Ben Reifel, a colleague from South Dakota whose mother was a full-blooded Sioux Indian, displayed on his office wall a message for everyone, especially those who seek to influence their Member of Congress: "Never criticize a Brave [an Indian warrior] until you have walked for two miles in his moccasins."

How to Win Support on Capitol Hill

I f you wish to visit a Member of Congress for the purpose of enlisting support for a particular cause, I offer these suggestions:

First, be considerate in phrasing your request for an appointment. Begin by mentioning something praiseworthy that the Member has done recently. Then, state briefly the purpose of your call, and, finally, recognize the hectic pace of Capitol Hill life by promising to take only ten minutes, not a second more.

Second, prepare carefully in advance of the visit. Find out what the Member has said or done on the topic of your concern. I remember vividly being visited by a lobbying group whose spokesman asked me to support three measures. He hadn't bothered to examine the public record where he would have found that I had already taken all the steps he wanted.

Third, on the day of the appointment, bring with you two copies of a brief summary, typed double-spaced and not more than one page in length, explaining the purpose of your call. Include your name, address and phone number. If the appointment fails to materialize, you can leave the outline with a staff member.

Fourth, be punctual but don't be surprised—or show irritation—if the Member is not there to welcome you. An unexpected roll call or important debate may have put the Member behind schedule. Offer to wait in his or her office, walk to the Capitol Building if the Member might wish to be called out of the chamber for a brief discussion, or return later in the day. Take whatever happens calmly and courteously. If a direct interview proves impossible, take the bad news gracefully. The assistant may try to connect you to the Member through a telephone located off the floor of the chamber.

Fifth, when the interview begins, after briefly complimenting the Member on some specific action, get to the point of your visit. If you promise to leave in ten minutes, do so, but leave with the Member the written summary of your objective.

Sixth, when you get home, write a brief note of appreciation, no matter what happened in regard to the appointment. Always address your letter and envelope to "The Honorable" –undeserving of this identification as the legislator may be. By being calm, courteous. and considerate, you will get high marks from the Member of Congress and his chief of staff, two people who may be important to your future success.

AIPAC's Keys to Success

For many years, the American Israel Public Affairs Council (AIPAC), the principal U.S. lobby for Israel, has been the most successful foreign policy lobby in American history. Unfortunately, the decent, professional salesmanship of the AIPAC team is often supplemented with strong-arm, intimidating tactics that are carried out by other elements of the pro-Israeli lobbying apparatus.

The effect is suffocating to cherished institutions of democracy. Free speech and open debate of issues that involve Israeli interests are the casualties. I can attest from personal observation that Capitol Hill has been devoid of balanced discussion of Middle East policy for nearly fifty years. The abuses, however, invalidate in no respect AIPAC's basic operating procedures. The organization's methods can be a useful guide to other advocacy groups. I. L. Kenan, who founded AIPAC in 1951, accurately described the organization as Israel's first line of defense because of its key role in winning policy battles in Washington. AIPAC has been victorious in every legislative tussle on Capitol Hill during the past twenty years and has lost only twice in the past forty years. Both times, it failed to block military aircraft sales to Saudi Arabia. Even then, it succeeded in securing changes that limited the range and effectiveness of the equipment.

For the most part, AIPAC attained this record by maintaining high standards of salesmanship and professionalism and operating carefully within public law. For AIPAC, "know your Member of Congress" is more than just a slogan. Most lobbies keep track of only a few key votes cast in the House and Senate chambers. For

Israel's lobby, that is just the starting point. AIPAC keeps detailed records on how Members of Congress respond to a wide range of issues, including how they vote and what they say in committees, the bills they introduce or co-sign, the public letters they sign, and their special interests beyond Middle East policy.

Each member of AIPAC 's full-time team of professional lobbyists is given responsibility for specific Members. This includes keeping personal files up to date but, even more important, establishing and maintaining a cordial relationship with each assigned Member and his or her principal assistant. While in Congress, I was one of the forty House Members identified as the special responsibility of AIPAC staff member Ralph Nurnberger. Even though my criticism of Israel's policies caused his employer to identify me as Israel's "Public Enemy Number One," he and I established a friendship of mutual respect that still survives. I believe he answered as truthfully as he could every question I posed, and he never misled me. His colleagues on the AIPAC staff maintained the same standards and, as a result, they generally had ready access to Members of Congress.

A congressional aide once explained why: "Professionalism is one reason. They know what they are doing, get to the point and leave. They are often a useful source of information. They are reliable and friendly. Most important of all, they are seen by legislators as direct links to important constituents."[1]

This professionalism enables AIPAC to provide thorough preparation to pro-Israel individuals and delegations before they visit Members of Congress and officials of the executive branch. When they arrive for scheduled interviews, they know exactly what the official has been doing and saying. One person does all the talking for the group and gets efficiently to the point of the visit.

A former high-ranking official in the State Department offers this appraisal of the discipline that exists within delegations lobbying on behalf of Israel: "When you have to explain your position day after day, week after week, to American Jewish groups—first, say, from Kansas City, then Chicago, then East Overshoe—you see what you are up against. These are people from different parts of the country, but they come in with the very same information, the same set of questions, the same criticism."

He said that other delegations lacked discipline: "When a group upset about U.S. bias favoring Israel would come in, more often than not those in the group would start arguing among themselves. I would just sit back and listen. They had not worked out in advance what they wanted to say."[2] I sense that Muslim advocacy groups are now following the AIPAC model.

Israel's U.S. lobby has an impressive apparatus that reaches beyond the tasks of monitoring Members of Congress and coaching delegations that visit Washington. One of its most effective but least known assets is a network of U.S. citizens—I call them loyalists—each of whom has developed a close political relationship with a U.S. senator from their state or the U.S. representative who serves their congressional district. They have established this relationship for the exclusive purpose of advancing and protecting the legislative interests of Israel. Loyalists have no desire for public recognition. In fact, they shun news interviews and try to stay out of the limelight.

The influence of these loyalists is a major reason for Israel's success in attaining and maintaining a powerful influence in Congress and the executive branch. They provide support to their Members of Congress that is uncritical and unconditional because they want congressional support of Israel to remain uncritical and unconditional. AIPAC is not the only lobby with a nationwide network of supporters. Other influential lobbies include the National Rifle Association, the American Association of Retired Persons, the lobby of the American Medical Association, and the National Right-to-Life Committee, but none matches AIPAC's success in dominating its field of policy. Muslim groups are steadily improving their lobbying apparatus, but, so far, none has developed a complement of loyalists who are as committed, responsive, and professionally prepared as the one serving Israel.

The AIPAC loyalists support their Members of Congress consistently. At campaign time, they make substantial financial contributions to help meet the ever-rising cost of candidacy, a challenge that not all Americans recognize. Mervyn M. Dymally, a former colleague from California, once observed that Arab-Americans seem to lack "a sense of political philanthropy."[3] I sense that many non-Arab Muslims are similarly handicapped. They are comfortable contributing generously for the construction of mosques and schools but have not yet recognized that substantial investments in political campaigns are also needed to advance the well-being of Muslims.

Former U.S. Senator Paul Simon once told me that, from his own experience, telephone calls from major donors routinely get returned ahead of others. Expressed another way, Muslims should recognize that generous campaign contributions, coupled with undeviating support and patience, can yield important advances.

Year in and year out, AIPAC-directed loyalists are eager to help. They are present with a warm welcome whenever the Member of Congress comes to their hometown for any purpose. They send notes of congratulations and support, and never express a word of complaint, no matter what the Member may say in a speech, and regardless of how he or she may vote on any subject. If the Member does or says something that could be considered unhelpful, the loyalist may ask for clarification but will do so in an uncomplaining way. Friends who always help and never complain are pure gold. In my congressional years, I had a number of such supporters.

AIPAC loyalists provide Israel with a built-in, durable, dependable support system on Capitol Hill that can be activated promptly and effectively, nationally or regionally, even in communities where one might expect supporters of Israel to be nonexistent.

AIPAC's Efficient Network

The network's efficiency was demonstrated to me one day in 1978 when the House Foreign Affairs Committee was considering a bill providing aid to Israel. I was in a somewhat mischievous mood and whispered to a colleague sitting next to me that I might offer an amendment to reduce the amount of proposed aid. I had not mentioned the amendment to anyone before that moment and had put nothing on paper. It was only a fleeting thought, because I realized that a proposal to cut aid to Israel would get no vote but my own. Offering it would have amounted to nothing more than a political statement on my part. I dropped the idea almost instantly and, without saying anything further about the amendment to my seatmate, I turned to other issues.

Now, to the remarkable part of this episode. Within thirty minutes two other members of the committee approached me with worried looks on their faces. They said that they had received calls from people in their home districts who had heard about my amendment and were concerned. By then, my half-humorous comment to my seatmate about an amendment was completely out of my thoughts, and the expressions of concern by my committee colleagues puzzled me for a moment. Then I realized that in just a few minutes, my whispered words had been swiftly relayed from a committee room on Capitol Hill to distant congressional districts, then back to the committee room.

Here are the links, I later learned, that created the rapid chain of events: First, my seatmate told other colleagues of my stated intention; second, this information was passed to an AIPAC staff member attending the committee session; third, the staff member called AIPAC headquarters about the rumor and provided the names of committee members who were present in the hearing room; fourth, employees at AIPAC called loyalists in the home districts of those committee members; fifth, the loyalists responded immediately with a call to their representatives, expressing concern; sixth, the two members of the committee brought their messages of concern directly to me.

It is noteworthy that AIPAC headquarters did not send a staff member directly to me or other committee members in the room to inquire about the rumor. The organization notified home district loyalists whom the organization knew would express concern swiftly, smoothly, and effectively to their Members of Congress. This indirect approach served AIPAC interests in several ways. It tested reaction time; it gave loyalists a specific, important job to do;

and it impressed all concerned, myself especially, with the efficiency of AIPAC's network. I was wondering if AIPAC also kept a stopwatch to record the time required to accomplish each step in the process. When I later asked Ralph Nurnberger about the fast reaction, he said: "These people are very good. They know just what to say."

AIPAC loyalists call requests to Members of Congress only when pending issues bear directly on Israeli interests, like my rumored amendment to cut aid. At such times, they place calls to their representatives or senators, and, because they are well known for the consistent, generous political support they provide, the calls go through directly and swiftly. When conveyed, requests are always expressed courteously and calmly. No threats. No hard sell.

The strategy works. It assures, with near certainty, the cooperation of the Members of Congress being approached. Israel's loyalists will get what they want every time, assuming there is no counter pressure from other helpful constituents who oppose unconditional aid to Israel.

This is effective salesmanship that other interest groups that seek influence in Washington can wisely emulate. AIPAC's network was not built in a day; it took nearly a half-century to complete. The creation of an effective system for influencing policy decisions in Washington that relate to Muslim stereotypes is a challenging objective. It will require sustained, patient effort.

Patience can be as important as money. If a Muslim, for example, begins to serve as a devoted and helpful loyalist, the Member of Congress may not change voting habits immediately or even soon, but it makes sense for the loyalist to remain patient, courteous, and supportive. The day will eventually come when these qualities of behavior pay dividends.

The goal is attainable and well worth patient effort. The progress that Muslims have already achieved is a promising start. In my travels around America, I find that Muslim committees-of-one are beginning to meet the challenge.

The Ultimate in Loyalty

Partisan lines are not always rigid. As a lifelong Republican, I am a firm believer in party affiliation. However, in Congress and elsewhere, I have often crossed party lines and worked closely with Democrats. Several of them are among my most cherished friends.

One of them, U.S. Rep. Thomas Foley, a Democrat who became House Speaker and subsequently ambassador to Japan, related a unique example of political loyalty several years ago.

As we sat together during a long flight one evening, he said, "I had a call today from a longtime supporter who is worried about the upcoming election. He told me not to worry, because, he said, my opponent is an awful man that nobody likes. Then he added, with a tone of condemnation in his voice, that my opponent is, to repeat his exact words, 'nothing but just another Irish Catholic lawyer from Spokane.'

He closed the conversation by saying, 'Don't worry, Tom, we're all for you. We're proud of you. We support you all the way.'" Foley chuckled. "My loyal friend forgot for the moment that I, too, am nothing but an Irish Catholic lawyer from Spokane."

Many Democrats helped in my campaigns for Congress. An elderly neighbor, Otis Hesley, a good friend and a lifelong Democrat who once held a political job in the county courthouse, could not bring himself to ask for a Republican ballot on election day even though he knew I faced stiff competition for the party nomination for Congress.

All through my primary campaign, however, he worked long hours as a volunteer in my headquarters. In the general election that November he "scratched" his customary straight vote for Democrats by voting for me.

Some of my most loyal and effective campaign leaders were newcomers to politics. Bill Carl, a Jacksonville, Illinois, businessman, although previously inexperienced in the political arena, served ably as my campaign manager all through my political career. He was expert in enlisting volunteers and keeping them enthusiastic.

A partner with his brother, Ted, in a dry-cleaning business located in the center of my district, he had the difficult challenge of defending my record in Congress, day in and day out, for twenty-two years. The son of a Greek immigrant, he never wavered in his support, even when I outraged the Greek lobby by defending U.S. aid to Turkey, a country that, at the time, was at odds with Greece over Cyprus.

The warm memories of failed candidacies that I report in Chapter 10 remind me of my own first campaign—also unsuccessful—for public office.

In 1952, when, as a young country newspaper editor, I announced my candidacy for the Republican nomination for state senator, I knew the odds were heavily against winning.

Before starting my campaign, I asked a venerable Democrat, Circuit Judge A. Clay Williams, for advice. I have never forgotten his words. "Campaign so that you win friends even if you don't win the office." I tried to follow his advice. I did not win the nomination, but, eight years later, people I met during the state senate campaign, including the woman who defeated me, Attorney Lillian Schlagenhauf, helped me win election to Congress.

In my campaigns, like Morshed Alam and Ali Alemi in later years, I knocked on doors no matter how bad the weather and never asked those I met about their party affiliation. I kept track of most of the people I met by writing their names and addresses on three-by-five cards and routinely made each a member of my advisory council, as I called it. From that ever-growing list emerged loyal supporters in the campaigns that followed, a technique that Alam has substantially refined.

One Person Can Make a Difference

Years ago, Paul Simon, a college drop-out, began his political career as a committee-of-one in a small southern Illinois town. His endeavors demonstrate that one person with determination and high purpose can succeed in the political arena without spending a lot of money or selling out to special interests.

Fifty years ago, when I first became active in public affairs,

Simon, although financially strapped and devoid of political support, had already revived a defunct weekly newspaper into a strong editorial voice and begun an enviable personal reputation in the political arena.

At nineteen, two years before he reached voting age, Simon left college to accept an opportunity in the newspaper business. Using the proceeds of a modest bank loan, he revived the *Troy Tribune,* a weekly that had ceased publication in the small village of Troy, Illinois. Although so poor he sometimes eased hunger pains by eating popcorn, he immediately began an editorial campaign attacking local officials for failing to enforce laws against prostitution and gambling, then broadened his assault, forcing the retreat of an organized criminal element nearby.

At twenty-five, aided by citizens who were impressed with his integrity and editorial zeal, he won election to the Illinois General Assembly, where he began a sustained but lonely battle against corruption at the state level. He even targeted a major force within his own Democratic Party, the political machine that controlled Chicago. At the time, I was editing a weekly newspaper in a small town near Simon's district and had become acquainted with him at an Illinois Press Association convention.

Simon's campaign against corruption brought scorn and resentment from some colleagues in both political parties. He worked diligently to protect his personal reputation. For years, like other editors in the region, I received mimeographed annual reports in which Simon volunteered full details of family income and expenditure. One report listed $12 he received from selling a used household item.

His legislative work led to legislative reforms and statewide recognition as "Mr. Clean." After a term as lieutenant-governor and two years in university teaching assignments, he began a long and distinguished career in Washington, elected first to the House of Representatives, then to the Senate.

Simon retired from the Senate in 1997, but not from the political arena. The following year, he campaigned for the Democratic presidential nomination. He outranked other

Democrats in the Iowa Caucus but shut down his campaign after disappointing results in early primaries. The same year, he became director of a public policy institute at Southern Illinois University where he leads worthy causes, writes books and teaches.

Whenever I hear cynical assertions that one person cannot make a difference in U.S. politics, Paul Simon's remarkable career comes to mind. Acting with determination and conviction—often alone—he set a high standard in personal conduct, idealism, scholarship, and leadership. No doubt some of the people reading these words have the integrity, intelligence and commitment to become, like Simon, stars in the political firmament.

Notes:
1. Paul Findley, *They Dare to Speak Out*, p. 37.
2. Ibid., pp. 163–4.
3. Ibid., p. 324.

Index